ULTIMATE GUIDE TO TAI CHI

Edited by
John R. Little and Curtis F. Wong

CONTEMPORARY BOOKS

Library of Congress Cataloging-in-Publication Data

Ultimate guide to tai chi / edited by John R. Little and Curtis F. Wong.
    p.   cm. — (Inside kung-fu magazine series ; bk. 2)
    ISBN 0-8092-2833-5
    1. T'ai chi ch'uan.   I. Little, John R., 1960–   .   II. Wong, Curtis.
III. Inside kung-fu.   IV. Series.
    GV504.U58   1999
    613.7'148—dc21   98-54248
                                                                                CIP

Cover design by Todd Petersen
Cover and interior photographs courtesy of CFW Enterprises
Interior design by Amy Yu Ng

Published by Contemporary Books
A division of NTC/Contemporary Publishing Group, Inc.
4255 West Touhy Avenue, Lincolnwood (Chicago), Illinois 60712-1975 U.S.A.
Printed in the United States of America
International Standard Book Number: 0-8092-2833-5

99 00 01 02 03 04 VL 19 18 17 16 15 14 13 12 11 10 9 8 7 6 5 4 3 2 1

Contents

PART III: ADVANCED TECHNIQUES

Preface

Philosophy as Martial Art

It is something of an irony that there endures a popular misconception in the West about martial artists that "those who *can*—fight," and "those who *can't*—talk about it." In some instances this may be true, which accounts for the fact that there will always be more fans than practitioners, but on the whole, the implication is erroneous.

For one thing, it's a self-incriminating statement implying that those who are fighters lack the intellectual wherewithal to discuss what they practice. This, in turn, suggests that they lack the ability to communicate or to formulate— to *think*, in short— about what it is they do when they fight.

Such an approach goes against the grain of reality—at least reality as expressed by the Taoist philosophy of yin-yang, or tai chi. Pure physicality is an extreme position and, as such, cannot be sustained for long before giving way to its complementary aspect—passivity. You see this whenever exertion is applied. For example, the faster you run, the less time you can spend running. Whereas you can walk, literally, for days, and jog for hours, the time you can spend in an all-out sprint is, of necessity, well under a minute. Intensity and duration exist in an inverse ratio; you can do something hard, or you can do something for long periods of time—you just can't do both simultaneously.

One of the few martial arts to incorporate this Taoist philosophy is the ancient Chinese art of tai chi chuan. Whereas many so-called hard schools of combat try to teach their students ways to dominate an opponent, the student studying tai chi chuan seeks rather to understand and complement—and thereby complete—the opponent's technique.

Students of tai chi chuan learn to cultivate the necessary emotional and tactile awareness and sensitivity to *react* in complete and appropriate concordance with nature. To do this successfully, you must first seek to understand nature's ways in order to fit in with them—and this requires an insightful perspective, or philosophy, by which to guide your thinking toward reality-based observation and reaction.

Whereas combat, by definition, is adversarial, philosophy is complementary—and yet this does not mean that philosophy and combat are mutually exclusive. A martial artist without philosophy is a dangerous individual—and more so to himself than to his opponent. So-called victories will be fleeting, for a martial artist who does not comprehend the environment that created and sustains him, nor the interrelatedness of all that it encompasses (including his so-called opponent or adversary), is walking into a jungle without a compass—a philosophy—to guide his actions. It is the intention of this book to provide you, the tai chi student, with just such a compass.

For more than a quarter of a century, *Inside Kung-Fu* magazine has provided its readers with some of the most exciting and historic reports on the growth and development of tai chi chuan. In addition to the insights and hard-hitting interviews with key tai chi figures for which *Inside Kung-Fu* is famous, this book features material from the archives of CFW Enterprises, the parent company of *Inside Kung-Fu*. The resulting compilation truly represents the best of the best writing on the subject of tai chi chuan.

Within the pages of this book, you will meet and get to know the present-day masters of "the art of moving meditation," in addition to learning the art's traditions and history. As the Yang style is the most popular and common form of tai chi practiced in the world today, you'll find a wealth of information on this branch of tai chi in this book. For example, Jane Hallander is one of the world's best-known martial arts writers, and with more than three hundred magazine articles and six books to her credit, she is certainly one of the most prolific. A teacher of Yang style tai chi chuan at her own school in San Rafael, California, Hallander is also a national and international champion in tai chi forms and push-hands competition at both tai chi and open tournaments. This experience gives her contributions a clear ring of purity and appreciation.

The articles included in this volume are the most inspirational and informative ever published in *Inside Kung-Fu*. They are of immense personal benefit not only to newcomers to tai chi chuan in search of a wonderful introduction to the art, but also to seasoned practitioners and masters who wish to evolve and deepen their understanding of tai chi chuan's intricacies and the higher principles that form the foundation of this art.

Let this volume serve as your training partner in tai chi, much like an old master who speaks to you when you are alone, solving your problems and stimulating your thinking in exciting new directions. As with any sessions spent with a true master, the rewards will be well worth the time invested.

John Little

A Brief Introduction to Tai Chi Chuan and Selecting a Tai Chi School

Dr. John Painter

What Is Tai Chi Chuan?

Few people know the truth about tai chi chuan. Is it a mysterious occult art, an exercise for old people, a Walter Mitty martial art for hippie types afraid to get involved with "real" martial arts, a magical ritual bringing secret inner strength to the initiates, or a deadly dance of death? At one time or another, all these labels and more have been applied to tai chi chuan, the popular but often misunderstood internal martial art of China.

Tai chi chuan is many things to many people. To some, it is an esoteric, dreamlike ballet. Many believe it is a unique technique of health, consisting of nourishing exercises for developing peace and harmony in mind and body, while to others it is a devastating martial art whose mastery endows the expert with the mysterious power to toy with one or more assailants as easily as a cat plays with a mouse.

Not only are there different interpretations—and five major styles of the art (each with its own set of forms)—but there also are many minor schools and little-known versions of the art, some of which are offshoots of the five major systems while others are independent family styles. Moreover, within tai chi chuan styles, there is often a great divergence in focus among teachers. Some stress the development of internal health only, while others emphasize the martial art. Still others place importance on the development of life force energy, or *chi*.

So, how does one go about finding the "real thing?" The best weapon you can have is knowledge. This introduction to the art distills the wisdom of some of America's influential and highly respected tai chi chuan instructors. I also have stirred into the pot my experience of watching tai chi chuan emerge from a cloud of secrecy and obscurity over the last fifteen years to a world-renowned internal health exercise and martial art. In selecting a school of tai chi chuan, it will help you to know what tai chi chuan was intended to be by its original creators. Examining the history and evolution of the art can often shed some light on its purpose and true intentions, as well as its relevance in our own quest to fulfill our personal needs.

Historical Origins

The history of tai chi chuan is fragmentary at best. Many stories exist concerning the founding and creation of this legendary art. Research by a famous martial arts master and scholar, Tang Hao, during the 1930s indicates that tai chi chuan, or "shadowboxing" as it is often called, originated in Wenxian County of Henan Province, China, about the middle of the seventeenth century.

This was a period of great social upheaval, when the Ming dynasty was being replaced by the Qing dynasty. The historical founder of tai chi chuan was Chen Wang Ting, a powerful warrior and Wenxian County magistrate. Chen fought many battles defending the county's borders. In later life, he retired from society, disillusioned by fame and the hard-style warrior arts, and entered into a life of solitude and Taoist pursuits.

He devoted his spare time to working in the fields and creating a new form of boxing art, which was later to become known as tai chi chuan, the "grand ultimate fist." Chen Wang Ting created his art by combining his martial arts skills with the Taoist philosophy of yin and yang, Chinese medicine, and physical therapy.

He wanted to create an all-purpose exercise and martial art for the benefit of mind and body as well as self-protection. To do this, Chen borrowed from two forms of Chinese yoga. The first was *daoyin*, a technique coordinating mental energy with the bending and twisting of the body to activate the internal energy of *chi*. The second method was *tuna*, a series of deep-breathing exercises to stimulate the abdominal area for the activation of *chi* in the body's center of energy, or *dan tian*.

This addition to the coordinated actions of Chen's shadowboxing routines produced the first

Chen style tai chi chuan, a complete system of exercise characterized by the creation of inner and outer power development. Further developments added spiral-like twisting actions, alternately extending and withdrawing the limbs and tightening and loosening the muscles while mentally directing the *chi* to spread throughout the body. The *chi*, originating in the *dan tian*, a point three inches below the navel, moves systematically through the body by the gradual twisting of the waist and limbs during exercise. When this intrinsic energy reaches the extremities it returns to the *dan tian*.

Chen Wang Ting discovered that martial arts exercises practiced slowly in a harmonious fashion not only stimulated the *Jingluo* (the channels of energy which circulate the *chi* to all internal organs, bringing about increased health and well-being) but also resulted in strengthening offensive and defensive forces of the body. This had the effect of creating dramatic increases in explosive force, power, and speed for use in martial arts applications.

The tai chi chuan designed by Chen Wang Ting thus was both a martial and health promotion exercise. Tai chi chuan's original form was a practical, down-to-earth martial art. Yet, it also contained esoteric Taoist medical principles for the preservation and development of internal energy and power, and was meant to be a physical exercise to strengthen and tone the body. It was one of the first of what we now call "holistic" arts.

The Creation of New Styles

The Chen style of tai chi chuan was kept within the family and not taught to outsiders. Through the years, it was adapted and modified into many variations by other masters.

Tai chi chuan did not truly come into prominence until the eighteenth century, through the efforts of Yang Lu Chan, a former martial artist. Having been soundly defeated twice in boxing matches by a young member of the Chen family, Yang resolved to give up the study of all hard styles and steal the Chen family art. Disguised as a beggar, he took up residence with the Chen family and secretly watched its practice. Unknown to Yang, the grand master was aware of Yang's intentions and was secretly watching him. The grand master was so impressed with Yang that he broke the family tradition and consented to secretly teach Yang the entire method during early morning hours while the household slept. He believed this would ensure the spread of the art outside of the Chen family.

The Yang Style

Yang became a superlative tai chi chuan master, defeating all challengers, including even the members of the Chen household. He modified the style and opened a school of tai chi chuan in Beijing.

Yang softened the art of Chen Wang Ting by removing many of the more vigorous jumping tactics and stamping of the feet. His son Yang Chien-ho improved on the techniques for health by extending and expanding the movements into what is now called the big-style. This is the most famous version of Yang's method and one of the most popular in China.

The Two Wu Styles

Yang Lu Chan and his second son, Yang Ban-ho, taught a set of tai chi chuan called the small-style. This method was learned by a Manchu known as Quan You. The son of Quan You took the name of Wu Jianquan and taught his interpretation of the Yang tai chi chuan small-style to others. The *Wu jin-quan* version now bears his name.

A third version, also called the Wu School, was created by Wu Yuxiang of Yongnian county around 1852. This version is a combination of the older Chen method learned from Yang Lu Chan and the new-style Chen method of Chen *quingping*. It is a compact set emphasizing body work and exertion of the inner power.

The Sun Style

The tai chi chuan of Wu Yuxiang was eventually absorbed by Sun Lu Tang, a superlative internal boxer already proficient in two other forms of the internal Taoist arts, *xingyiquan* boxing and *baguazhang*, the eight-diagram palm boxing. Sun combined the strong points of all three schools into his personal style.

Today, these styles and many other versions are taught in China, Europe, Australia, Japan, and North America. Each of the styles differs in appearance and sequence, yet all are essentially the same in structure and principles.

Total Tai Chi Chuan Training

According to the Chinese masters, learning the total art takes many years, and true training will contain the following elements:

Meditation

The purpose of tai chi chuan meditation is to cultivate the *chi* force of the body. Most styles practice the standing forms of meditation, sometimes called "posting" or *jan-chung*. The student assumes a posture from the form or stands as though holding a large barrel. While the student is holding the chosen posture, the breath is controlled and the mind concentrates on the alchemical process of mixing and summoning energy in and around the arc of the *dan tian*.

Seated meditation, *ching-tso*, is optional in many schools. This technique is practiced by sitting on the floor or in a chair and centering the mind upon the navel point as in the standing method.

Chi Kung (Qigong)

Tai chi chuan styles often incorporate breathing techniques to blend the powers of the body/mind/spirit into a harmonious whole. The simplest forms are methods of deep breathing. One form is known as "postnatal breath," in which the diaphragm muscle is pressed downward as the student inhales and flexed upward on the exhalation. A second method, the "prenatal breath," reverses the postnatal breath. This method is said to be the way a fetus uses its abdomen in the womb to obtain energy from the mother. Other forms of *chi kung* involve coordinated arm movements, waist twisting, and vocal sounds, all used to increase the life forces.

The Tai Chi Form

A series of body movements linked together is a "set," or *hsing*. Depending on the style, the set may consist of approximately 44 to 108 separate movements. Each style has its own number of linked postures. The postures may vary greatly from style to style, but visually they all have a similar and distinctive effect unique to tai chi chuan. Some styles have more than one set, with each more advanced than the preceding.

With the exception of Chen style, almost all tai chi chuan beginner's forms are characterized by slow, even movements, often resembling someone swimming underwater or moving in slow motion. Chen also does this, but the set is punctuated with quick motions and stamping of the feet.

Later training can also involve faster practice. Fast practice of the form is designed to give those in the upper levels an understanding of the martial arts application as well as for aerobic benefit. No matter what level one achieves, the basic foundation of the tai chi chuan form is slow, even practice.

Push-Hands

Push-hands is a two-person exercise used to develop sensitivity and awareness of energy flow. By developing push-hands skill, one can neutralize and guide the force of another without opposing it. This is invaluable as a defensive technique; however, the principle also applies to learning to manage stress in everyday life. Push-hands teaches that it is not necessary to fight against an opposing force. One learns to go with the flow, borrowing energy from an attack and using only a small amount of force to topple a larger, more powerful one.

Push-hands is the beginning of martial arts skills, and excellent skills they are. The well-trained student who excels at push-hands after five to ten years should be quite capable of neutralizing and controlling the aggressive actions of an assailant. Masters of the technique can often toy with one or more trained attackers as easily as a cat playing with a cricket.

Weapons

Most schools teach weapons training as a method of developing extra power and extension of energy; the focus of weapons training is not on fighting or fencing in tai chi chuan. Students learn to use the saber, or "big knife," to develop waist strength and flexibility. The sword, a double-edged weapon, trains power and control in the wrists and forearms, while the spear, or lance, is used to enhance the ability to project intrinsic energy.

Benefits of Tai Chi Chuan: Fact and Fiction

Health and Serenity

The essential principle underlying claims of increased health and stress reduction is the mental attitude pervading all tai chi chuan practice. Practitioners are taught to develop a serene heart with a concentrated mind. As students learn to relax during performance of the form, they begin to develop an awareness of mind/body control. This results in increased self-worth and confidence. Tai chi chuan players discover that they create their own emotions and are responsible for their actions. Such knowledge allows a student to change undesirable aspects in his or her character, which can have wide-ranging benefit.

A decrease of physical and emotional tension resulting from regular tai chi chuan practice also stimulates certain areas of the brain responsible for controlling the body's immune system, thus promoting resistance to illness and infection. Clinical studies have shown the art to be effective in reducing high blood pressure and a host of other stress-related ailments. Tai chi chuan also is used as physical therapy, in China as well as in a number of progressive clinics in the United States, for the treatment of stress-related disorders.

Strength and Fitness

Teachers who claim that tai chi chuan training will develop aerobic fitness and muscular development should be avoided. No clinical evidence exists to support this claim. Aerobic capacity can be achieved only through an exercise form that places progressively increasing workloads on the cardiovascular system. The slow versions of tai chi chuan will not supply this benefit beyond a moderate range unless the speed and difficulty of the form are continually increased to match the student's personal aerobic target zone. Lowering the stances to increase resistance in the slow form will not, as some people claim, increase the cardiovascular benefit significantly to produce a training effect of sufficient duration to qualify as an aerobic activity.

However, some aerobic benefit can be realized by tai chi chuan beginners who are in poor physical condition. They may see gains in aerobic capacity and overall strength, but only until the body adjusts to the workload provided by the form. The increases will then level off, and no further gains in strength will take place without an increase in the intensity of the workload. Some tai chi chuan advocates claim they have seen little, "skinny" tai chi chuan players who were much stronger than a well-muscled athlete.

Tai chi chuan players who have practiced well for five to ten years appear stronger because they use their bodies in a kinetically correct fashion and therefore make full use of the body's power through existing muscular strength, correct leverage, and a knowledge of momentum. Athletes with large muscles who have not had the benefit of the tai chi chuan principles often employ only brute force. They are frequently using their own muscles against themselves when performing feats of strength.

In the practice of tai chi chuan, overall muscular power in the upper torso does not increase a great deal as a result of forms practice. However, the kinetic efficiency of the body increases dramatically. This increase in ease of motion and correct posture alignment allows tai chi chuan practitioners to utilize up to 85 percent of their natural strength, in contrast to the untrained person, who utilizes only about 45 percent of available muscle efficiency. What appears to be an increase in muscular power to some observers is merely the process of learning to use the body correctly.

Selecting a Tai Chi School

With the knowledge base from the preceding discussion, to find a school that will suit your needs, you should first decide just what you expect to gain from studying tai chi chuan. Do you simply want better health, or do you want to learn tai chi chuan to defend yourself, or to enhance your internal power? Or all of the above? Getting in touch with your needs is a good idea before your start your quest.

Where to Look

In most large cities across the United States, there are usually several teachers available. Look in the yellow pages or ask around to compile a list of candidates. Checking with the local community college programs is another option. Anyone who wishes to study this art should identify as many teachers as possible in the area. Then go visit the training sites of each. Some may be in a commercial building, a church hall, or a college gymnasium, while other classes are taught in parks. The authenticity of the art does not rely on the place in which it is practiced. However, for the beginner, it generally is best to have a quiet and serene environment in which to train.

If the site matches your needs, call the instructor and ask to visit an actual class. It's most helpful to observe both a beginner's and advanced class to determine how you might progress as a student of that particular school. Avoid a teacher who will not allow visitors during class time. Legitimate teachers have nothing to hide and do not conduct "secret" classes.

The "Master Teacher" Stereotype

Once you have located a teacher to visit, do what the Chinese say: "Empty your cup." Let go of any expectations about how a competent tai chi chuan teacher should look, act, or sound.

Good and bad teachers come in all shapes, sizes, and nationalities and in both sexes. A teacher does not have to be Chinese to have a command of the art. A good teacher has to communicate the basic principles in a clear and concise manner—this is essential.

The hallmark of excellence in teaching is not how the teacher performs, but how he or she gets you to perform. No matter how many awards and trophies have been won or how perfectly the forms are executed for the class, if the person in question cannot explain in simple terms, or communicate in some way how you can do the technique, you are not looking at a good teacher!

Is Age Important?

The age of a tai chi chuan instructor is purported to make a difference in imparting the art. A survey of a large cross section of teachers in America found that, generally, the younger teachers say "no," and the older teachers say "yes."

Chong Teh, a well-respected teacher of the Tai Chi Ch'uan Association in Atlanta has been studying the art for forty years and teaching since 1970. He states, "The age of the instructor makes a difference in the quality of instruction. An instructor needs to be mature in mind and body before teaching the internal arts. Such maturity requires a few years to develop."

Larry C. Eshelman from Butler, Pennsylvania, who has studied for nineteen years and taught Yang style for eight, responds, "Age is not as important as maturity. Instructors must know not only form, but also the essence of the art. Some people can learn at twelve, or even younger, and comprehend everything, while others cannot comprehend at forty-two. The quality of the lineage is the dominating factor. If the student who becomes a teacher had a good teacher and learned from those teachings, that person will mature in the art as well."

A practical approach is to look for an instructor with experience and maturity in the arts, placing less importance on chronological age than on the maturity of the instructor's skill. In other words, how long has the instructor been practicing and teaching the art to others on a daily basis? Most Chinese and Western teachers responded that a student can be considered for instructor level only after a period of daily practice, under the watchful eyes of the master, of from five to ten years.

The State of Tai Chi Chuan in America

Tai chi chuan is developing rapidly in America. It is being practiced by different people for different reasons. When you're looking for a school to fit your needs, one reason for your site visits is to determine the category of the school. The major divisions of schools can be grouped under three classifications, from conservative to ultramodern.

The Orthodox School

The orthodox school is the do-it-by-the-numbers school. It usually will have all the requirements for complete tai chi chuan training. Progress in this type of school is quite slow, depending on the degree of perfection and strictness of adherence to the rules insisted upon by the teacher. The advantage to this method is that one learns the style as it was taught by the teacher's teacher, and his teacher before him. The disadvantage is that the method often is "frozen" in time, innovation, and change. The founding principles of the tai chi chuan philosophy are not encouraged. "We do it this way because it has always been done this way," is often the motto of the orthodox approach. Orthodox teachers come in two basic varieties. The first is usually an older person who learned the system in China or from a family member and has practiced it this way for most of his or her life. The second type is one to avoid, and that is the Western teacher who has become fanatically obsessed with the art and wants to talk, act, and live like the "old masters" of ancient China.

Kenneth Cohen has been teaching tai chi chuan for more than fifteen years. One might think a Westerner such as Cohen, who has taken the time to become an ordained Taoist priest, would fit into the latter category. Nothing is further from the truth. Cohen comments: "Beware of orthodoxy in the martial arts. Once, when I was teaching in a park, there was another tai chi chuan group nearby. The instructor announced in a rather loud voice, 'We believe that our tai chi chuan form is the only correct one. Once you know this, you have learned all you need to know.' In response I used a Taoist technique called 'put him on a pedestal of ashes and watch him sink.' I turned to my class and said, 'Our tai chi chuan form is the worst. If you want real, true, orthodox tai chi chuan, study with someone else.'"

The Liberal School

The liberal school of tai chi chuan thought is becoming more prevalent with the opening of China's cul-tural floodgates. Teachers and masters from China, both those from the *wushu* teams who teach the art for sport form competition and traditional old-world masters, are taking on a new policy of openness, sharing, and willingness to adapt to change when change is necessary.

Practitioners who fit into this category tend to be better educated and more open-minded. Often interested in the science behind the art and what it can do to promote friendship, goodwill, and health, these teachers and students are the pioneers of the latest innovations and research on tai chi being conducted around the world.

Liberals are often good teachers, with new and innovative methods, as well as explanations of how and why something works. The disadvantage is that liberal schools often do not encompass the whole art. Some place a strong emphasis on form and appearance and not internal development. There are liberal schools that offer all aspects, so it is best to shop around if liberal sounds like the place you want to take your empty cup.

Avant-Garde School

The avant-garde school is the school of "tai chi chuan beatniks." This category is composed of those who want to use the art as a method of spiritual enlightenment and divorce themselves totally from structured forms and any mention of martial arts, weapons training, or serious physical exercise. The avant-garde school usually makes up its own rules, forms, and meditation exercises, blending its brand of tai chi chuan with various forms of occult practices, from astrology to channeling.

Advocates of this style of practice are well-meaning, gentle souls who mostly are just waving their arms about and trying to experience the "good vibes." Although it's basically harmless, I cannot think of any advantages to joining this group if you are seeking real tai chi chuan instruction.

Recognizing the Essentials of Form

When you visit a tai chi chuan class, you cannot see the internal energy, or whether or not the meditation is effective. So, you are left with observing the forms and the participants. Here are a few things to look for.

Hallmarks of Good Form

Slowness. Beginners will execute all movements as slowly as possible. The form can be properly learned only if attention is paid to control of each muscle group, which makes working slowly essential. Chen style tai chi chuan will have some fast techniques throughout the form, but overall, the moves are slow and continuous.

Continuity. The teacher's moves should flow continuously and without pause, from one to another, in an even interchange of postures. Pausing to adjust feet or body position during the form is not a good sign in a teacher.

Relaxation. The instructor's body should appear to be almost floating. Shoulders are never tensed, and the chest is never arched. The waist, shoulders, and arms should appear to move as though they were more liquid than solid bone and flesh. The face should appear calm and serene. There are no grimacing, teeth-gritting facial expressions. Each move should appear to give off waves of deep, quiet strength without a feeling of restrained tension.

Weight Distribution. With the exception of the beginning of the form, the body weight will never be equally distributed on both legs for any length of time. The body will be erect. As the practitioner moves, the upper body is carried, riding above the hips. Weight is carried so that it presses directly into the earth through one foot at all times. There should be a great impression of being well centered.

Breathing. The breath should be natural, in through the nose and out through the mouth. Exotic breathing methods or the rapid expulsion of breath have no place in the practice of the tai chi chuan slow form. The breath should be easy and not labored. Watch to see if the demonstrator is holding his or her breath during the performance. If the person appears winded after the form, something is amiss.

Posture. The body is held erect, with knees bent. The head is up, with chin tucked slightly. The eyes are focused on the forward hand and do not glare. The chest is relaxed and not expanded, and the coccyx is tucked slightly. Actions should not look sleepy, limp, and listless. There should be an overall impression of relaxed yet alert energy permeating the entire posture.

Movement. All movement will appear to be emanating from the waist and flow outward to the fingers in a smooth, uninterrupted flow. The feet are placed firmly in contact with the earth before weight is shifted to the front or back, and the knees never extend beyond the toes during a lunge. Look to see if the knees are kept in alignment over the toes, not twisted in or out over the instep or outside edge of the feet. The front foot will point in the direction the performer is facing at the completion of each move.

In good tai chi chuan, if you carefully watch the shoulders and arms, you will see that only one joint moves at a time. This movement will be executed so smoothly that it will appear to be a continuous flow, like that of a whip cracking in slow motion, with the momentum beginning in the handle, which is the waist, and proceeding in an orderly, almost undulating, action into the fingertips. The palms, when kept open, should have the fingers slightly spread and extended, with no exotic hand or finger formations.

In punching, the closed fist is kept perpendicular and not parallel to the ground.

Taking the Pulse of the Class

When visiting the school, talk to the students and find out what they like about the program. Watch the classes and see if the students are having fun learning. It is best to avoid teachers who run their classes like a military camp or who never smile. Discipline is important and should be part of the class, but remember that tai chi chuan is based on Taoism, and Taoists do not take things as seriously as many of their Zen-oriented brothers in *budo*. Look for laughter.

Price Structure

Prices vary from school to school. Some teachers charge nothing, as they have no overhead and merely want to share the art, while others with commercial schools have to pay the overhead and can charges fees ranging from $30 to $80 a month. The average price is around $60 per month in a commercial school.

My last research turned up a few unscrupulous teachers in Canada who were so inflated with greed and self-importance that they had the audacity to charge up to $150 or more for each technique. A student who learns the first three or four moves has to come back and pay again to get the next set of movements. All I can say is, "A fool and his money are soon parted."

Larry Eshelman explains the marketplace dynamics: "There are many traditional teachers who feel that ancient knowledge is sacred and no fee should be charged, while others charge a minimal fee and teach after finishing their day's work in their chosen professions. Both types often condemn the commercial schools, claiming that it is best to have only a few quality students who prove their worthi-ness to learn by enduring long hours of hardship and servitude to the master.

In our Western society, we have a different method of proving to the teacher the value of the instruction, by paying what we feel the instruction is worth to us individually. Money is just another form of energy and has no value until it is used to purchase something that is considered valuable. Of course, if an exceptional prospect comes along who has no money with which to pay, rather than lose a good student, I will set up some form of barter with him to pay for his instruction.

All in all, you should pay what you think the instruction is worth, although if you are lucky enough to find a truly good teacher, the reward you receive will be beyond price."

Memberships

Some schools require students to sign a membership contract. In most cases, this is for the legal protection of the commercial school and to act as a guarantee of the students' sincerity. I would advise anyone to avoid signing any contract of more than four months' duration. And do not sign anything until you have read and understood every word of the agreement.

The best advice is to first go see the class. Then, if there is a contract, read it over and go home and think about it, and in the morning if you still want to join, go ahead. In most states, you have from 48 to 72 hours to change your mind on a contractual arrangement with service-type businesses. So, if you get into class the first night and decide it is not for you, you can still legally back out. Check with your county courthouse or attorney on the regulations for your state.

Run, don't walk, out of any school claiming to teach traditional tai chi chuan that offers you a pay-up-front belt or sash program as in indication of your ability. There are no belts or sashes in "real" tai chi chuan, just what you know—and that should be enough, as it speaks for itself through your every action.

Reality Checks

The only way to truly tell if the art is for you is to get your feet wet and keep your eyes and feelings open. Rex Eastman of the Kootenay T'ai Chi Ch'uan Center in Nelson, British Columbia, advises the beginner to "buy a book, such as T. T. Liang's *Tai Chi and Self-Defense*, and read the guiding points to help direct your tai chi chuan school search."

Ken Cohen sums up succinctly: "In looking for a good school, follow this rule: Do not believe your ears—what people say about this school or that school or what one instructor says about himself or others. As Emerson said, what you *are* speaks so loudly that I cannot hear what you say. Trust your own intuitive sense. How do you feel when you observe a class?"

Ask yourself if you feel enthused, playful, and inspired, or do you sense anger, stress, and fear? Look at many different schools and find one with which you feel comfortable. Look to the students of the class. Have any of them come close to the level of the teacher? Is there an atmosphere of learning and mutual respect? Does the instructor use his or her own words to express the principles, or merely quote some other authority?

Finally, observe the instructor in daily life. Is he speaking with controlled *chi* mind, living a tai chi life, or is the person "pushing the river"? To me, the real mark of mastery is ease and effortlessness, with precision in movement and a realization of one's own limitations and willingness to continue learning.

PART I
Histories and Traditions

A History of Tai Chi Chuan
The Oral Tradition

Kenneth S. Cohen

There have always been two histories of tai chi chuan, one a written history, which changes with every advance in scholarship, and the other an oral tradition, passed from master to disciple, and which remains fairly constant within any particular school of tai chi chuan.

Owing to the modern bias for the written word, we have usually called the former the "real" history, and the latter "legend" or "fiction." And yet we know that these "legends" are far older than documented materials on tai chi chuan. The first books written about tai chi chuan are all from recent times.

So, what I propose to do here is assume that the oral tradition is the "real" one. I will expose for the first time (in Chinese or English) the oldest of these oral traditions, which comes from Chinese Taoism, the original religion of China. (The Taoist church founded by Chang Tao-ling goes back to the second century A.D., Taoist philosophy to the fourth century B.C., and Taoist yoga, *tao yin*, to long before that.) I shall draw on Chinese legend and scholarship

only when it adds to this oral tradition. This may suggest something of the beauty and complexity of the history of tai chi chuan.

The Most Guarded Secret

There are numerous reasons for the inaccuracy of many written sources and for the secrecy shrouding both the history and techniques of tai chi chuan. In old China, martial arts were usually kept within a family or school and rarely communicated to outsiders in any way. This would prevent your enemy from learning a deadly technique and either discovering its weakness or using it against you. It should be understood that Taoist monasteries were not always havens of peace. When Taoism became the state religion during the Tang dynasty, there were great battles between the Buddhists and Taoists. So, this secrecy was a real concern.

Likewise, both knowledge and technique were

sometimes guarded out of economic self-interest, to eliminate competition and ensure continued patronage by the court. Also, knowledge was held back to test the sincerity and patience of the students, or to determine which students were ethically ready to use martial arts wisely.

Unfortunately, some masters had their egos invested in their arts. As long as they kept even a little bit to themselves, the students might assume that the masters knew far more than they actually did. Taoists especially committed little to writing. When a monk received ordination, he had to copy by hand the master's manuscripts and then keep them to himself. The few things written down were meant as mnemonic devices to recall what one already knew.

Many of the standard histories of tai chi chuan are misleading because of indiscriminate research. An example is all the books that take the story of Chang San-feng, reputed founder of tai chi chuan, to be historical fact. Few realize that Chang's name appears in none of the registers of ordained Taoists of his period, or that his biography (and the books ascribed to him) had been written 400 years after Chang supposedly died. These authors draw heavily on the Taoist oral tradition, perhaps without realizing it.

The problem is compounded by the Chinese love of exaggeration, which goes all the way back to the Taoist philosopher Chuang-tzu, who lived in the third century B.C. A tale is often exaggerated in order to impress us with its value or to make its basic truth sink in more deeply.

Taoist monasteries were primarily places for spiritual training. Martial arts were practiced as a way of strengthening, disciplining, and unifying body and mind. The masters did not want outsiders to know about their martial arts, lest they be swamped with students and their spiritual life disrupted.

Unlike the United States, where one can learn martial arts almost anywhere, in China, *where* one learned was almost as important as *what* one learned.

Holy arts had to be learned in holy places and rarely went beyond the boundaries of their place of origin. This is why the Taoist tai chi styles (from the Sacred Peaks of China) have remained relatively unknown.

Some yoga and martial arts techniques are even believed to be the creation of gods. For instance, the famous "eight pieces of brocade" (*pa tuan chin*), a series of stretching and meditative exercises popular throughout China, is believed to have been created by Lu Tung-pin, one of the "Eight Immortals." Such arts might be "learned" in one of three ways:

First, the Taoist master might leave his body to travel in another realm of existence. (One of the classics of Chinese literature, the *Yuan Yu* chapter of the *Ch'u Tzu*, third century B.C., is a poem of astral travel!) There he observes the movements of the gods and imitates them when he returns to earth. The Taoists believe that much of tai chi chuan was created in this way—that tai chi chuan is actually the dance of the gods! One illustration is the Tang-dynasty stone rubbing of the "Cloud Dance," excavated in 1973–74. On it are three pairs of female figures, all in a posture remarkably similar to the tai chi chuan form "part the wild horse's mane." (Other movements that might have a stellar origin are "jade lady at the shuttle"—the "jade lady" is a star goddess—and "step up seven stars.")

Second, the techniques may have been seen in dreams. There is a story that the god of the polestar, Hsuan Tien Shang Ti, taught the principles of tai chi chuan to Chang San-feng in a dream. Taoist monasteries had special chambers devoted to the art of dreaming.

Finally, Taoist masters are said to have the ability to draw the gods down to earth, causing an individual to become possessed by the spirit of a great martial artist. Whether fact or fiction, cases of this type of "spirit possession" are said to be known to anthropologists the world over.

The Patriarchs of Tai Chi

We can see that nobody created tai chi chuan. It was, rather, synthesized from various systems of movement and meditation that were already present in China. The history of Yang, Chen, and Wu style tai chi chuan has already been eloquently detailed by Huang Wen Shan in his book *Fundamentals of T'ai Chi Ch'uan*. Therefore, this discussion traces the origin of Taoist tai chi chuan and how it influenced the modern styles.

The first tai chi chuan form was practiced by Cheng I Tao Jen, a celibate Taoist priest (*Tao-shih*) of the Chuan Chiou period (722–480 B.C.). Nothing is known of his life or art, yet the Taoist priests of the Sacred Peaks (*Wu Yueh*) still credit him as the first patriarch. By the end of the Tang dynasty (590–906 A.D.), there were various modifications and styles of tai chi chuan, often attributed to Hsu Hsuan Ping, Cheng-ling Hsi, Yin Li Hsiang, and, most important, Li Tao Tzu, a Taoist from Mount Wu Tang who named his martial art *hsien tien chun* (prenatal boxing).

The Taoist styles of tai chi chuan were greatly refined by the Sung-dynasty Taoist master Chang San-feng (c. 1000 A.D.). Although the first documents on Chang San-feng's life are found no earlier than in the biography of the famous sixteenth-century boxer Chang Sung-chi, the Taoist priests have, right to the present day, maintained a long and colorful oral history. Master Chang is described as being over six feet tall, with enormous eyes and ears, a bristling beard, and long hair tied in a topknot. It is said that he wore only one robe, summer or winter, could eat tremendous quantities of food, and could climb high mountains as though flying.

The Taoists of Mount Hua and Wu Tang trace the lineage of Master Chang back to the founder of Taoism, Lao-tzu (fourth century B.C.). Lao-tzu is said to have transmitted his doctrines to Yin-hsi, guardian of the pass, in the Chung-nan Mountains. Yin-hsi taught Ma-I, "the Hemp-clad Taoist." From

Ma-I there is a gap of several hundred years until the doctrine came to Chen Hsi-I, the famous recluse of the Sung dynasty, mentioned earlier. Chen Hsi-I studied Taoist yoga on both Mount Wu Tang and Mount Hua. On Wu Tang he taught Huo-lung, the master of Chang San-feng. These six masters—Lao-tzu, Yin-hsi, Ma-I, Chen Hsi-I, Huo-lung, and Chang San-feng—are the six saints of the sect of Taoism known as the "Sect of the Hidden Immortals" (*Yin-hsien Pai*), which flourished in the Lo-Shan District of Szechwan Province during the eighteenth century.

The history of tai chi chuan is intimately bound up with this Taoist sect. Chang San-feng is said to have taught on Mount Hua, Wu Tang, and O-Mei both during his lifetime and by either his disciples or apparitions until the 1800s. Just as Taoist masters believe they might be visited by immortal spirits, after the historical Chang San-feng died, they believed that he too became such a spirit. We have records of individuals who met Chang San-feng through a period of more than 500 years! This prompted one emperor to say that Chang San-feng had left his traces "throughout the empire." Why is this spirit cult important to our history? Because according to Abbot Pan Ssu-lin, of Liang Hsien Monastery on Mount Hua, it was a disciple of Chang San-feng from Lo-Shan District who taught Yang Lu Chan (1799–1872), the founder of Yang style tai chi chuan.

As the story goes, Yang was dissatisfied with the tai chi chuan he learned from the Chen family master, Chen Chen-Xing. The unique Yang style of tai chi chuan is not a modification of the Chen family style, but rather a completely different style, the Taoist tai chi chuan called *yu chou* tai chi chuan (universal tai chi chuan). Yang Lu Chan learned this style either directly from Chang San-feng or, much more likely, from a disciple of the Hidden Immortals sect.

According to the Taoists, the history of Chen style is nearly independent of Taoist tai chi chuan. A Buddhist priest who was also an expert at close-range fighting taught the traditional Taoist health exercise *tai chi pa fa* (eight ways of tai chi) to two martial artists, one from Chekiang and one from Shan-hsi. I believe these two can be identified as Yen Chin-chuan and Wang Tsung-yueh.

Yen Chin-chuan was the disciple of Chang Sung-chi, the sixteenth-century proponent of *nei chia chuan* (inner family boxing), a method of military training based on principles similar to tai chi chuan. (This art may also have been developed by Chang San-feng.) Wang Tsung-yueh was the famous boxing instructor of Chenjiagou Village, home of Chen style tai chi chuan. He is not to be confused with Wang Tsung, the twelfth-century disciple of Chang San-feng. Together, Yen Chin-chuan and Wang Tsung-yueh developed the first 108-posture tai chi chuan form

which later became known as Chen family style. In short, the Chen style probably derives from Buddhist Shaolin, *tai chi pa fa*, and the training methods of *nei chia chuan*.

Kenneth Cohen is the director of the Academy of Taoist Healing Arts in Berkeley, California, and Boulder, Colorado. A contributing editor to the Yoga Journal, *Cohen now makes his home in Flushing, New York. This material was published in the November 1991 edition of* Inside Kung-Fu.

The Emperor's Long Fist
Was It Tai Chi's Predecessor?

Dr. David E. Kash

According to one theory, tai tzu chang chuan *emerged
nearly three hundred years before the advent of tai chi chuan.
Today, the ancient art is in the capable hands of Chao Yuh Feng.*

In the year A.D. 960, the first emperor of the Sung dynasty, Chao Kuang Yin (also called Tai Tzu), founded a system of personal health and combat exercises called *tai tzu chang chuan* (great ancestor's long fist). This system covered all aspects of tai chi, Hsing I, and *paqua*, the original internal systems of northern China.

Tai tzu was perfected soon after, and journals in 984 documented the style's effectiveness. This system was further refined by the Chao family, making note of the eight original movements derived from *tai tzu: peng, ni, ji, an, cai, nieh, cho,* and *kao*. The famous Yang Cheng Fu learned this ancient style and forms of long fist, and it commonly became known as tai chi chuan.

Knowledge Survives Destruction

Contrary to popular belief, Chang San-feng was not the actual founder of tai chi chuan. History records

the birth of Chang San-feng in 1247, almost three hundred years *after* Chao Kuang Yin's presence in China. The term *tai chi*, thus, is a generic term coined well before the emperor created the long fist system known as *tai tzu chang chuan*.

Chao Kuang Yin, having a keen interest in the martial arts, is credited in Chinese history with collecting and documenting all available manuscripts on the subject, including those from the Shaolin temple. It is said he stored these manuscripts in his library in a tower behind the temple. When the temple was destroyed, most of the records were lost. Fortunately, the emperor passed on his knowledge of *tai tzu chang chuan*, and today we see the fruits of his labor in Chinese parks and martial arts schools. Most of the Northern systems of martial arts, including all styles of tai chi chuan, have their origin in the emperor's long fist.

General Chen Wang Ting utilized the extensive information available on *tai tzu chang chuan* to create Chen style tai chi in 1618. In 1799, Yang Lu Chan created the Yang style from the Chen style and passed this art on to Yang Cheng Fu, who was famous for his tai chi prowess. This brings us to Chao Yuh Feng, the thirty-fifth-generation descendant and inheritor of the system. A friend of Yang Cheng Fu, he was entrusted with maintaining the integrity of the one-thousand-year-old system.

Born in 1911 in the small town of Wan Hsien, near the San Chang River in the Szechwan Province of western China, Chao Yuh Feng studied his family's style of martial arts and received his tutelage in *wu tang ti pai* from Master Lee So Chien. Chao was appointed captain in the nationalist army under General Chiang Kai Shih and was bestowed the honor of hero after being captured by the Japanese during World War II. In 1949, he moved to Taiwan, Republic of China, and worked for a sugar company as well as teaching tai chi chuan at various community centers.

The Republic of China's T'ai Chi Ch'uan Association appointed Chao director of Yongnian Lin County around 1979. This ministry of education post employs only the highest-level masters practicing the original and traditional tai chi systems. Masters must have more than fifty years' experience in tai chi chuan to qualify for the position. The association is primarily concerned with public health and the promotion of tai chi, including publishing books and journals, to which Chao has contributed extensively. The T'ai Chi Ch'uan Association sponsors culturally enlightening tournaments annually in which directors such as Chao Yuh Feng are honored judges.

Seeing Is Believing

Meeting Chao Yuh Feng during 1983 was not by chance; it resulted from a visit with one of the Orient's most prominent martial arts leaders, Dr. Huang Sien Teh, of the Taipei Kuo Su Association. While discussing with him the martial arts and its growth in America, I requested learning a rare style called *tze men chuan* or *tai tzu chang chuan*. "I will teach you," Dr. Huang replied.

I returned to the United States and continued training with a small group of students at a park in Burbank, California. A few months later, a Chinese master named Chao Yuh Feng approached the class and introduced himself. He said he had spent the previous month observing us. Somehow we could tell his knowledge was great. It was then I realized that he had been sent from Taiwan, although it took me a full year to learn that he was the direct descendant of Emperor Chao Tai Tzu.

At our first meeting, Chao demonstrated an uncanny breathing technique called *nei gong*, developed through two special exercises called *tiao shi wan chi* and *kun yun chuan*. A visiting student was told to place his hands on the master's head. Chao made a high-pitched humming sound and sent the student's hands flying off his head. He was showing how he could reverse his *chi* while controlling the energy.

At the age of seventy-six, Master Chao Yuh Feng displays the flexibility and agility of a man much younger. While demonstrating *gin ji tu li* ("golden rooster" posture), a posture difficult for the most experienced master, he is at ease. His knowledge of practical application is astounding, and on numerous occasions he related specific details to enhance a form's application and function. Master Chao is strict when it comes to perfection of mind, movement, and form; he insists that each move be performed slowly and without error for the student to receive the total benefit of the life-giving energy known as *chi*.

He teaches original *chi kung* and *nei gong* exercises which date to Emperor Chao. Performed with relaxed intention, they create a circuit of energy which produces first heat, then *chi*. When the exercises are properly performed, one realizes the eight secret words, or postures, necessary for mastery. This system of *tai tzu chang chuan* is simple, with the preparatory exercises designed for internal strengthening and protection.

The pure eight moves develop into eight characteristically different energies. From these eight movements, Chao has developed a sixty-four-movement form called *tai tzu chuang*, which connects all moves and utilizes the four directions and eight gates.

Simple as this may seem, only through years of study can the practitioner hope to master the system's profound secrets. The system contains a depth of knowledge and understanding of life through the forces of nature. And through it all, one realizes that just one pure move can replace a host of ineffective moves. Chao Yuh Feng's message likewise is simple yet profound:

Walk on clouds. Sit like a bell. Lie like a bow.

David Kash is a tai tzu chang chuan *practitioner based in southern California. This was his first contribution to* Inside Kung-Fu *and appeared in the December 1987 edition.*

Yang Family Tai Chi Chuan

Scott M. Rodell

Yang Lu Chan is the most well known Chinese martial artist in the tai chi world. The story of his obtaining the secret art of tai chi chuan in the remote village of Chenjiagou and his fame as "Yang the Unbeatable" are common legends among tai chi players the world over. The art he created—Yang style tai chi chuan—is the most popular form in the world today and is practiced around the globe. What is surprising is that he made a little-known Chinese family art into a common exercise practice in America in less than one hundred years.

The familiar story of Yang Lu Chan's being challenged by the emperor's head guard gave him lasting fame overnight. In the conflict, he stood in a no-win situation: To lose would mean instant obscurity; to win would meant that the Imperial Guard would someday make his family pay. The master reasoned that the only way to preserve his reputation as "unbeatable," yet avoid retribution, was to fight to a stalemate. To do this, Yang felt, a fighter's skill must be three times greater than his opponent's. History records that the bout did indeed end in a draw.

Two Yang Styles

There was still another major obstacle in Yang Lu Chan's path. The Imperial family decided Yang would teach them his art. Today it may be difficult to see how this created a problem for the master, but China's rulers at the time were Manchus from the north. The Chinese thought of them as invaders and outsiders. With patriotism in mind, Yang did not want to give his art to outsiders.

Yet, an emperor's wish is dangerous to deny. So, Yang Lu Chan created a new Yang style similar in posture to the Chen family's style, but devoid of many parts of his personal style. This was the beginning of what we now know as the *mi chuan* (hidden tradition) or *lao* (old) Yang style and the *zin* (new) Yang style. One style was kept within the family, and the other was open to the public.

Later, when Yang Lu Chan's sons, Chien-ho and Ban-ho, and grandson Cheng Fu began to teach all Chinese, they secretly continued this two-form tradition out of necessity; if the Imperial family were to learn of Yang Lu Chan's earlier deception, trouble would soon arrive.

Many martial artists (particularly non-Yang stylists) claim that the new Yang style is useless, and that

Yang Lu Chan purposely made it so. This claim is without basis, as even a quick review of Chinese martial history and contemporary masters shows.

Yang Lu Chan's grandson, Yang Cheng Fu, never studied the older *mi chuan* form, yet he was well known as a skilled boxer. Many of Cheng Fu's students, notably Chen Wei Ming and Cheng Man Ch'ing, are tai chi legends today. And America's most well known exponent of tai chi chuan's martial component, William C. C. Chen, studied the new Yang style form exclusively, learning only the *mi chuan* push-hands from Wang Yen-nien.

The Old Form

So, what remains of the Yang tradition, and what does the *mi chuan* form hold that the new form lacks? Amazingly, the *mi chuan* part of the Yang style came within one teacher of extinction. The story of its preservation is typical of the twists and turns of Chinese martial history.

Yang Lu Chan had long been dead when his son Chien-ho decided to pass the secret art outside the family for the first time. In that era, reputations were made through challenges, not workshops. Yang Chien-ho fought with a master from the *zi ran men* (natural style school), DuXing-wu, which ended in a draw. A student of Du decided to challenge the Yang family for his teacher. This student, WanXing-wu, was fast becoming known in China for his successful challenges.

When Wan arrived at the Yang family training center, the students inside were all concerned that they would be called on to face this challenger. As they stood in the courtyard looking at each other, Zhang Qin-lin spoke up. "Oĸ, I'll go see what Wan wants," he said.

To everyone's amazement, Zhang returned in a few minutes unhurt. Wan was gone. Zhang told them Wan had "asked for a lesson so he could learn of the Yang style" (the polite way of issuing a challenge), to which Zhang agreed. Knowing that the *zi ran men*

fighters were particularly good with their feet, Zhang was on his guard when Wan began with a right kick. Zhang swept it to the side and threw his punch into the opening. Wan immediately threw a strike, and their hands collided. Wan stopped and shouted, "*Gao ming*" (great). Zhang assumed Wan's wrist had been so badly hurt that he could not continue.

Zhang's Training

At the time, Zhang had been studying the new Yang style with Yang Cheng Fu. Chien-ho, having seen Zhang's loyalty and love of his teacher, called him into his personal quarters to look him over. Chien-ho noted that Zhang truly had the body of a martial artist. He was short and heavy, with hands and feet that were twice as big as normal. He had ventured to the Yang family's home at the age of fourteen after his parents' death to pursue his love of martial arts. Chien-ho decided to secretly teach Zhang the *mi chuan* form, which never before had been seen outside the Yang family.

Zhang Qin-lin later become famous by winning the All China Fighting Championships in 1929 in the unarmed division. T. T. Liang (Cheng Man Ching's senior student) described Zhang as having amazing abilities. During World War II, Cheng ran into Zhang in Nanjing. They had both studied under Yang Cheng Fu, and the younger Cheng, wanting to test himself, challenged Zhang to push-hands.

Liang described the encounter with a wave of his hand, "Zhang just pushed him down." The story goes that Cheng bowed to Zhang and then studied push-hands with him for nine months. In the end, Cheng challenged Zhang to a fight and was knocked out.

Mountain Strength

What made Zhang so strong? Liang said, "He learned something in the mountains from a Taoist." It was Zhang's Taoist beliefs that led him to choose a docile life instead of one teaching martial arts. In all, Zhang taught only seven students (Cheng Man Ching, Wang Shan-zhi, and Li Yunlong of Hebei, and Liu Yao-zhen, Liu Zhi-liang, Su Qi-geng, and Wang Yen-nien of Shan-hsi). Of these seven, only two remain alive. And only Wang Yen-nien, living in Taiwan, teaches the *mi chuan* form.

Wang studied with Zhang only after he received an introduction from his father, who was studying Taoist meditation at the same *Tao Guan* (Taoist study center) as Zhang. Today at seventy-six, Wang is the last and youngest of Zhang's students. No one knows what became of Zhang Qin-lin.

Scott Rodell competed with the U.S. team at the International T'ai Chi Ch'uan Tournament in Taiwan, placing second in the push-hands division. He currently teaches both new and mi chuan *Yang family tai chi chuan and Taoist meditation at the Great River Taoist Center in Washington, D.C., and Baltimore, and recently taught in Russia and Estonia at the request of the Soviet Wushu Federation. This material appeared in the March 1993 edition of* Inside Kung-Fu *magazine.*

Tai Chi's Secret Weapon
Tranquillity

Bob Mendel

The fluid, sinuous movements of tai chi chuan are almost hypnotic, like the swaying of a king cobra in the sunlight. The hands and arms moving evenly, as though drawing silk thread from a cocoon, forming graceful, curving lines in space.

The legs shift body weight back and forth evenly, in the alternating rhythm of surf pounding on the beach. But hidden within the flowing movement is a series of individual forms that make up a sophisticated art of self-defense: strike, parry, punch, and kick.

Of the millions of people around the world who practice tai chi chuan today, the number who know it as a self-defense system is relatively small, and those who can teach its application are fewer still. One teacher who does is Kai Ying Tung, third-generation master of the art.

Using Stillness to Contain Movement

Born in Peking (Beijing), Master Tung began his own practice at the age of eight, taught by his grandfather, Tung Ying Chieh. At seventeen, Tung began teaching, and today, at thirty-five, he continues to teach his family's system here in the United States. The Tung family system, passed down from Master Yang, has always included self-defense, since tai chi chuan is a martial art "by mere definition," says Tung.

We're sitting in a coffee shop on a sunny Saturday morning several blocks from Master Tung's studio in Los Angeles. Tung has taught in the United States for the past seven years, prior to that traveling and teaching in Hong Kong and Southeast Asia. What is it, we ask, that makes tai chi chuan unique among martial arts? "The use of stillness to contain movement," answers Master Tung. "You wait for the other person to move, and you use the other person's force. So, you are using stillness to contain movement."

Tung emphasizes that the word *waiting* is misleading. In tai chi chuan, you don't wait for attack and then react. The idea is to anticipate the opponent. "When they want to move, you sense it and move faster," says Tung, "as though you hear their movement and move first." A simple description to sum up the goal of tai chi chuan self-defense. But it also calls for an extraordinary combination of sensitivity and speed, and the ability to act decisively. This is the goal of all martial arts systems.

In the feudal society of old Japan, the *bushi* who trained for the life of the warrior made *zazen* meditation an integral part of his practice. The reason? He sought a state called *mushin no shin* ("no mind attitude"), which permits one to act spontaneously when confronting attack. Advanced stages of kung-fu and karate systems also deal with perception and stillness. What makes tai chi chuan unique is that despite its reputation for slow development of the student, it is a very direct and simple way toward stillness and its use in containing movement. Tai chi chuan is called a "moving meditation" because it begins by stressing tranquillity in the midst of movement. And it does the same in the face of attack. The *T'ai Chi Classics* say: "If he does not move, I do not move. At his slightest stir, I have anticipated it and move first."

Push-Hands Practice Builds Relaxation

How does tai chi make this possible, we ask Master Tung. "When you are relaxed you can move faster," he says, "and you can tell what your opponent is going to do more easily. It's also important to be relaxed because you feel better. Many movements in tai chi chuan help the student loosen up. The pushing movements help limber up the wrists. When you do tai chi chuan, you should be relaxed but not limp. It is relaxed with energy. This is softness on the out-

side but energy or hardness within—like an iron bar wrapped in cotton."

To cultivate relaxed energy when facing an opponent, tai chi chuan uses the exercise called *tuo shou*, or push-hands. In push-hands practice, students pair up, in rows or a line, and circle their hands in a pattern, each sensing the partner's balance, energy, and movement. At first glance, push-hands practice doesn't look like practical training for self-defense.

"Some people don't know the value of push-hands," admits Tung, "and they think that if you're sparring with someone from another school, or in self-defense, the opponent would not use the push-hands form. But that's not the point. If the opponent does not make contact with you, there is no real danger. If there is contact, then it is the same as push-hands."

Tung sees many students who try to rush their progress in this part of tai chi chuan training. "The way to practice correctly is not to try to push too soon, although most people do. It's better to spend six months just circling the hands until there is real smoothness in your movements," he says. Tung also sees other problems with pushing early. "It makes the student too tight," he says, "rather than relaxing him and loosening him up. The same is true with sparring too early. When you spar you get away from the forms and just fight. When you do that, you don't use the forms and learn the principles behind the movements. It's better to wait longer and understand tai chi and the forms in more depth."

Balance Through Alternating Yin and Yang

Master Tung suggests even more patience, along the lines of what tai chi chuan often calls investing in loss. "In push-hands most people want to win," says Tung, "but you shouldn't worry about that in practice. If they push you, you learn more. If you don't look at it that way, it will be hard for you to be good in tai chi later." Push-hands practice itself requires a foundation in posture. Tung says simply, "You can't do push-hands if you're off balance when you move."

Balance is what tai chi chuan is all about, and what makes it a uniquely Taoist art is the alternation of yang and yin, as substantial and insubstantial. This shifting of weight smoothly is learned gradually, through the slow and careful repetition of the eighty-one-movement slow set in the Yang system. The various postures strengthen the legs, build balance, and circulate the *chi* through the body. According to tai chi chuan tradition, the energy is "rooted in the feet, develops in the legs, is directed by the waist, and moves up in the fingers."

These individual forms of the slow set serve as a foundation for push-hands practice in another way. The original movements of tai chi were thirteen in number, corresponding to the eight directions and eight trigrams of the I-Ching, plus the Five Elements. These basic postures are woven into the continuous patterns of push-hands. And just as in the slow set, in movement, double-weighting is always avoided. "You're able to move faster," explains Master Tung, "with your weight on one leg rather than two. All the movements in tai chi chuan are partially solid and partially empty."

This alternation of solid and empty, soft and hard, is part of the Taoist tradition in which the art came into being. The story is well known, of the sage Chang San-feng observing the battle of a snake and a bird, the snake's elusive movement illustrating the Taoist principle of yielding to force. Tai chi chuan attracts much interest in the yielding. Yielding and absorbing the momentum of attack, yielding and deflecting a thousand pounds with a trigger force of four ounces, yielding and bending and then snapping back.

Cultivating Force, Extending the *Chi*

But what kind of force is used in the snapping back? Does tai chi chuan use only "four ounces" of force?

we ask. "The idea of four ounces of strength refers only to deflecting the attack to ward off the opponent," says Tung. "Otherwise, you use as much force as possible."

Tai chi chuan cultivates more than one kind of force, claims Tung, noting that there is "a long power, where the movement extends outward for a long way. There is short power, like an explosive burst. There is attaching power, lifting power—all based in *chi*." Tung adds, "You should know yourself and your own power. And you may know other people, how much they have. But if they don't know you, it's better."

Although tai chi power is based in *chi* and stresses circulation of this energy by relaxation and an erect posture, Tung doesn't believe in teaching exercises to build *chi*. "There is no need to focus on building chi," he says, "because it is there. Tai chi chuan focuses on what you do with it." Master Tung points out that as students develop in training, they find freedom in the forms. He says, "In the beginning, you have to think about doing the form—Is it correct? Later, you don't have to do that; it's just *chi*. Then you can extend the *chi* outward, beyond the movement.

This is similar in a way to weapons training because weapons are essentially an extension of the hand. We teach the knife, sword, and staff, each being a different length and requiring different focus. You can look at the length of a sword as being about the same distance as you might extend your *chi* without it. But in using weapons, you focus only on the tip of the weapon; with empty hand movements, you can extend the *chi* beyond the hand."

Tung Family Tradition

The stress on use of the *chi* is also found in kung-fu systems, but rarely is it at the heart of training, as in the internal systems, and this fact made tai chi chuan a departure from existing martial arts at its founding. The stress on toning the inner organ systems for balanced energy and basic health and vitality was an intrinsic part of Taoist yoga tradition, with which Chang San-feng, the founder, was known to be well versed.

According to accounts, the art was preserved by Chang San-feng's students and then by the Chen family in Henan, who kept the techniques a secret within the family for generations. Eventually a man named Yang Lu Chan heard rumors of the art and worked his way into the Chen household to learn it. He was discovered, but his skill was so great that the Chen family taught him willingly.

Yang Lu Chan then went to Peking, where he was called "Yang the Unsurpassed" for his fighting skill, and taught tai chi chuan. Yang's two sons continued to teach, and their sons in turn continued the system, now known as Yang style. Among the pupils of Yang's grandson was Tung Ying Chieh, who came to be known for his writing on tai chi and for developing a fast set complementing the Yang style. This was Kai Ying Tung's grandfather, and the fast set is taught as part of the Tung family tradition.

The Tung family fast set gives the student a chance to feel something of the self-defense application of the slow set forms and to develop a sense of issuing energy. The fast set is based on the Yang style slow set but executed briskly, more compactly, and

with energy. Tung likes to see the fast set done with spirit, moving, breathing, sweating, but always in balance, centered and controlled, because it is in the midst of this movement that tai chi chuan seeks stillness.

To be able to use stillness as a tool, either in confronting an opponent or in everyday life, we must become familiar with it. So, tai chi chuan is, says Master Tung, truly an exercise of the mind. Master Tung stresses concentration, and attention on the forms, whether it be fast set or slow, beginner or advanced student. Attention and care in details of execution are encouraged to the limit of the student's ability. Tung's traditional approach to tai chi chuan reflects the search for inner stillness at the heart of Asian philosophy and experience. As reasonable and pragmatic as any modern style, and unlike some of them, it offers a sense of balance and completeness.

This material was published in the December 1976 edition of Inside Kung-Fu *magazine.*

The Quest for *Chi*

Lawrence Tan

The quest. What was the philosophers' stone to early alchemists, or the Holy Grail to knights of the Round Table, is *chi* to many serious martial artists. *Chi*, that mysterious energy with almost magical qualities, is one of the highest goals for dedicated practitioners to attain—few ever succeed.

The Wonders of *Chi*

To cultivate *chi* means to transcend the physical limitations of the body and to pierce into a rarefied realm that goes beyond the five senses to develop keen intuitive powers; consequently, it means the ability to achieve superhuman feats impossible through ordinary training.

Amid the oral traditions of many martial arts are numerous tales that describe the wonders of *chi*. Defensively, *chi* can be willed to almost any part of the body to make it impervious to injury or pain from powerful hand and foot blows—some believe, even against bladed weapons. Offensively, *chi* can be directed to inflict tremendous injury seemingly by a mere touch —it's even said injury can be inflicted without bodily contact! Such colorful claims, stretching from the astonishing but credible to the further limits of the imagination that most would regard as sheer fantasy, provide mystique to the art and, no doubt, appeal to our thirst for the exotic and esoteric.

The Reality of *Chi*

What is *chi*? The Chinese term can be translated to mean "breath," "air," "gas," and the like, but it is also a metaphysical notion that means "cosmic energy" or "intrinsic force" that, according to Chinese philosophy, pervades the universe comprising Heaven, Earth, and Man.

Chi is usually related to internal systems or inner styles, in contrast to external systems or outer styles.

This dichotomy is a traditional method of categorizing systems, based not so much on differences in techniques, since they are essentially similar, but rather in the way of executing the technique and generating power. Internal systems rely on *chi*, while external systems utilize muscular or brute strength. Proponents of internal systems claim they are superior, though more difficult to master than external, since the practitioner is not subject to the limitations of personal physique for power. A skinny, smaller person can deliver as devastating a force as a stronger, larger one who otherwise would win out of sheer size and brute strength.

As a philosophical concept, *chi* is not unique to East Asian philosophy; it is found in other world philosophies: in Hinduism it is similar to *prana*, in Greek thought it is like *pneuma*, and in Judaism it is *ruakh*. Although Greek and Hebrew thought—which lay the foundation for Western civilization—have similar concepts, *chi* is not readily accepted by many Westerners, who may regard it to be superstition or, at best, scientifically unvalidated.

In terms of traditional marital arts, however, *chi* is a reality. This intrinsic energy as it is related to the Chinese martial arts is a psychological and physical force that is a combination of breath and blood circulation, and the mind. There also may be a relationship to adrenaline and the central nervous system. What particular combinations of these elements make *chi* or what it is exactly in scientific jargon is unknown. This vague definition is one reason why this notion often has not been taken seriously by the Western empirical mind.

As elusive as *chi* is to define, it is even more elusive to attain—if it does in fact exist. In the contemporary martial arts world, those who have supposedly nurtured *chi* to a significant degree are a rare anomaly. Still, the inevitable stories circulate of "old masters" in hiding who perform amazing feats like extinguishing a burning candle from a distance of ten feet by using their *chi*. Unfortunately, few people have actually witnessed these deeds, and what

reaches our ears is usually an exaggerated version of an eyewitness report from a "friend of a friend of a friend" who is the cousin of the "old master's" sister-in-law.

Then there are the "circus stunts"—breaking cement blocks on the body of someone lying on a bed of nails, or breaking bricks or ice with a soft strike. While these have been passed off as genuine demonstrations of *chi*, many are simply stunts that do not require any internal powers and can be explained by ordinary physics (such as the bed-of-nails stunt, which was performed by muscle men in the West who had never heard of *chi*). Still other so-called feats of *chi* have been specially "prepared" prior to the demonstration (such as tampering with ice or bricks so that they would break at a soft strike). The majority of these demonstrations often are not viewed critically by the audience; the viewer's secret desire to believe abets in the credibility of these bogus demonstrations.

Even in ancient dynasties, when China's military training was at its zenith, *chi*, or inner strength, was not very common. Thus, the average warrior was also awed by the stories of martial feats achieved through the powers of *chi*. Often, truly devoted warriors, dissatisfied with their achievements and wanting to explore further frontiers of the mental and physical aspects of the fighting arts, sought to cultivate intrinsic energy. To do so, they first sought teachers—monks or retired military experts—who forsook the world of men to return to nature. These personages had become recluses and had left behind only their names and the records of their heroic exploits or legendary feats of skill.

Enticed by stories of these extraordinary masters who knew the secrets of *chi*, fighters traveled the rugged terrains and seldom-traversed paths up to mountaintops bathed in mist seeking a Taoist or Buddhist temple hugging a cliff, or perhaps a small hut swallowed up by the vast landscape, or even a secluded cave that had become the abode of such a master. Here the seeker stayed with the master to study—if he was accepted as a disciple, and only after he had proved his sincerity.

Romance and Mastery

In my quest to find *chi*, I went to Hong Kong. Instead of trekking up to mountaintops bathed in mist to find a master, I ascended to the roof of an apartment building. I seemed to have transcended both the magnificence and squalor of one of the world's most crowded cities. Here I could see the clear blue sky, the mountains of Hong Kong, and the harbor with ancient junks and modern ships side by side—a sight one is apt to miss in the bustling streets below.

In a sense, this master's rooftop abode was similar to a mountain retreat. The walls were lined with potted plants, trees, flowers, and a weapons rack. There was the sound of chirping birds in cages, and two huge German shepherds wandered around. A diagram of the *baguazhang* was painted on the floor. I entered a small room with calligraphy and paintings hanging on the walls between shelves filled with books. Here I met a smiling Chan Yick Yan, who dwells in this rooftop apartment and is a master of *chi*.

Master Chan appeared to epitomize the romantic version of a master: kind, learned, humble, and wise. I was especially honored to be able to see him, since up to then, he had refused to be interviewed by Hong Kong's leading martial arts magazines. He answered our questions simply yet thoroughly without bragging about his style or overwhelming us with his knowledge, as seemed to be a habit of so many so-called masters. Occasionally, when words were inadequate for explaining detailed points or subtle theories, he demonstrated on me. A day earlier, Kam Tung, one of Chan's favorite disciples, also demonstrated some of their style's techniques, and I was fairly impressed with his abilities. But this time, I was truly amazed.

Now that I could compare the movements of a top disciple with those of the master himself, I was able to "feel" the difference between one who is highly skilled in a system and one who has mastered the system. While both Kam Tung and Chan Yick Yan's blocking and striking hand techniques were precise and deft, a gulf separated them. Master Chan's motions were impeccable and by far more polished. When he blocked my punches, I could not detect any muscular force (which at times was apparent with some of Kam Tung's powerful blocks), and my blows seemed to simply fall short of their targets; evidently Chan was using the barest amount of energy to deflect them. When his arms, which seemed acutely sensitive to all my motions, came in contact with mine, they seemed to stick, so that I was unable to penetrate his defense to hit his head or body.

Throughout this free-flow exchange of techniques, his hands and arms remained relaxed and soft, yet when they rested on or followed my arms, they felt heavy. I was aware of the tremendous latent power which he seemed to be able to explode through his arms; fortunately for me, he unleashed this force only occasionally (and lightly, at that) against my shoulders.

As if Chan were aware of my doubts, he told me to punch again. This time I "cheated" a bit—for the sake of scientific inquiry, of course—and used a tiger claw thrust instead of a clenched fist. This way, perhaps I could get a better "feel" of what was going on. After thrusting, I grabbed at his flesh; it definitely was not hard, tensed muscle. In fact, the sense was more like clutching fat. Then suddenly a surging force erupted from the depths of Chan's stomach, and my tiger claw came flying out like a missile.

Before I got over my amazement, Master Chan, using both of his hands, held my forearm and pulled my tiger claw into his *dan tian* region. A bubbling-out type of force was generated against my tiger claw (again holding on to his flesh). Chan regulated the duration and intensity of the force: light, light, strong, medium, strong, and so on. My arm felt as if it would be bouncing in and out like someone on a trampoline were his hands not holding it into his stomach.

Finally the spastic spurts became a strong, steady surge of force that pressed against my tiger claw. Because his hands prevented my hand from coming out of his stomach, the pressure on my bent wrist was tremendous. Had he not released my arm—when he noticed my pain—I believe my wrist would have been sprained or perhaps even broken. He smiled warmly and massaged my wrist. My skepticism was appeased.

This last demonstration of *chi* established that Master Chan had achieved an advanced level of internal strength that surpassed the "receiving" energy stage. Known as the "returning" energy level, this is the ability to return the same amount of energy that the attacker expends on his attack; in other words, if the attacker hits you with 200 pounds of force, his fist would automatically bounce out with 200 pounds of force. At this "returning" energy level, all self-defense motions of attack or defense are thoroughly unconscious; they are expressed by the body instinctively without premeditation. At this stage, when the *chi* is strong and "in tune" with the external environment, the body will spontaneously and naturally respond to the external stimuli.

Toward Spiritual Development

Having reached such levels, one has little to worry about as far as self-defense and fighting is concerned, but does that mean one's quest has ended? If this were so, many masters like Chan would have forsaken the art long ago.

On the contrary, the quest has no more ended for them than the quest for knowledge has ended for someone who receives a doctorate degree. In fact, reaching this level means the real journey has begun.

This is because seeking perfection in the martial arts is only a microcosm of perfecting one's self. Finding a master, cultivating *chi*, and learning to harness its power for individual combat are considered phases in the endless process of developing the self.

It is true that in the beginning the quest for *chi* is usually directed toward less lofty goals such as perfecting fighting skills. However, once this basic need for self-preservation, or self-protection, is fulfilled and one has achieved confidence, a sense of well-being, and health, one does not have to dwell on the lower aspects of the self. The energies previously devoted to physical well-being through self-defense can instead be channeled to higher elements of one's self; at this point, one seeks spiritual development.

Having attained fighting proficiency with one's *chi*—assuming the equivalent degree of insight and maturity on the mental level—one realizes that the search for *chi* within a fighting context has limitations. Hence, the concern is no longer with conquering the enemy; one is now concerned with conquering one's self—for one's true enemy is *within*. The search for *chi* in the martial arts context should bring the student to such an insight at an appropriate point along the path of development. In essence, the martial ways of utilizing *chi* are only a temporary vehicle to find and reach the spiritual ways of *chi*.

For Master Chan, daily practice is no longer aimed at fighting—he long ago fulfilled that lower need of his self—but rather is used as spiritual exercise that has become a way of life. Practicing internal forms is to be meditating in motion.

When Chan is doing a form, he relaxes his mind and body; his breath is slow, deep and rhythmic; and he centers himself—his ego is forgotten, and his mundane cares drift away. He is peaceful, just as if he were doing seated meditation, but he is moving. *Chi* permeates his body and pours out into the universe where it flows between Heaven, Earth, and Man and then returns to him, in a cyclical give-and-take exchange of the "life force." During this active meditation, in a sense, Master Chan is dancing with the universe and playing with the energy of the cosmos. He is balanced on the edge.

To the initiated, the alchemists' quest for the philosophers' stone was not for the sole purpose of converting base metals into gold (as our grade-school chemistry books misinformed us), but was instead a symbolic term for the alchemist's search for spiritual transformation. Similarly, the knights' search for Holy Grail was, in fact, a spiritual expedition. So too, the quest for *chi* is undertaken not only for the purpose of developing energy to beat the hell out of somebody, but also for the martial artist's spiritual growth. Chan Yick Yen has attained astonishing skills with his *chi*, but to him, his journey has just begun: he can use his *chi* to conquer an enemy, but now he must use it to cultivate himself spiritually.

This material appeared in the August 1976 edition of Inside Kung-Fu *magazine.*

6

A Contrast Between *Wushu* and Traditional Tai Chi

Jane Hallander

The most popular tai chi style in the world today is Yang. Coming originally from the Yang family in China, this style gets its popularity from its large circular movements that are guaranteed to improve your health. Unlike the martial art–oriented Chen style, anyone of any age can practice Yang tai chi and benefit from it.

Although many different so-called Yang forms exist, only one is the actual Yang family form. Known as the long form, or 108-movement form, this is the only tai chi sequence the Yang family taught. The small-circle form was simply an advanced way of doing the original sequence.

That 108 form is known in today's China as the 88 form. However, while the sequences of the 108 and 88 forms are very close, there the resemblance ends. The 108 form is traditional Yang tai chi, practiced the original way by Yang stylists in China and elsewhere. The 88 form is a contemporary way to interpret Yang tai chi, practiced as a competitive *wushu* art or strictly for health purposes.

Simplification by Decree

China's government-run Physical Education Department decided to shorten, or simplify, the traditional Yang family form. Thinking the 108-movement form was too long, with many movements repeated, they came up with a five-minute-long, 24-movement form. This they made into a government-standardized tai chi form that could be taught to anyone.

The 24, or short form, became so popular that *wushu* tournaments adopted it as their Yang competition form. However, people soon wanted something longer than just five minutes, so the government again put its twenty-to-thirty-minute version of the 108 Yang long form in its tai chi curriculum. The

24-movement short form stayed on as a *wushu* competition form and the most widely taught tai chi form in China.

Tradition and Application Versus Health and Competition

Anyone who competes in or judges tai chi tournaments will notice a big difference between competitors who do the traditional form and those with *wushu* background. Los Angeles tai chi instructor Wen-Mei Yu knows firsthand why *wushu* and traditional practitioners vary so much in their interpretations of the Yang tai chi form.

"Basically, *wushu* stylists who use the short form or 88-movement form are never taught any applications to their tai chi movements. *Wushu* tai chi is taught only for health and competition. Every movement is designed to be easy by anyone to learn in a very short amount of time," she explains.

While Wen-Mei Yu has done both types of Yang tai chi, her primary training comes from some of China's top traditional tai chi masters. Originally from Shanghai, Yu learned her Yang tai chi directly from Fu Zhong Wen, nephew of Yang Cheng Fu, the grandson of Yang tai chi's founder. She was voted China's top tai chi coach by a panel of her peers and has won first place many times in tai chi forms and sword divisions in traditional and *wushu* tournaments in her native Shanghai, an area that contains many of China's best tai chi competitors. She has spent most of her life learning, competing in, and teaching tai chi.

According to Yu, the differences between *wushu* and traditional Yang tai chi are most notable in the weight distribution and footwork. For instance, when moving forward into the common "bow" stance, where the weight is distributed 70 percent on the front leg and 30 on the rear, *wushu* stylists who do the 88 form are taught to lean back before pivoting the forward heel 45 degrees to the outside. Traditionalists either don't move the weight back at all or shift back no farther than about an inch.

Because they carry their body weight slowly over one leg at a time in low stances, traditional Yang stylists build impressive strength in their legs. Those who practice the 88 form stand much more upright, taking shorter steps. While much easier, it never develops the kind of strength needed for martial arts or more rigorous sports.

Remember, tai chi was originally, and still is with some teachers, taught for martial arts purposes as well as for health. However, the government of today's China rejects the fighting aspects of most martial arts. Only recently have traditional tai chi and other Chinese martial arts made a comeback in China. Since the original tai chi body actions were designed for martial applications, government *wushu* coaches, who cannot teach those applications, change the form to achieve similar body movements.

Shortcutting the Learning Curve

One of the principles of correct tai chi practice is that the waist and hips carry or propel the hands. In other words, the hands don't move independently of the body. Maximum relaxed power comes from the hips, not just the arms and shoulders. For example, in the "brush knee" movement, the forward pushing hand should be pushing directly in front of the body's midline. You can achieve this position by either placing the arm in front of your nose, or turning your waist and hips to the opposite side of the pushing hand. Turning the waist is correct: if you're pushing with the right hand, the waist turns to the left. Simply moving the right hand over to your centerline is incorrect.

For the average person, it usually takes considerable practice and experience to learn correct waist flexibility. *Wushu* tai chi stylists shortcut practice and experience by shifting their weight completely off the forward leg as they initiate the "brush knee and twist" movement, looking 90 degrees to the side of the pushing arm. This makes it easy to turn the waist in the opposite direction as they complete the "brush knee" movement.

Those who practice the traditional 108 form barely shift back and turn no farther than 45 degrees to the side when starting "brush knee." As they finish, they unwind and turn the waist back the other way. *Wushu*'s exaggerated turning and looking 90 degrees, or even backward, as in "repulse the monkey," also helps a novice learn to relax the hips—another must of correct tai chi practice.

The hips should always be relaxed, meaning they collapse slightly inward, rather than protruding forward. Again, this takes time to develop—unless you cheat by changing the form movements enough to force the body into the correct position. Before you run out to make easy changes, remember that by cheating, you lose the meaning and applications of the tai chi form.

Traditional Yang stylists look forward when doing "repulse the monkey"—that's where the opponent is located. Looking back to make it easier to turn the waist and relax the hips is a good way to learn if you don't have much time to practice and care only for the health benefits.

Another example of correct waist and hip movement is seen in the "single whip" movement from the traditional 108 form. As the hands are drawn back before forming the whip position, they make a level circle caused by waist rotation. In the 88 form, the hands operate independently from the body, making two separate, meaningless circles as they form the whip and push outward.

The "bird's tail" posture also looks very different in the two forms. In the 108, "ward off," the first position, is formed with the left hand about eight inches behind the right hand —acting as a protective hand behind the blocking right hand. "Ward off" in the 88 has the left hand down by the hip as if it had no use. Lack of knowledge of the application causes incorrect form like this.

A final example is "needle at sea bottom," a wrist-locking technique. It is formed traditionally by using waist and hip action to lift the hand, prior to the actual joint lock. In the application, this lifting helps pin the opponent's grabbing hand in place. Since *wushu* tai chi lacks applications, there's no hip rotation. *Wushu* stylists simply turn to the side and raise the hand to the ear, simulating the position from traditional tai chi.

Because *wushu* stylists and coaches do not learn the applications of form movements, they must use exaggerated body movements to obtain look-alike postures. Those who do know the actual applications also know that Yang tai chi fighting applications look like the form movements.

No End in Sight?

There are no secrets in authentic traditional Yang tai chi. "If you understand what you are doing, every time you practice the 108 form, you are also practicing self-defense movements," says Wen-Mei Yu.

Even the completion of each movement differs between the 88 and 108 versions. According to Yu and other Yang tai chi experts, traditional Yang tai chi positions all end with a slight pause at the imaginary point of contact with the opponent. You may not notice this end point, because good Yang practitioners look beyond their hands. Although the hand and body motion stops, vision continues onward, making the motion appear continuous.

Those who practice *wushu* tai chi run their movements together. There is no imaginary point of contact. Each movement is taken up to a point of completion but is never ended—just run continuously into the next position.

Obviously, if you want a martial art, you shouldn't look toward *wushu* Yang tai chi. Even those who want tai chi for health only will probably find traditional Yang tai chi better for them. It's more difficult than *wushu*'s 88 form, which makes the body stronger and healthier.

This material appeared as "Wu Shu vs. Traditional Tai Chi: A Contrast Between China's Two Major Martial Arts" in the Spring 1994 edition of Inside Martial Arts *magazine.*

A Comparison of Yang and Chen Styles

Kenneth Cohen

The ancient practice of Chen style tai chi chuan is beginning to generate considerable excitement within the martial arts community. Longtime proponents of the style point to three reasons for its resurgence: the changing political climate in China, which now allows Chen style to flourish and welcomes Americans eager to study the art; new access to information about this style through knowledgeable instructors such as Adam Hsu, Hus Ku-ming, and B. P. Chan; and the belief that Chen style is the signature fighting style of tai chi chuan and is most applicable in self-defense situations.

While Chen style is an excellent system for self-defense, utilizing low stances, a variety of movements, and a precise method of generating power, it is certainly not the only tai chi style with applications in battle situations.

Numerous stories record the prowess of the early Yang family members. It's reported that Yang Lu Chan once asked a man to grab the end of his spear. With a slight movement of his waist, Yang cat-apulted the man onto a rooftop. In another account, Lu Chan's son Yang Chien-ho is said to have once rested his palm lightly on a student's shoulder. The student mysteriously collapsed in a heap.

In more recent times, Yang style tai chi chuan master William Chen has demonstrated his "inner power" by taking full-force punches and kicks to his torso. In the 1950s, in Taiwan, Chen became one of the first tai chi chuan masters to win a full contact inter-Asian tournament. Nor should such examples of Yang style self-defense be taken as exceptions. There are probably as many proficient martial artists in Yang style as in Chen or Wu style.

Common Principles

All styles of tai chi chuan share common principles of self-defense. For one, any movement in the tai chi chuan solo exercise should have a clear line of power, integrating a shifting of the weight, turning of the waist, and relaxed breath. Tai chi chuan is characterized as *yao nu li* (waist, leg strength) as opposed to the *shou li* (arm, hand strength) so common in other styles.

In the Yang style, the body leads, and the arms follow the turn of the waist. In the Chen system, there also is a form in which the hands lead the body, as though the body is pulled and turned by the force of the strike. Regardless, in both styles, the waist and lower back play the central role. In all tai chu chuan styles, the whole body attacks. Thus, the stances are fluid, adapting to the situation and following no fixed pattern.

Tai chi chuan practitioners defend themselves by *hua* (neutralizing, blending) with an opponent's force. One moves out of the way, allowing the opponent to fall into the counterattack. And all tai chi chuan stylists practice *chan* (adhering) to the attacker, staying in close to control the opponent's balance and to better sense the next move.

Don't confuse the speed and aggressiveness of a form with its applicability. Practicing a form is never the same as usage. One becomes a good fighter only by practicing single movements at full speed in realistic situations. The by-product is proper timing, footwork, power, and the relaxed attitude that allows for quick reaction. The tai chi chuan form is merely a possible repertoire of techniques and a training in the principles of efficient, effective motion. The form provides a vocabulary, but it is up to the student to create various sentences in the self-defense situation.

Yin Versus Yang

In fact, Yang style has certain self-defense advantages over the Chen style. An important principle of Yang style is "from slowness comes speed; from weakness, strength." The extreme slowness of the Yang form develops a high level of balance and control and helps you sense where you are tensing inappropriate muscle groups—such as raising the shoulder when punching, or tensing the neck and face when kicking. Excess tension reduces speed and power in a martial art strike.

In one a tai chi chuan self-defense class, a young man was grimacing and tensing his body while practicing a basic punch. The instructor commented, "Who are you trying to impress? Are you fighting yourself or the opponent?" The alert relaxation (weakness) of Yang tai chi chuan helps one recognize and correct inappropriate movement before it becomes chronic and habitual.

Relaxed movements are also an excellent means of reducing stress and improving health. Yang style tends to slow the heartbeat, deepen respiration, and in general, lower the metabolic rate. This may indeed increase one's reserve of *chi* (internal energy) and ultimately lead to increased fighting stamina. Relaxed movements are also the best way to cultivate "fighting sensitivity," the feeling the *T'ai Chi Ch'uan Classics* refers to as *tung ching*. It is also called "comprehending force"—the ability to sense the angle, direction, and power of an opponent's attack.

A simple experiment will illustrate this claim. Stand and face your partner about one arm-length apart. Extend your right arm forward at chest level and allow the backs of your hand or wrist to make light contact. Your partner then moves his arm up, down, right, left, and in circles at varying speeds. Your goal is to follow his movements, while never losing physical contact with his wrist or hand. To sense and follow your partner's motion, you must remain relaxed, particularly in the waist, shoulder and elbow areas.

Now try tensing any muscle in your body while still following your partner. You will find that you have a slower reaction time. Try tensing the wrist and elbow. It becomes almost impossible to stay with your partner. As the experiment shows, *tung ching* requires one to be *chin* (light), *ling* (alert), and most important, *sung* (relaxed).

In the past, many Chen tai chi chuan stylists have criticized Yang style for its slowness and gentleness. However, Yang Lu Chan, the founder of Yang style, may have preferred the Chen slow set, realizing it was truer to the principles outlined in the tai chi chuan writings. *Tai chi* means "the blending of yin and yang"; *chuan* means "boxing art." The basic significance of yin and yang in tai chi chuan is "up and down, slow and fast, soft and hard, inside and outside (man and nature)." Many martial artists believe Yang style has only the slow and soft, only the yin. But in Yang style, as in most profound arts, the truth is neither superficial nor obvious. Movements are exceedingly slow in practice and lightning fast in application.

Slowness removes the "kinks" from the joints and teaches one to move more efficiently. Postures are soft on the outside, but hard—yang—on the inside, like a steel bar wrapped in cotton. Hardness is felt in the bones. Yang tai chi chuan theory states that through relaxation and "sinking of the *chi*" (abdominal breathing), internal energy accumulates in the *dan tian* (lower abdomen). Eventually this *chi* overflows and enters the bones. The molten *chi* cools and solidifies, making the bones as hard as steel.

The "softness" of Yang style also states that the body should show only minimal tension until the actual moment of contact. Then, the fist tightens and the body tenses just enough to maintain stance and transmit power through the fist. Proficiency as a fighter can be measured by the ability to quickly change poles —from yin to yang to yin, or relaxation to tension to relaxation. But it is the yin that is most difficult to cultivate and therefore requires the most training.

Evolution of the Art

The historical record indicates that Yang Lu Chan was an excellent fighter when he met Chen Chen Xing. The famous scholar-author Chen Wei Ming writes that it was only after Yang had defeated all of Chen's advanced students that the elder instructor agreed to teach him. If Yang then studied only the slow set, it is likely that he believed it to be practical and applicable. When Yang returned to his native Yongnian County in Hebei, he termed his art *mien chuan* (soft boxing), or *hua chuan* (neutralizing boxing). The combat effectiveness of this "soft" martial art soon earned Yang the title Yang *wu-ti* (Yang the undefeatable). Eventually Yang became an instructor to the royal family in Peking (Beijing).

There is evidence that the early Yang style did have several quick, vigorous movements in the solo form. In the 1920s, a Chen style author, Shen Chia-chen, invited Yang Cheng Fu (grandson of Yang Lu Chan) to his home in Peking to teach tai chi chuan. Although Yang's form was generally soft, relaxed, and even, there were also several explosive techniques, which Shen admitted he didn't understand until he had studied *pao chui* (the quick, advanced Chen form) under Chen Fa-ke. Many early Yang stylists were said to sweat profusely while practicing tai chi chuan.

Today the Yang style has evolved into the most relaxed of all tai chi chuan styles. The separation of slow form (for health and proper technique) from quick application can only be considered an improvement. Also, it has led to the immense popularity and appeal of Yang style, which can now be practiced for relaxation, health, *and* self-defense. Unfortunately, such a drastic evolution has not occurred in the Chen style, probably because of its local character and greater emphasis on family and lineage.

Meditation in Movement

From a spiritual aspect, the modern Yang style is truly meditation in movement. As the *Classics* say, "In movement seek tranquility." The even tempo and constant relaxation allow the mind to become empty, receptive, and alert. The constant height of the body (there is little up-and-down motion as opposed to Chen) stills the "waves" of thought, so the senses become a calm lake, reflecting the image of the world. According to Yang style tai chi chuan master Paul Gallagher, "The four stages of tai chi chuan practice are form, function, feeling, and forgetting." The progression is as follows:

- **The form**—The student learns the principles of tai chi movement.
- **The function**—The student learns the self-defense application of each movement.
- **The feeling**—The student simply observes himself or herself and nature while practicing tai chi chuan—watching the flow of breath, the changing of scenery, the inner feeling of the form.
- **The forgetting**—At this stage, the body will automatically perform the exercise. The form has been programmed into the cortex.

When you reach the final point, you may feel that self-defense is not particularly important. Many of the older masters of Yang style drop sparring from their repertoire. This does not mean it doesn't exist. It's just that many find it hard to fight when tai chi chuan becomes a vehicle of the Tao and, in the words of Master T. T. Liang, "an excursion into paradise."

Kenneth Cohen is a martial artist and freelance writer in Nederland, Colorado. This material was published as "The Gentle Style of Yang Tai Chi" in the July 1986 edition of Inside Kung-Fu *magazine.*

PART II

Basic Techniques

8

The Yang Family Tai Chi Form

Doc-Fai Wong and Jane Hallander

Preparation: First frame of Yang tai chi form. Feet together, hands at sides.

Step out with left foot to shoulders-width distance.

Raise hands to shoulder level.

Lower hands to hip level. Bend both knees while lowering hands.

Left ward-off: Turn right 45 degrees, stepping into a left ward-off position.

"Grasp the bird's tail." Note: the following positions—ward-off, rollback, press, and push—all comprise "grasp the bird's tail."

Step forward with right foot to a right ward-off position. Left hand protects at the right elbow.

Roll back. Turn waist to the right.

Using your waist, draw both hands back 45 degrees to the left.

Press: Center your hips forward, placing the palm of the left hand against the pulse of the right arm.

Press forward, using the hips for power.

Push: Straighten both arms, keeping the elbows slightly bent.

Draw slightly back.

Push forward, using hip power.

"Single whip." Turn 180 degrees to the left.

Draw your right hand back to the whip position, with the left hand protecting at the right armpit. Look in the direction of the whip hand.

Step out to "single whip." Left hand pushes straight ahead.

Raise hands and step forward. Turn 90 degrees to the right, right hand raised, left hand opposite the right elbow.

"Stork spreads its wings." Pull back with both hands, using waist action.

Hands close together, with the right hand protecting the lower body and the left hand protecting the upper body.

Step out with right foot to strike with the right shoulder.

Right hand pushes up and to the front. Left hand pushes down.

Left brush knee and twist step: Turn the right arm inward, palm toward the face.

Drop the right hand down while raising the left hand to shoulder level.

Turn the waist 45 degrees to the right. Right hand circles to a position at ear level.

Step forward with left foot. Left hand brushes over left knee as right hand pushes forward.

"Play the fiddle." Shift body weight back to the right leg, raising the left toe. Left hand extends forward, with the right hand positioned opposite the left elbow.

Left brush knee and twist step: Turn the waist 45 degrees to the right. Left hand follows waist action. Right hand circles to ear level.

Left foot steps forward. Left hand brushes down over left knee, while the right hand pushes forward.

Right brush knee and twist step: Turn waist 45 degrees to the left. Right hand follows wrist action. Left hand circles to ear level.

Right foot steps forward. Right hand brushes down over the right knee while left hand pushes forward.

Left brush knee and twist step: Turn waist 45 degrees to the right. Left hand follows waist action. Right hand circles to ear level.

Left foot steps forward. Left hand brushes down over left knee while right hand pushes forward.

"Play the fiddle." Shift body weight back to the right leg, raising left toe. Left hand extends forward, with the right hand positioned opposite the left elbow.

Left brush knee and twist step: Turn waist 45 degrees to the right. Left hand follows waist action. Right hand circles to ear level.

Left foot steps forward. Left hand brushes down over left knee while the right hand pushes forward.

Step forward parry and punch: Turn waist 45 degrees to the left, drawing the right fist back. Shift weight to the right foot.

Shift weight back to left foot, allowing right foot to take a forward twist step, turning the body 45 degrees to the right. Right fist comes diagonally across the body. Left hand circles to a position level with the left ear.

Step forward with left foot, as left hand reaches forward in parry position.

Punch with right fist while drawing back left hand to protective position opposite right elbow.

Apparent close-up: Turn right palm upward. Left hand slides forward under right arm.

Draw back with both palms facing downward.

Push forward, using hip power.

Cross hands. Turn 90 degrees to the right.

Close hands, right hand on outside. Feet shoulders-distance apart.

"Carry the tiger to the mountain." Turn 45 degrees to the right. Left hand circles to position next to ear.

Step out diagonally with right foot. Right hand brushes down over right knee while left hand pushes forward.

Shift weight to left leg. Right hand scoops upward.

Shift weight forward to right leg. Right hand chops diagonally to imaginary opponent's throat.

Diagonal "grasp the bird's tail." Roll back, using waist action.

Press forward, placing left palm against right wrist.

Straighten both hands.

Draw back.

Push forward, using hip power.

Turn 90 degrees to the left.

Shift weight to right leg, while drawing arms back.

Left foot takes a 45-degree twist step.

Right foot follows to side. Shift weight to right foot, left toe raised. Left elbow is positioned directly over right horizontal fist.

Right "repulse the monkey." Pick up left foot. Turn left palm upward. Right hand circles to position level with ear.

Left foot steps back. Left hand withdraws as right hand pushes forward.

Left "repulse the monkey." Pick up right foot. Turn right palm upward. Left hand circles to position level with ear.

Right foot steps back. Right hand withdraws as left hand pushes forward.

Right "repulse the monkey." Pick up left foot. Turn left palm upward. Right hand circles to position level with ear.

Left foot steps back. Left hand withdraws as right hand pushes forward.

"Slanting flying." Turn 90 degrees to the right, with right hand scooped under left hand.

Step out with right foot. Right hand extends forward.

Raise hands and step forward. Shift weight back to left leg. Right arm extends forward. Left hand positioned opposite right elbow.

"Stork spreads its wings." Pull back with both hands, using waist action.

Scoop under, right hand protecting lower body and left hand protecting upper body.

Step out with right foot into a right shoulder strike.

Right hand pushes up and to the front. Left hand pushes down. Pick up left foot, replacing it with the toe down.

Left brush knee and twist step: Turn right arm inward, palm toward the face. Lower right hand while raising left hand.

Raise left hand to shoulder level. Turn waist 45 degrees to the right. Left hand follows direction of waist. Right hand circles to position at ear level.

Step forward with left foot. Left hand brushes down over left knee as right hand pushes forward.

"Needle at sea bottom." Shift weight back to right leg. Right hand pokes downward. Left hand is at left side, palm down.

"Fan through the back." Step out with left leg. Raise right arm next to head. Left hand follows its motion upward.

Shift weight forward, pushing forward with left hand. Right hand stays positioned next to head.

"Chop opponent with fist." Turn 180 degrees to the right. Right hand drops down to waist level in fist position. Left arm follows body movement in a blocking action.

Right backfist.

Shift weight forward, pushing with left hand. Right fist is withdrawn to right side.

Step forward parry and punch: Turn body 45 degrees to right, reaching forward with right grabbing fist.

Pull back diagonally to the left, using waist action.

Right foot takes a twisting step forward. Left hand circles to position level with left ear.

Parry: Left foot steps forward. At same time, left hand moves forward in parry position.

Shift weight forward to left leg. Punch with right fist. Left hand is positioned opposite the right elbow.

Left ward-off: Open hands slightly to a left ward-off position.

"Grasp the bird's tail." Scoop under hand position, right hand protecting lower body, left hand protecting upper body. Left foot steps forward.

Ward-off. Right hand comes up to ward-off position. Left hand positioned opposite right elbow.

Rollback: Turn the waist 45 degrees to the right, reversing palm positions at the same time.

Roll back diagonally, using waist action.

Press: Shift weight back to left leg. Center hips forward. Place left palm on right pulse point.

Shift weight forward, using hip power.

Push: Straighten arms, keeping elbows slightly bent.

Draw back.

Push forward, using hip power.

"Single whip." Turn 180 degrees to the left.

Draw right hand back to the whip position, with left hand protecting at the right armpit. Look in the direction of the whip hand, but not at the hand.

Step out to "single whip." Left hand pushes straight ahead.

"Wave hands like clouds." Shift weight to the right leg, dropping the left hand down in a circular motion.

Turn the waist to the left, shifting the body weight to the left foot. As the weight shifts left, the left hand circles to a position in front of the face, palm toward the face. The right hand protects the lower body.

Right foot closes with the left. Shift body weight to the right foot while turning the waist to the right. Right hand circles to front of face.

Step out with left foot. Shift body weight to left foot. Turn waist to the left. Left hand circles to front of face.

Right foot closes with the left. Shift body weight to the right foot while turning the waist to the right. Right hand circles to front of face.

Step out with left foot. Shift weight to left foot. Turn waist to the left. Left hand circles to front of face.

"Single whip." Draw right hand back to the whip position, with left hand protecting at the right armpit. Look in the direction of the whip hand.

Step out to "single whip." Left hand pushes straight ahead.

"High pat on the horse." Shift weight back to right foot. Right hand starts pushing forward.

Right hand extends forward, with hand angled upward. Left hand positioned with palm upward in front of waist.

Separation of right foot. Step out diagonally 45 degrees to the left. Look toward the right.

Cross hands, and prepare to kick with right foot.

Separate hands, keeping both elbows slightly bent. Kick to the right corner with right toe.

Separate of left foot. Step down diagonally 45 degrees to the right. Look to the left.

Cross hands, and prepare to kick with left foot.

Separate hands, keeping both elbows slightly bent. Kick to left corner with left toe.

Turn and kick with left sole. Pivot on right foot 135 degrees to the left. With left foot still raised from previous kick, prepare to kick with left heel.

Open arms and kick with left heel.

Left brush knee and twist step: Step forward with left foot. Left hand brushes down over left knee, while right hand pushes forward.

Right brush knee and twist step: Turn the waist 45 degrees to the left and step forward with right foot. Left arm follows direction of waist. Left hand circles to ear level.

Right hand brushes down over right knee while left hand pushes forward.

Step forward and punch downward: Step forward with left foot. Left hand brushes down over left knee while right hand punches downward.

"Chop opponent with fist." Turn 180 degrees to the right. Right hand drops down to waist level in fist position. Left arm follows body movement in a blocking action.

Right backfist.

Shift weight forward. Push with left hand while withdrawing right fist to side.

Step forward parry and punch: Turn body 45 degrees to the right, reaching forward with right grabbing fist.

Pull back diagonally to the left, using waist action.

Right foot takes a twisting step forward. Left hand circles to position level with left ear.

Left foot steps forward. At same time, left hand moves forward in parry position.

Shift weight forward to left leg. Punch with right fist. Left hand is positioned opposite the right elbow.

Kick with right sole. Both hands open equally.

Hands circle into a prepare-to-kick position.

Kick with the right heel. Both hands spread apart equally.

"Hit the tiger" left. Step down with feet together, right hand extended to the right in a fist. Left hand is in fist position at right elbow.

Step out 45 degrees to the left. Right fist crosses in front of face, then drops to waist level. Left fist circles upward to position opposite eyebrows.

"Hit the tiger" right. Drop both hands down while shifting weight to right foot.

Shift weight back to left foot, turning body 45 degrees to the right.

Right foot steps out. Right fist circles upward to position level with eyebrows. Left fist stays at waist level.

Kick with right sole. Shift weight back to left foot. Cross arms, preparing to kick.

Kick with the right heel.

Strike ears with double fist: Pivot 45 degrees to right corner. Keep knee up. Drop hands to position parallel with right knee.

Step forward with right leg. Hands reach forward to double-knuckle strike to temple.

Kick with left sole. Shift weight to right leg. Cross hands, preparing to kick.

Kick with left heel.

Turn and kick with right sole. Pivot 180 degrees to the left.

Prepare for kick position.

Kick with right heel.

Step forward parry and punch: Step down, pulling back
with the right hand.

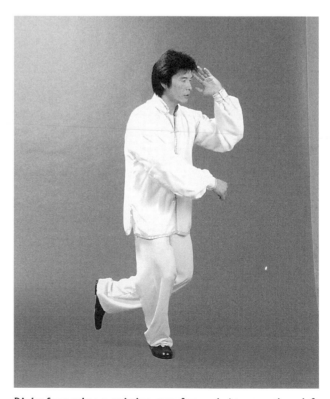

Right foot takes a twisting step forward. At same time, left
hand moves forward in parry position.

Right foot steps forward. At same time, left hand moves forward in parry position.

Shift weight forward to left leg. Punch with right fist. Left hand is positioned opposite the right elbow.

Apparent close-up: Turn the right palm upward.

Left hand slides forward under the right arm.

Draw back.

Push forward, using hip power.

Cross hands. Turn 90 degrees to the right.

Close hands, right hand on outside. Feet shoulders-width apart.

"Carry the tiger to the mountain." Turn 45 degrees to the right. Left hand circles to position next to ear.

Step out diagonally with right foot. Right hand brushes down over right knee. Left hand pushes forward.

Shift weight to left leg. Right hand scoops upward.

Shift weight forward to right leg. Right hand chops diagonally to imaginary opponent's throat.

Diagonal "grasp the bird's tail." Roll back, using waist action.

Press forward, placing left palm against right wrist.

Straighten both hands.

Draw back.

Push forward, using hip power.

Horizontal "single whip." Turn left 135 degrees, pivoting on the right heel.

Shift weight to the right foot, drawing left foot back. Draw hands past body, with right hand in the whip position, left hand protecting next to the left armpit. Look in the direction of the whip hand.

Step forward to horizontal "single whip," pushing forward with the left hand.

Right "part the wild horse's mane." Turn right 90 degrees. Hands close together, right hand protecting the lower body, left hand protecting the upper body.

Step forward with right leg, opening both hands outward at the same time.

Left "part the wild horse's mane." Turn the right toe outward 45 degrees, turning the body with it, and close hands, with the left hand on the bottom.

Step forward with left leg, opening both hands at the same time.

Right "part the wild horse's mane." Turn the left toe outward 45 degrees, turning the body with it, and close hands, with the right hand on the bottom.

Step forward with right leg, opening both hands at the same time.

Left ward-off: Step out to the left, approximately 90 degrees, to a left ward-off position.

"Grasp the bird's tail." Scoop under hand position, right hand protecting lower body, left hand protecting upper body. Left foot steps forward.

Ward-off: Right hand comes up to ward-off position. Left hand positioned opposite right elbow.

Rollback: Turn waist 45 degrees to the right, reversing palm positions at the same time.

Roll back diagonally, using waist action.

Press: Shift weight back to left leg. Center hips forward. Place left palm on right pulse point.

Shift weight forward, using hip power.

Push: Straighten arms, keeping elbows slightly bent.

Draw back.

Push forward, using hip power.

"Single whip." Turn 180 degrees to the left.

Draw right hand back to the whip position, with left hand protecting at the right armpit. Look in the direction of the whip hand.

Step out to "single whip." Left hand pushes gently ahead.

Right "fair lady works the shuttle." Turn 135 degrees to the right, dropping left hand down. Right foot takes a small twist step forward.

Step forward with left foot. Left hand blocks upward.

As the body weight shifts forward to the left foot, the left hand finishes its upward block. Right hand pushes straight.

Left "fair lady works the shuttle." Close hands, right hand on the bottom. Pivot 315 degrees to the right on left foot.

Step out with right foot. Right hand blocks upward.

Left "fair lady works the shuttle." As weight is shifted forward, right arm finishes its upward block. Left hand pushes straight.

Right "fair lady works the shuttle." Pivot on right heel 90 degrees to the left. Right hand drops to side.

Step out with left foot, blocking upward with left arm and pushing straight with right hand.

Left "fair lady works the shuttle." Close hands, right arm on bottom. Pivot 135 degrees to the right.

Step forward with right leg, blocking upward with left arm.

As weight its shifted forward, right arm finishes its upward block. Left hand pushes straight.

Left ward-off: Step out 45 degrees to the left.

Left hand in ward-off position.

"Grasp the bird's tail." Scoop under hand position, right hand protecting lower body, left hand protecting upper body. Left foot steps forward.

Ward-off: Right hand comes up to ward-off position. Left hand positioned opposite right elbow.

Rollback: Turn waist 45 degrees to the right, reversing palm positions at the same time.

Roll back diagonally, using waist action.

Press: Shift weight back to left leg. Center hips forward. Place left palm on right wrist's pulse point.

Shift weight forward, using hip power.

Push: Straighten arms, keeping elbows slightly bent.

Draw back.

Push forward, using hip power.

"Single whip." Turn 180 degrees to the left.

Draw right hand back to the whip position, with left hand protecting at the right armpit. Look in the direction of the whip hand.

Step out to "single whip." Left hand pushes straight ahead.

"Wave hands like clouds." Shift weight to right leg, dropping left hand down in a circular motion.

Turn the waist to the left, shifting the body weight to the left foot. As the weight shifts left, the left hand circles to a position in front of the face. The right hand protects the lower body.

Right foot closes with the left. Shift body weight to right foot while turning the waist to the right. Right hand circles to front of face.

Step out with left foot. Shift body weight to left foot. Turn waist to the left. Left hand circles to front of face.

Right foot closes with the left. Shift body weight to right foot while turning waist to the right. Right hand circles to front of face.

Step out with left foot. Shift weight to left foot. Turn waist to the left. Left hand circles to front of face.

"Single whip." Draw right hand back to the whip position, with left hand protecting at the right armpit. Look in the direction of the whip hand.

Step out to "single whip." Left hand pushes straight ahead.

"Snake creeps down." Shift weight back to right leg. Left arm and hand follow the body's backward movement. Keep the knee slightly bent.

Right "golden rooster stands on one leg." Shift the body weight forward, with right hand following along the center line.

Raise right leg, toe pointing down. Right arm is poised directly over right knee.

Left "golden rooster stands on one leg." Right leg steps back. Raise left leg, toe pointing down. Left arm is poised directly over left knee. Right "repulse the monkey." Pick up left foot. Turn left palm upward. Right hand circles to position level with ear.

Left foot steps back. Left hand withdraws as right hand pushes forward.

Left "repulse the monkey." Pick up right foot. Turn right palm upward. Left hand circles to position level with ear.

Right foot steps back. Right hand withdraws as left hand pushes forward.

Right "repulse the monkey." Pick up left foot. Turn left palm upward. Right hand circles to position level with ear.

Left foot steps back. Left hand withdraws as right hand pushes forward.

"Slanting flying." Turn 90 degrees to the right, with right hand scooped under left hand.

Step out with right foot. Right hand extends forward.

Raise hands and step forward. Shift weight back to left leg. Right arm extends forward. Left hand positioned opposite right elbow.

"Stork spreads its wings." Pull back with both hands, using waist action.

Scoop under, right hand protecting lower body and left hand protecting upper body.

Step out with the right foot into a right shoulder strike.

Right hand pushes up to the front. Left hand pushes down. Pick up left foot, replacing it with the toe down, heel up.

Left brush knee and twist step: Turn right arm inward, palm toward face. Lower right hand while raising left hand.

Raise left hand to shoulder level. Turn the waist 45 degrees to the right. Left hand follows direction of waist. Right hand circles to position at ear level.

Step forward with left foot. Left hand brushes down over left knee as right hand pushes forward.

"Needle at sea bottom." Shift weight back to right leg. Right hand pokes downward. Left hand is at left side, palm down.

"Fan through the back." Step out with left leg. Raise right arm next to head. Left hand follows its motion.

Shift weight forward, pushing forward with left hand. Right hand stays positioned next to head.

"White snake puts out its tongue." Turn 180 degrees to right. Right hand drops to waist level in open-hand position. Left arm follows body in a blocking action.

Right back-of-the-hand strike.

Shift weight forward, pushing with left hand. Right hand is withdrawn to the right side.

Step forward parry and punch: Turn body 45 degrees to the right, reaching forward with right grabbing fist. Pull back diagonally to the left, using waist action.

Right foot takes a twisting step forward. At same time, left hand moves forward in parry position.

Left foot steps forward. At same time, left hand moves forward in parry position.

Shift weight forward to left leg. Punch with right fist. Left hand is positioned opposite right elbow.

Left ward-off: Open hands slightly to a left ward-off position.

"Grasp the bird's tail." Scoop under hand position, right hand protecting lower body, left hand protecting upper body. Left foot steps forward.

Ward-off: Right hand comes up to ward-off position. Left hand positioned opposite right elbow.

Rollback: Turn waist 45 degrees to the right, reversing palm positions at the same time.

Roll back diagonally, using waist action.

Press: Shift weight back to left leg. Center hips forward. Place left palm on right pulse point.

Shift weight forward, using hip power.

Push: Straighten arms, keeping elbows slightly bent.

Draw back.

Push forward, using hip power.

"Single whip." Turn 180 degrees to the left.

Draw right hand back to the whip position, with left hand protecting at right armpit. Look in the direction of the whip hand.

Step out to "single whip." Left hand pushes straight ahead.

"Wave hands like clouds." Shift weight to right leg, dropping the hand down in a circular motion.

Turn the waist to the left, shifting the body weight to left foot. As the weight shifts left, left hand circles to a position in front of the face. Right hand protects the lower body.

Right foot closes with the left. Shift body weight to right foot while turning the waist to the right. Right hand circles to front of face.

Step out with left foot. Shift body weight to left foot. Turn waist to the left. Left hand circles to front of face.

Right foot closes with the left. Shift body weight to right foot while turning the waist to the right. Right hand circles to front of face.

Step out with left foot. Shift weight to left foot. Turn waist to the left. Left hand circles to front of face.

"Single whip." Draw right hand back to the whip position, with left hand protecting at right armpit. Look in the direction of the whip hand.

Step out to "single whip." Left hand pushes straight ahead.

"High pat on the horse." Shift weight back to right foot. Right hand starts pushing forward.

Right hand extends forward, with hand angled upward. Left hand positioned with palm upward in front of waist.

Plain crossed hands: Left elbow crosses right hand diagonally.

Turn and cross-kick: Turn 180 degrees to the right. Left arm blocks across.

Cross arms, right arm on outside.

Cross-kick outward, using right hand as target.

Brush knee and punch low: Pull back with right fist, using waist action.

Right foot makes a twisting step forward. Left hand circles to position level with ear.

Left foot steps forward. Left hand continues down in brush-knee position.

Punch low with right fist.

Left ward-off: Step out to the left to a ward-off position.

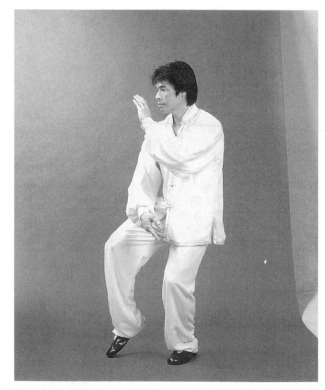

"Grasp the bird's tail." Scoop under hand position, right hand protecting lower body, left hand protecting upper body. Right foot steps forward.

Ward-off: Right hand comes up to a ward-off position. Left hand positioned opposite right elbow.

Rollback: Turn waist 45 degrees to the right, reversing palm positions at the same time.

Roll back diagonally, using waist action.

Press: Shift weight back to left leg. Center hips forward. Place left palm on right pulse point.

Shift weight forward, using hip power.

Push: Draw back, with arms apart.

Push forward, using hip power.

"Single whip." Turn 180 degrees to the left.

Draw back right hand to the whip position, with left hand protecting at the right armpit. Look in the direction of the whip hand.

Step out to "single whip." Left hand pushes straight ahead.

"Snake creeps down." Shift weight back to right leg. Left arm and hand follow the body's backward movement. Keep left knee slightly bent.

"Step up seven stars." Make a fist with left hand. Shift the weight onto left leg. Right hand in fist position at right side.

Step forward with right leg, heel up, and weight on left leg. Right arm crosses under left arm. Both hands are fists.

Step back to "ride a tiger." Step back with right leg. Left heel up, weight on right leg. Separate hands, with right hand protecting the head, and left hand at left side next to thigh.

Lotus kick: Drop right hand down. Bring left hand up, above right arm.

Pivot on right foot 180 degrees to the right.

Place weight on left leg, turning body another 180 degrees to the right. Bring both arms to right side.

Lotus-kick to the right (crescent-kick to the right).

"Shoot a tiger." Place right foot down at 45-degree angle to right corner. Both hands on left side.

Shift weight to right foot. Drop both hands down, carrying them over to right side, left fist at right armpit and right fist next to right ear.

Punch 45 degrees to left corner with right fist. Left fist draws slightly back.

Step forward parry and punch: Shift weight to left foot, pulling back with right hand.

Right foot takes a twisting step forward. At same time, left hand circles to position next to left ear.

Left foot steps forward. At same time, left hand moves forward to parry position.

Shift weight forward to left leg. Punch with right fist. Left hand is positioned opposite right elbow.

Apparent close-up: Left hand slides forward under right arm.

Turn right palm upward.

Draw back.

Push forward, using hip power.

Cross hands. Turn 90 degrees to the right.

Close hands, right hand on outside. Feet at shoulders-distance apart.

Conclusion. Hands come down to sides. At same time, straighten up.

Left foot closes with right.

Yang Style Traditional Training

Daniel Y. Wang

Translated by Mark Cheng

The traditional training methods of tai chi are slowly becoming extinct. These days, many instructors are teaching either great form and no application, average form and some questionable application, or altogether poor form and incorrect application. The rarest few are those who teach both proper form and function.

This situation is due to a number of factors which all students should clearly understand. Otherwise, you may not know what you're missing. One contributor is the fact that many people learn tai chi purely for health reasons. These individuals typically begin their training either to recover from an illness or simply to maintain physical (or mental/spiritual) fitness. With this outlook, the practitioner is unlikely to take the time to learn the proper fundamentals.

Also, people who undertake serious training in tai chi as a martial art are exceedingly rare. The fundamental training exercises (ji ben gong) are not the stereotypical effortless exercises often associated with tai chi. Because so much noise has been made about the differences between internal and external styles (nei, wai jia), many people fail to understand that real tai chi incorporates training exercises that would be labeled "hard style" and are physically quite challenging at the deeper levels. Many students also fail to realize that the deciding factor in whether or not one is doing tai chi is not the speed, but rather the embodiment of sung (suppleness) as well as other key characteristics.

These misunderstandings make it difficult for students to find teachers who understand tai chi training to such depth, and make it even harder for those serious teachers to acquire students who know what they're looking for in tai chi. The truth is that many people like the idea of doing martial arts, but almost nobody wants to put in the thorough effort it takes to really understand art on all levels: beginning, intermediate, and advanced, as well as physical, mental, emotional, spiritual, and cultural.

The Beginnings of Skill

Perhaps the first and most important step in tai chi training, after finding a teacher who's a master in skill and not just in name, is *zhuang gong*, or standing skill. Before a student can begin the form, it is imperative to learn how to stand correctly. Without the correct physical framework, a practitioner's tai chi is fragile, unstable, and incomplete.

The proper stance (*ping xing bu*) is more than just having the two feet parallel and knees slightly bent. The pelvis must be tucked in under the torso, while the spinal column remains vertical to the ground. This also bends the knees to their proper depth. The head must then rest on top of the neck, with the chin sunken slightly to prevent the head from tilting backward. This assemblage, in turn, must rest vertically on top of the shoulders and the torso.

This gives the body the proper structure for the *chi*, or internal energy, to sink down to the *dan tian*, or lower abdomen region. Thus, proper standing technique becomes a kind of *zhan zhuang*—a standing meditation *chi kung* exercise in which students learn to feel their *chi* circulate inside while they are standing still. The effect is stillness in movement and movement in stillness.

Building on Basics

After a student has learned *zhuang gong*, the next order is to begin learning the form. In this step, the student must first learn all the stances of the movements, as a continuation to the *zhuang gong* training. The front and back stances (*gong bu*, *xu bu*), in addition to more advanced stances such as the drop stance (*pu bu*) and one-legged stance (*du li bu*), are practiced by learning the form. The student must bring the hands, eyes, body, and footwork (*shoo*, *van*, *shen*, *fa*, *bu*) together with proper theory or method.

Here, the concept of body unity comes into play, teaching the student to coordinate the stance, hips, and torso in one focused movement. This body-unity training focuses the body's power by teaching the body to begin and end each movement at the same time, just as the light through a magnifying glass comes together at one point. To accomplish this unity, it is critical to clearly understand which parts of the body are empty or full, and when. That is so that you can distribute your weight, *chi*, and intention (*yi*) to the appropriate parts. For example, doing the "white crane spreads its wings" posture without placing all the weight on the back foot constitutes poor form, which leads to poor function.

Another key point often overlooked is what is called *wai san he, nei san he*, which means "three external and three internal harmonies." The three external harmonies are:

- Hands in harmony with the feet (*shoo yu zu he*)
- Elbows in harmony with the knees (*zou yu yi he*)
- Shoulders and hips in harmony (*jian yu kua he*)

An example is the movement for "Single Whip": Taking as the starting point the body balanced over the right foot and limbs close to the body, the first principle of *wei san he*, that of hand-foot harmony, applies when the right-hand crane's beak and left foot go out together, allowing the body to counterbalance itself as well as teaching proper self-timing. (Another example is the ending form after the "raise hands" movement, which requires elbow-knee and hand-foot alignment on the lead side.)

Self-timing is important because one most know where the parts of the body are every stage to avoid fumbling in close spaces. The second of the three external harmonies in "Single Whip" applies at the completion of the movement, in which the elbow and knee should be vertically aligned on the left side.

As provided in the third of the external harmonies, the shoulder and hip should never be out of line with one another, as that would tighten the muscles in the back unnecessarily and dissipate power from the legs to the hands.

The *nei san he*, or "three internal harmonies," come next. They are:

- Mind (*xin*) with intention (*yi*)
- Intention with *chi*
- *Chi* with force (*li*)

These all come into tight focus when you apply tai chi in fighting. The mind and intention are not one and the same, as most would assume. The mind must focus its intention on whatever part of the body is being used as a weapon at that time (e.g., the left arm of the "single whip," or the foot during the "separation kick"). This focused intention calls the *chi* to the weapon in use. Thus, the saying "Where the *yi* goes, the *chi* will follow." With proper *chi* direction, the student gains the ability to exert force (*li*) out of the body and into the target, uniting energy and force.

The student must also learn the three main sections of the body: arms, legs, and body proper. Each of these sections can be further divided into three subsections: the arms into the hand, forearm, and upper arm; the legs into the foot, lower leg (shin), and upper leg (thigh); and the body into the head, chest, and abdomen. Each of these nine subsections has two terminals, the root and the tip, as the table shows.

The Parts of the Arms, Legs, and Body

Section	Root	Tip
Hand	Wrist	Fingertips
Forearm	Elbow	Wrist
Upper arm	Shoulder	Elbow

Section	Root	Tip
Foot	Ankle	Toes
Lower leg	Knee	Ankle
Upper leg	Hip	Knee

Section	Root	Tip
Head	Shoulder	Crown
Chest	Floating ribs	Shoulder
Abdomen	Hips	Floating ribs

Every root and every tip has a purpose in fighting, and the power is expressed when each of these nine sections learns to move independently but together in harmony.

Daniel Wang has trained extensively in Beijing since his childhood, eventually becoming one of the most respected instructors of tai chi. He trained under Master Jiang Yu-Kun to learn the Yang style tai chi system in its entirety. He also learned traditional baguazhang, Hsing I, chi kung, and Muslim longfist (Cha Quan). Wang, with help from Mark Cheng, is currently preparing a book on the traditional training methods of tai chi and a biography of Yang Lu Chan. This material appeared in the October 1998 edition of Inside Kung-Fu *magazine.*

10

Tai Chi Martial Stances

Doc-Fai Wong and Jane Hallander

While tai chi standing meditations and breathing exercises develop *chi*, tai chi forms practice and martial arts stances develop fighting habits. Realizing that fighting ability takes more than *chi* development alone, Yang family teachers added focus and intention training to the forms practice. Rather than mindlessly practice the form, tai chi practitioners were taught to visually penetrate an imaginary target. Then, when a real adversary presented himself, tai chi stylists used their relaxed, but still intent, focus against the opponent. This added more penetration to their striking power.

Intention and focus also are important parts of tai chi stance training. Don't confuse martial arts stances with standing meditation. They are not meditative positions; the eyes are kept open to further a fighting focus and spirit. Tai chi martial stances also are not the same as forms postures. While forms postures represent actual fighting techniques, stances are passive positions that develop specific parts of the body. For instance, the "spear and shield" stance

strengthens the upper and lower arm and wrist for future use with the ward-off technique.

Tai chi stances also develop a fighting gaze, or focus. Unlike standing meditations, the stances are done with the eyes looking purposefully into the distance. According to the ancients, a fighter's spirit (*shen*) comes out through his eyes, uniting with his *chi* to double his strength.

There are ten tai chi fighting stances, each serving a specific training purpose.

Mao Dun

Mao dun translates to "spear and shield." This stance resembles a fighter holding a shield in one hand and a poised spear in the other.

To execute *mao dun*, place one foot forward in a cat-stance position. Your weight should be directly over the other leg. If you have your right foot forward, your right arm will be rounded, with the hand

Mao dun

Zheng shen pu hu

directly in front of you as if holding a shield. Your left arm will be at your side, with the elbow slightly protruding to the rear of your rib cage. The palm of your left, or spear, hand faces your body. The spear hand is held vertical, with the fingers pointing straight ahead and the forearm parallel to the ground.

Turn your body sideways, with your chest facing 45 degrees to the left. Look straight ahead without blinking. Quietly breathe. Put your intention on *chi* coming out of your hand, like a spear thrusting forward, and flowing through the curved arm like a shield repelling an enemy.

Spend ten minutes in this position, then change sides, repeating the stance for ten minutes with your left leg and arm forward. Your body, arms and legs should have energy running through them. The force isn't tense; it is closer to the soft, unyielding energy you see when a garden hose is filled with water. If

someone pushes on your arms, you should meet that resistance with equal resistance, not force. Do not buckle under the push.

Mao dun has several purposes. Besides developing your fighting intention through a relaxed, penetrating gaze, the cat-stance position conditions and strengthens your leg muscles. The forward shield arm is strengthened for future defensive ward-off (*peng jing*) use. The back arm (spear arm) represents both an offensive elbow strike and a forward finger poke. This conditions the muscles in your shoulder, arm, wrist, and hand. *Mao dun's* health benefits are the same as for all other tai chi martial stances. It strengthens your back muscles and *ming men* pressure point area, completing your upper-body and lower-body connection. You also learn to send *ti chi* out through your hands, adding more penetration to your strikes and strength to your grabs and joint locks.

Ce shen pu hu

Tuo ying

Zheng Shen Pu Hu

At first view, "front body pouncing tiger," or *zheng shen pu hu*, appears the opposite of its intended purpose. This stance places tai chi practitioners in an uncomfortable, tiring position that forces them to relax their shoulders while strengthening their arms.

Start in a cat stance, with one leg forward and heel raised. Slightly raise both hands above and in front of your head, hands at a 45-degree angle to your wrists, with the palms angled downward. Your upper arms should be level with your shoulders. Look straight ahead. Your body should be facing an imaginary opponent, with your hips positioned forward.

Stand for ten minutes with one leg forward, then switch to the other leg forward for ten minutes. The arm muscles strengthened are used for pushing or pressing downward. Your leg muscles also benefit

from this stance. As your shoulders relax, *chi* flows easily into your hands.

Ce Shen Pu Hu

Ce shen pu hu is very close to *zheng shen pu hu*, except that *ce shen pu hu* is the "side body pouncing tiger." Instead of strengthening your arms for a front press, *ce shen pu hu* develops one arm at a time.

Again from a cat stance, if you have your right foot forward, slightly raise and extend your right hand above head level and directly in front of your body. The fingertips are bent into a relaxed position, as if pressing down or pouncing on prey. The other hand stays in a protective position to the inside of the right hand's elbow. Both hands are at 45-degree angles to their wrists, with the palms down. Unlike the "front body pouncing tiger" stance, this one has

Zi wu

Lohan bao ding

your body at a 45-degree angle to the imaginary tar-get. If your right hand is raised, your body will be angled 45 degrees to the left. Keep your eyes open and your intention focused.

Practice *ce shen pu hu* for ten minutes daily with each leg forward.

Tuo Ying

Tuo ying, or "lifting the baby," actually looks as if you are hoisting an infant with both hands. Its benefits are improved wrist flexibility and strength.

From a specific martial arts standpoint, *tuo ying* simulates catching someone's leg or arm with a for-ward thrust, throwing the opponent off balance. Like the other stances, *tuo ying* also strengthens your legs and relaxes your shoulders.

Start with one leg forward in a cat stance and your body weight resting over the other leg. If your

right leg is forward, extend your right arm in front of you, twisting your wrist until your palm is up. Your left arm should be rounded and positioned next to your right elbow, with the hand also twisted up. Turn your waist until your chest faces 45 degrees to the left. The visual effect is of carefully lifting a baby in front of you. Look straight ahead, with purpose in your eyes. Keep your shoulders relaxed and your back straight.

Hold the position for ten minutes on each leg. When you change to left leg forward, extend your left arm out in front, with the right arm by your left elbow.

Zi Wu

Zi wu means "day and night." It's a stance specifically designed for stretching and loosening joints, such as the hips and knees. You will need a chair or table for *zi wu* practice.

Zi wu is done by placing one foot on top of a chair back or table approximately waist high. If the right foot is on the chair back, the toe points right. Look to the right, with your right hand behind your back and against your *ming men* pressure point. The palm is outward. The left hand pushes away from your forehead in a protecting position.

In the past, this stance was done for up to an hour, rotating from leg to leg on the chair or table. Now ten minutes per leg each day is adequate. Besides stretching joints, it helps strengthen leg muscles and improve kicking power.

Lohan Bao Ding

Lohan bao ding, or "carrying an incense burner," is another tai chi one-legged stance. Lift one foot straight up as high as possible, with the knee bent and the calf of the raised leg parallel to the ground. Turn the toe of the raised foot upward as far as possible. Both arms are evenly rounded and level with the chest, with the fingers pointing toward one another. This makes a connection with your *chi*.

Look straight ahead, and maintain your balance. When you get tired, change supporting legs. At first, you will have trouble holding each leg for more than thirty seconds. However, if you practice ten minutes a day, you will be able to stand for more than four minutes without changing supporting legs. This stance strengthens the legs and improves balance.

Tui Mo

Tui mo, or "pushing the grinder," has the feet in a cat stance, with one foot forward and heel raised. Keep your arms level with your waist, with both palms pushing forward.

Your fingers should point up, with the wrist slightly bent, as if pushing the long handle of a grain grinder. Your elbows point down. Your body and hips should face forward. The distance between your hands is approximately two and one-half feet. Again, the eyes look into the distance. *Tui mo* develops wrist energy from imaginary forward pushing force.

Da Peng Zhan Chi

Da peng zhan chi, which translates to "eagle spreads its wings," starts from a cat stance, one leg forward almost level with the shoulders and extended at a 45-degree angle to the body. Your palms should be facing downward. The cat stance is used, rather than having both feet parallel, to further strengthen the legs.

Parallel stances are meditation stances good only for *chi* development and health. True martial arts training requires more difficult cat or one-legged stances. When practicing *da peng zhan chi*, place your body and hips forward. Besides conditioning the legs, this stance strengthens shoulders and arms, while sending *chi,* or energy, to fingertips and out to the arms. This improves left and right pushing energy.

Qing Ting Dian Shui

Qing ting dian shui, or "dragonfly skimming the water," is also done from a cat stance. If your right leg is forward, the right hand is positioned forward and angled upward forehead high, with the palm straight ahead.

The left hand pushes to the rear, with the elbow and wrist slightly bent. Look straight ahead, your body at a 45-degree angle to the imaginary target. Relax your waist and chest, focusing your attention into the distance. *Qing ting dian shui* develops power on both sides.

Tui mo

Da peng zhan chi

Qing ting dian shui

Fo yuan

Fo Yuan

"Floating on top of the cloud," or *fo yuan*, is the only moving tai chi martial stance. From a cat stance with your right leg forward, your right arm will be slightly rounded and extended forward at chest height. Your left arm also is rounded but not extended as far forward as the right. The left arm is held at waist level. Keep both palms down.

While looking straight ahead, slightly rock your body forward and backward. Stay relaxed, but be aware of the energy moving your body from side to side.

This stance develops forward energy and intention. Do it for ten minutes on each side.

Note: Each one of the ten tai chi martial stances requires that your lower back be straight, not swayed with the hips out. This is critical to your success with any internal system. If you correctly practice these stances with your hips tucked and lower back straight, you eventually will have a strong, naturally connected posture. You will find it hard to be uprooted.

"Grasp the Bird's Tail"
Yang Tai Chi's Signature Technique

Jane Hallander

All martial arts have certain techniques that characterize the particular discipline's fighting principles and theories. In the case of China's internal martial arts, interesting stories are often built around a technique that has great value to the art. "Grasp the bird's tail" is a classic example and—even as far away as Italy— is emphasized in tai chi training.

Among the several Yang tai chi techniques that repeat themselves often during the form, "Grasp the Bird's Tail" stands out because of its variety of uses. Sometimes translated to "grasp the sparrow's tail," it forms the foundation for tai chi double-hand *tui shou* (push-hands) practice, while also teaching four of the most important self-defense techniques in tai chi's arsenal.

The story behind the name centers on Yang Lu Chan, the founder of Yang family tai chi, who was said to be so relaxed and subtle with his internal power that he could prevent a songbird from flying off of his hand. According to legend, one day, a sparrow landed in the palm of Yang's hand while he was in the "right ward-off" position. Knowing that the bird had to push off with its feet against his palm before it could fly away, Yang concentrated his internal energy in circles, giving the bird nothing solid in his palm on which to push. In this way, he kept the bird from flying almost as though he had grasped its tail. Since right ward-off is the first of the four tech-

niques of "Grasp the Bird's Tail," the entire movement became representative of the famous story. The other three are rollback, press, and push.

One of the top Yang style instructors in Italy is Geneva-based Mirco Corrarino, a student of Doc Fai Wong who traces his Yang tai chi lineage directly back to the Yang family as a sixth-generation practitioner. Corrarino explains the importance of "Grasp the Bird's Tail": "Every kind of *jing* (power) is expressed in the four movements that make up 'grasp the bird's tail.' Besides, these four movements are the key movements in tai chi push-hands."

Ward-Off

As noted, ward-off is the first of the four techniques that make up "Grasp the Bird's Tail" and means literally what it says—ward off or redirect oncoming force, from either a push or a punch. A defense scenario might look like this: There isn't enough time to step aside to avoid an oncoming punch. Instead, the tai chi practitioner brings his forearm up to fend off and redirect the punch and its power. He turns his waist with the ward-off movement to add extra strength to his ward-off block.

The ward-off arm is always curved into a half-circle position, with the palm facing the tai chi stylist. This allows *peng jing* (expanding energy) to further reinforce the arms' strength and help redirect the opponent's straightforward force off to one side. It's easy to position your arm correctly for ward-off. Hold both arms in front of you, rounded, with the middle fingertips of one hand lightly touching the middle fingertips of the other. Then drop the elbows slightly, and drop the left arm to your side. The right arm and hand are now in a correct ward-off position.

Ward-off plays an important role in tai chi push-hands as a vehicle for the expression of *peng jing*. This is important because *peng* energy is a major factor in preventing someone from pushing you off balance. *Peng* is literally expanding energy, since the roundness of your arm and distance from your body provides a strong buffer zone between you and your opponent.

Rollback

Rollback follows ward-off. Again, the name accurately describes the movement. The tai chi stylist's hands look as if he were grabbing someone's arm and pulling the opponent off balance diagonally in front of his body. Actually, it's an elbow lock, commonly called an "arm bar" by other martial arts, done by using your own forearm as a lever for downward pressure on the opponent's upper arm above the elbow. Your lower hand lifts up, against the opponent's wrist, while your right arm presses downward, creating an elbow lock.

Likewise in a defense situation, rollback easily follows ward-off. After deflecting a punch with

ward-off, you must do something, since the attacker will likely use his other hand. Following the "grasp the bird's tail" form, your wrists twist as if you were encircling the opponent's punching arm, trapping that arm and placing it in position for rollback. With your hands in place, you need only shift your weight back and turn your waist away from your opponent. Your body becomes a giant lever, pressing down on the opposition's arm and locking the elbow.

In a friendly push-hands match, rollback is used to guide or redirect your partner off balance, especially after a failed push attempt that you have foiled with your ward-off technique.

Press

After rollback is press. Press is an interesting technique, because the pressing hand is the hand pushing forward against the other arm's wrist. As the Yang family taught press, the palm of the pressing hand should rest against the pulse point of the other forearm. This strengthens the wrist of the other hand—the actual weapon in this technique. The back of the wrist is pressed forward with a snapping *fa jing* (explosive energy) action if this technique is used for self-defense. Targets are usually sensitive pressure points, such as those located in the sternum area.

When used for self-defense, press is always a sudden explosive technique designed to do great damage. The tai chi stylist usually takes a step forward when launching the press technique. If you follow the sequence of "Grasp the Bird's Tail," the press technique becomes a way to release an opponent who has already been trapped with the rollback technique. In this instance, the target is a pressure point on the opponent's upper arm that, when stimulated, may cause numbness, as well as initial pain, in the arm.

Press in tai chi push-hands practice uses far less force than in its self-defense applications. It is a milder, forward pressing action, with an uplifting motion toward the end of the technique. You might first fool the opponent by pressing downward to pull him off balance, then as he leans forward into the downward press, change your pressing motion to an upward moving technique. This usually propels your opponent backward, off balance.

Push

Push uses both hands to push the opponent off balance. In the Yang tai chi form, the heels of both hands make contact with the target. It is necessary for your elbows to be pointed downward to position your hands correctly for this technique. Your hands should be no farther than shoulders-width apart. Farther apart or closer together than shoulders-width doesn't allow the joints in the arm to align correctly for maximum power output.

The fighting application of push can be a strike with both hands to the lung one and lung two pressure points, located at the junction of shoulder to chest, or it can be a strike to other sensitive pressure points in the chest area. No matter where the target area is located, push as a self-defense technique is not a simple push: it is a jarring strike, made by stepping toward the opponent and using the arms as if they were battering rams directed by a whiplike body action.

The push-hands application of the push technique may be a subtle forward push with both hands to uproot your opponent, or it can be wed with a small mount of *fa jing* (explosive energy). If powered with *fa jing*, the push should not be forceful enough to cause injury. In push-hands practice, the push technique is best used to take an opponent off balance and is often targeted to your push-hands partner's ward-off arm, rather than his chest.

In "Grasp the Bird's Tail" the push technique always follows press and is the last of the four component techniques. In push-hands practice, it naturally follows press, since you may start with press and easily move into push. You can also follow rollback with a push technique.

"In Italy, there is a great interest in tai chi," Corrarino notes, "and we want to learn all facets of tai chi, including the martial aspects. For that reason, I emphasize the importance of technique sequences such as "Grasp the Bird's Tail" in both the form and push-hands applications."

This material appeared in the July 1998 edition of Inside Kung-Fu *magazine.*

12

Tai Chi Push-Hands

Doc-Fai Wong and Jane Hallander

Tai chi *tui shou*, or push-hands, is as important to the martial art of tai chi as meditation, stances, or form practice.

It is said that practicing the form teaches you to know yourself, while push-hands lets you know your opponent. There's nothing mystical in this statement. It simply means that when you correctly practice forms, you are teaching your body to relax and react in its most mechanically efficient manner as a single connected force.

Push-hands practice teaches you to feel your opponent's strong and weak points, instantly knowing where you should attack or defend. Eventually, when your push-hands technique is developed well enough, you will know your opponent's next move or weakness as soon as you touch hands or arms with him. Push-hands is the sparring part of tai chi.

Although push-hands gives you an opportunity to try out your tai chi training under sparring circumstances, don't expect to start with the freestyle version. First you must become familiar with *shou*

patterns, developing your sensitivity and what the Chinese call listening ability.

The most common pattern in Yang tai chi is double-hand, in which you and your partner alternate defense and offense, with the action moving smoothly from one person to the other. However, the two-handed push-hands pattern is not easy to learn. For this reason, it's better to start with a single-hand *tui shou* pattern which develops sensitivity, continuity, and relaxation.

Single-Hand Push-Hands

Start with the right leg forward. Your weight should rest over your left leg, with the foot pointed 45 degrees outward. For stability, turn your right foot inward about 15 degrees. Place your right arm into a ward-off position, lightly touching your opponent's right arm, which is also in a ward-off position. You and your opponent have the right legs and right arms forward. You may place your left arm behind your back or out to the side, whichever helps with balance. As with the double-hand pattern, you and your partner now exchange attacking and defending postures, waiting for the opportune moment by shifting your weight over your forward foot, while still keeping your spine straight.

When you shift your weight forward, your opponent leans back by moving his weight over the rear leg and sinking his hips to deflect your push. He rotates the waist to the right if he has contact with his right arm and to the left if *tui shou* is done left arm to left arm. Unlike in Wu style, you should not lift the toe of your forward foot when shifting back your weight.

Then it is your partner's turn to come forward, attacking if he wants. The pattern is a continuous exchange of offensive and defensive movements. Of course, you won't try to push each time you shift forward into attacking position. Wait until you feel a weakness in your opponent's defenses or balance. Keep in mind that contact between you and your partner is not wrist to wrist: it should be the first third of your forearm to the first third of your partner's forearm. This gives both of you more wrist flexibility and a slightly longer reach.

One reason to start with single-hand push-hands before double push-hands is to develop relaxation and waist action. If your shoulders get sore, you are too tense. The other reason is to learn to "stick." When your opponent moves, your arm should move with him and never lose contact. If you break contact, you create a weakness in your own defenses and allow the opponent to use sudden force against you. Practice single push-hands equally on both sides.

Double Push-Hands

When you are comfortable doing single push-hands, you can start practicing the double *tui shou* pattern with a partner. Place your right arm up in a ward-off position. It makes no difference which leg is forward,

but if your right foot is forward, your partner's right foot also should be forward, and vice versa.

Your partner will place both hands on your ward-off arm, in a pushing position—the right hand on your wrist and the left on your elbow. Now he pushes forward. Place your left arm inside your right arm in the same ward-off position, and exchange it for your right arm, creating a "bridge" between your chest and your partner's pushing hands. Drop your right arm down and around in a half-circle to a position with the palm against your partner's left elbow. Push your partner's left arm up by pushing against his left elbow and wrist, using your right hand against his left wrist. You are now in the attacking position, ready to push forward against your partner's ward-off arm.

Repeat, with you now pushing and your partner defending as you just did. In this direction, you are defending with your right arm and your partner with the left arm. When you become adept at this direction, smoothly change directions by simply reversing the pushing direction. After you change directions, your left arm is the ward-off arm, while your partner's right takes on that responsibility.

Reversing directions is a valuable defense tactic against a straight push, redirecting the attacker's force away from you. Don't try double push-hands sparring until you are proficient in both directions.

The Four Training Stages

When you know both single and double push-hands patterns, your training naturally evolves into four distinct stages, each with its own special kind of energy, called *jing* in Chinese.

Stage One

The first stage is *dong jing*, or "understanding energy." For instance, when someone uses either the neutralizing or discharging force against you, you must recognize and understand its type. At this level, then,

Single push-hands pattern—ward-off position

Defend by withdrawing and deflecting the opponent's forward momentum.

Push forward.

The opponent defends.

Single push-hands pattern and push

you begin to understand the different types of force and resistance used against you. *Dong jing* knowledge is a must before you can move on to the next stage. You may not know how to deflect or neutralize an attack, but you should understand the differences among sticky (*nian jing*), adhesive (*zhan jing*), connecting (*lian jing*), and following (*sui jing*).

Stage Two

The second stage is called *ting jing*. It means "listening" or "feeling energy." *Ting jing* helps you feel how strong or weak, tense or limp, your opponent is at the moment of contact. When you develop *ting jing*, you'll instantly know whether the opponent's elbow is tense, or if he's off balance. Well-trained tai chi practitioners feel these sensations through the entire body at the initial touch, as if the opponent were broadcasting on silent radio waves. *Ting jing* is practical knowledge, used to feel the opponent's intentions and weaknesses.

Stage Three

After *ting jing* comes *hua jing*, or "dissolving energy." *Hua jing* is just what it implies. When people push or attack you, once you make contact, you neutralize their forceful *jing*. You do that by slightly yielding, then redirecting the force. *Hua jing* requires relaxation and sticking ability. You must learn to follow your opponent's force, using it to your own advantage.

Stage Four

The final stage is *fa jing*. *Fa jing* is "discharging" or "releasing energy." After you use *hua jing* to neutralize your opponent and put him off balance, it is your chance to discharge *jing*. *Fa jing* is that discharging power and is characterized by sudden explosive force.

The Four Basic Fighting Tactics

Tai chi push-hands patterns use the familiar four basic fighting tactics within the *hua jing* and *fa jing* levels. These are:

- Ward-off (*peng*)
- Rollback (*lu*)
- Press (*ji*)
- Push (*an*)

An example of ward-off: After contact with your opponent's arm during double push-hands practice, both hands and elbows stick together. If you move, your opponent moves. If you don't, he doesn't. Ward-off is the physical connection that establishes *ting jing*, or listening energy.

Rollback is a "following" action. If someone pushes straight against you, you will turn your waist from your rollback arm, rotating and rolling your arm along his pushing arm as you redirect or deflect the force of his push. In the end, you are still balanced, while your opponent is off balance.

Press is an offensive tactic used when you try pulling your opponent or rolling back, and your opponent pulls back against your pulling force. At that tensed moment, follow your opponent's movement, pressing the palm of one hand against the inside of the wrist of the other hand. Attack straight forward.

Push is another offensive technique. If your opponent is weak, push straight forward with both hands. For tense opponents, neutralize the push by sticking to the opponent's hands, circling downward, and pushing forward.

After double push-hands patterns comes push-hands sparring and *da lu* practice. Remember, don't try freestyle push hands until you are good at pattern *tui shou*. If you try freestyle sparring too soon, it can easily turn into force-against-force pushing or wrestling.

Double push-hands pattern

Da Lu Practice

Da lu, or "great pull," adds four more techniques to the basic ward-off, rollback, press, and push. Those four techniques are *cai* (pull), *lie* (bend backward), *zhou* (elbow strike), and *kau* (shoulder strike). *Cai* is a sudden downward pull, like jerking someone's arm. *Lie* is a joint-breaking action that hyperextends the opponent's joint by bending it against its natural direction. *Zhou* is used by placing leverage against someone with your elbow, as in a joint lock. It also is a strike that takes the opponent off balance or injures him. *Kau* is a leaning action or a direct shoulder strike. Leaning against someone is usually done to take him off balance.

Da lu footwork is different from the regular push-hands pattern. It is footwork that moves diagonally forward and backward in four directions. Nowadays, push-hands sparring is becoming popular in tournament competition. Some tournaments allow only stationary footwork, while others let opponents travel at will within twenty-foot circles, using tai chi freestyle sparring tactics.

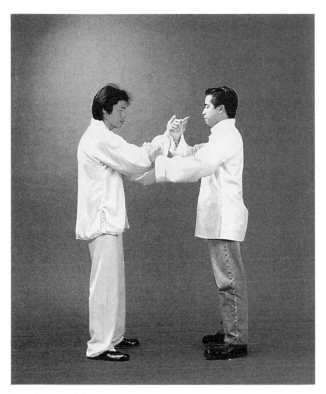

Starting position

The opponent does *kou*, a shoulder strike.

Cai, a straight downward pull

Lie, leverage against the shoulder joint

Zhou, an elbow strike

13

Tai Chi's *Cheng Hsin* Rollback

Jef Edwards

Pure and simple, this tai chi technique combines joining, leading, and neutralizing to produce power nonexistent in other styles.

Perhaps the most powerful technique of its kind, tai chi's *cheng hsin* rollback technique demonstrates the utmost purity in an art form. The rollback is one of the four techniques of the basic tai chi double practice called *tui shou*, which uses *peng, lu, ji,* and *an*—ward-off, rollback, press, and push. At once a joining, leading, and neutralizing technique, the rollback manifests each of these principles without compromising one for the sake of the other. The *cheng hsin* rollback is a great fighting technique as well as a powerful teaching tool.

The purity of joining, leading, and neutralizing is always maintained throughout any *cheng hsin* rollback. This not only yields the power inherent in each of these principles, but also combines each to create an even greater functional effectiveness.

Joining is the skill of blending and being connected with the activity of another. Joining with the movement and energy of an opponent puts you in touch with all the information needed for leading or neutralizing; the opponent's timing, speed, and balance already are accounted for as an aspect of joining. In leading the adversary to a position where he can do less harm, you can effectively neutralize him. The continued neutralization of the opponent's power leaves the leader unaffected by the opponent. In this way, you follow the principles of leading, joining, and neutralizing until the upper hand has been gained. The power of the *cheng hsin* rollback technique comes from lending oneself unconditionally to the purity of functional principles.

Principles of Workability

In martial arts, as well as in other walks of life, we often get in our own way by looking for what seems to be an immediate or quick solution. For example, suppose you want to drive to the grocery store to do some last-minute shopping before your dinner guests arrive. In this example, you are in such a hurry that you do not want to take the time to actually get into your automobile. Instead, you endeavor to drive the car while running alongside the door of the vehicle. If this were to become a common occurrence, think of the skill you would develop—the coordination required to manipulate the clutch, brake, and throttle while steering at the same time as running. The footwork required would be magnificent and the endurance tremendous. On the other hand, any beginning driver could get to the store and back much more quickly.

The truth is, when we are rushed or under pressure (in a fighting situation, perhaps), we tend to follow our habitual way of doing things. To a master fighter, the unworkable approach that many people have to fighting appears just as ludicrous as trying to drive a car without getting inside, doing what is familiar instead of what holistically works.

The internal martial arts teach that we must first endeavor to change the state of being to one in which all techniques are more powerful. To follow the most appropriate and workable methods of fighting, we need to come from a state of being where such methods can emerge. If our fighting method depends on relaxation, then we must come from a state of being relaxed. However, if we are continually in a low-energy state of being, it is unlikely that we will magically meet the demand in a tight situation. If we are narrow-minded and insist upon fighting our own way, then a powerful opponent with a radical method will gain the upper hand. The most powerful thing would be to fight from a context that can handle any situation.

How, then, can we shift to an appropriate state of being? Two methods are available; both are classical and both are essential. One way is through intense contemplation or questioning of being, such as the study of Zen. This study can put one in touch with the context from which states of being arise. The other method is through disciplined training of a particular state of being. The practice of a technique such as the *cheng hsin* rollback presents us such an opportunity.

The Value of Leading

It's important to understand the value of leading in the fighting arts. Blocking isn't the best way to keep a force off its target. In extreme cases, the drawbacks of blocking and using force are obvious. For instance, look at the incredible mass and expense of energy required to dam a river or even dike its banks. Compare this with the force required to lead it off via aqueducts. Or consider a bullfight. You may say the odds favor the bull's being killed. After all, this is almost always the outcome. However, there is one basic rule that the matador must follow without fail if he is to survive: He must never pit his strength directly against the bull's. The matador would never in a thousand fights consider blocking the bull to prevent an attack. That is a no-win situation. What this artist has studied for years is the skill of leading the bull away from his body with seemingly little effort. Olé!

Not only does blocking take a heavy toll on the blocker, but it also fails to completely neutralize the force. If you are a big strong guy, then you may not be affected very much by stopping the blow of your opponent. But this is not absolute; if you are moved even slightly off balance, a skillful fighter can take advantage.

Professional boxers are experts in the art of leading. They understand that their bodies are targets and that they can lead their opponent's desire to hit them, and thus set the opponent up, keeping him off balance, exposed, and in a position where he cannot make a powerful attack. This is all done without laying a hand on the adversary.

So, how does one accomplish leading? As in the case of the proverbial "carrot before the horse," leading is created by offering some prize and then taking it away. The boxer offers a target, such as his chin, to manipulate the challenger. A matador offers himself and the cape to lead the charge of the bull just out of reach of his body. In the *cheng hsin* rollback technique, an arm in the ward-off position is offered to attract the force of the push.

Keeping the aforementioned images in mind, follow this simple description of the *cheng hsin* rollback. Here the ward-off is offered to the push, as an alternative target to the body. It must be handled by the pusher if he doesn't want to be smacked in the face.

- Standing with one foot forward, at a comfortable length of stance, with the width approximately that of the shoulders, one holds the arm out in front of the chest, with the shoulder relaxed and the forearm horizontal as though it is floating in water. The wrist is in front of one side of the body, while the elbow guards the other.
- Receiving the push, the ward-off yields the whole arm and simultaneously pulls the wrist inward toward the opposite side of the chest from where it was originally stationed (left wrist moves toward the left side, right toward the right), immediately changing the direction the push must take to stay in contact. Shifting the weight to the back foot further neutralizes the push, and with a turn of the waist it is led to the outside.
- Then the other arm reaches up and, joining the motion of the push at the side of the pusher's arm, escorts the redirected push to where it is being led. The word *escort* is used because in no way should this second arm be forceful. There should be no more than a very few ounces of pressure on the pusher. Keep the example of the matador in mind, and remember that the force is redirected only through the use of leading. Although variations must sometimes be used, according to the direction of the push as well as other moves, the principles remain the same.

Practice the big things first and the subtle concepts later. Spend plenty of time training the gross movement and the feeling of leading. Go through the steps of the rollback in a deliberate manner, being sure to stay in touch with your partner from the beginning to the end of the technique. Trying to make a slick and quick movement out of the rollback in the beginning stages can lead to cheating—using strength or tricks—to accomplish the result. That won't improve your ability.

Here's a helpful technique to improve your joining ability: With your arm over the shoulder or around the waist of your partner, walk with him toward a predetermined destination, such as a doorway. Walk toward the doorway a number of times simply to get a feeling for walking with another person; this is following his movement. Then, taking your partner into account, try joining and directing him just off the mark of his goal. This should be done without pushing him or having him feel manipulated. Instead, the leading partner sets up the walk so that it is he who enters the doorway and the other is led incidentally into the wall. Practice this until you can lead your partner so that he feels as though he missed the target by his mistake.

When handling the push, do not push back against it. Even in taking it to the side, do not push it away; this is unnecessary and is not nearly so effective as the leading. When someone is pushed away from his target, it becomes that much clearer to him where the target is. Leading, on the other hand, takes the opponent where he wants to go; as a result, he doesn't put up a fight.

Learning Through "Listening"

When correctly done, the *cheng hsin* rollback technique is extremely workable. There are no shortcomings in the technique; it works off absolute principles and not relative ones. It does not matter how strong your opponent is because no strength is being used against him. Speed is not an issue because the rollback is already in touch with the movement of the partner. Any breakdowns that occur functionally while doing the rollback are handled continually through adherence to the principles of leading, joining, and neutralizing.

Cheng hsin techniques require no muscular strength and no exceptional speed. What is required is an acute sensitivity to what is happening right now. An opponent may not shout out your name before he charges, so to make use of such sophisticated techniques as joining, leading, and neutralizing, you have to pay close attention at all times. This is called "listening."

Obviously, the rollback described won't handle every situation and energy. Sometimes the opponent will push across your body, anticipating a rollback, and try to pin your arm against your chest to counteract the technique. This case calls for leading in another direction, and a different body movement. The principle and the appropriate joining movement are apparent through "listening." The body feel and sensitivity is trained by doing the basic rollback, from which variations can be handled.

The *cheng hsin* rollback is considered the most powerful technique of its kind, in part because it has martial ramifications that go well beyond the form of the technique. The neutralization of the opponent's force is created without any compromise to the one doing the rollback. Because he hasn't allowed any of the force to come onto his own body, by resisting or blocking, he is stable, grounded, and in charge of the situation. As a development for a more workable way of fighting, it is a training of the functional skills of listening, joining, leading, and neutralizing.

The form of all *cheng hsin* techniques arises from the principles of true workability. The martial *Classics* point to the necessity of making this kind of shift; when a fighting situation arises, it would be foolhardy to go into battle with nothing more than a catalog of techniques. What is called for is truly a different way of being.

Jef Edwards is an instructor at the Cheng Hsin School of Being in Oakland, California. This was his first contribution to Inside Kung-Fu Presents *magazine, and appeared in the July 1991 edition.*

14

San Shou: Tai Chi's Dispersing Hands Set

Stuart Alve Olson

Renowned tai chi master T. T. Liang refers to the *san shou* form as the "two-person dance." This appellation may strike the tai chi student or martial artist as a bit contradictory, considering that this is a sparring set. But Master Liang's reasoning for calling *san shou* a dance lends a much broader meaning and basis than what might usually be attributed to this term.

In the late 1940s, Master Liang went to live with Master Hsiung Yang-ho at his mountain retreat in Taiwan, specifically to learn the tai chi chuan *san shou* (dispersing hands) set, as well as tai chi sword fencing and push-hands. He soon observed that most of the students, especially the beginners, could not complete the two-person form without using force and struggling to keep their balance. Master Liang jovially likens the performance to "All-Star Wrestling." He relates that Master Hsiung would often simply tell everyone to stop and go off on his own to practice the solo form. This was because, as

Master Liang often explains, "Nobody wants to lose; everyone wants to win."

To keep tai chi partners from struggling clumsily through the two-person set, Master Liang developed a more dancelike approach. He incorporated music, beats, and distancing between the partners. This produced several benefits for the practitioner: greater conciseness of movement, an increased ability to relax, and a better sense and understanding of the three basic aspects of *san shou*—neutralize, seize, and attack. The "dance" also aids in developing the skills of "receiving" and "interpreting" energies. All this gave the set a dancelike appearance.

However, there's another reason Master Liang refers to his movements in musical terms. He explains, "When dancing, one is relaxed, agile, and in good spirits. You're having fun. There is no attitude of winning, only of enjoyment with your partner—it's like playing together as children do. This is what tai chi sparring should be like. Otherwise, you'll become competitive, and all the *chi* will go up into your head and upper body, creating tension and stiffness, lack of breath control, and confusion of mind and spirit.

Master William C. C. Chen once related a similar philosophy with real-world applications. On being confronted by an assailant, his response, to paraphrase, was "Oh, good—practice time." With this attitude, he claims he can remain both relaxed and focused.

Master Liang believes that through the dance interpretation, a practitioner can better apply and understand the fundamental principles of tai chi chuan, which are learning to lose, yielding, and giving up oneself in order to relax. With the idea of dancing, we don't carry the baggage of competition, the tension of having to win, or the ego of being number one. This psychology appears consistently throughout Master Liang's teaching.

Another example is a principle that Master Liang teaches in connection with push-hands. When you are being pushed by an opponent, he says, imagine that you are pulling him toward you; when pushing an opponent, act as though he were pulling you toward him. The analogy is to being almost magnetic, in order to give yourself greater control and to eliminate the idea—and fault—of resistance. The *T'ai Chi Ch'uan Treatise* says, "Because I know myself, I then know my opponent, but he does not know me."

In contrast, as we consistently make use of terms such as "sparring" and "fighting," or when we think "push" when we're pushing, we will take on the physical aspects and expressions of those terms, which results in resistance and tension, and so end up employing only external muscular force rather than the real source of tai chi strength, the intrinsic energy.

The *san shou* set, as well as *da lu* (great rollback) and *tui shou* (pushing hands), which are explained in the next section, can serve as a gauge by which to measure and test our ability to relax and be sensitive. Many people practice the solo form and acquire

a false sense of relaxation (*sung*); it isn't until someone actually pushes on us that we can begin to know whether or not we are truly relaxed. Those who just practice the solo form and experience a state of relaxation must therefore be aware that this is a subjective experience.

Mr. Liang notes also that the problem of becoming relaxed is compounded by the differences in meaning between the English idea of "relax" and the Chinese term *sung*. Relaxation, he says, is only one aspect of *sung*; it also denotes such qualities as sensitive, alert, preserving energy, awareness, and active.

Formation of the Two-Person Set

Within Master Liang's two-person sets are a variety of other sets, including *da lu* and *tui shou*. However, the main body of the set is the Yang family original eighty-eight *san shou* postures. Basically, *tui shou* involves use of the four cardinal directions, employing ward-off, rollback, press, and push postures to develop sensitivity. *Da lu* deals with the four diagonal directions, employing pull, split, elbow-strike, and shoulder-strike postures to develop nimbleness. *San shou* employs the applications of all the postures in the solo form, encompassing all the aspects of the art. Master Liang has augmented the original Yang family *san shou* set's eighty-eight postures for each partner with the following sets:

- Yang style *da lu*
- Wang Yen-nien's *da lu*
- Cheng Man Ching's four-corner *da lu*
- Fixed-stance push-hands
- Active-step circling push-hands

By adding these to the original eighty-eight postures, master Liang's two-person set becomes 178 postures for each partner, which provides in a more extensive practice and broader experience of tai chi application.

Historical Roots

San shou is not found within the tradition of Chen family tai chi chuan. The applications were practiced individually, not within the confines of connecting postures. *Tui shou* appears to be the mainstay of Chen style two-person practice, with much emphasis on a *fa-chin* (issuing energy). It was Yang Lu Chang, the founder of the Yang style of tai chi chuan and the first nonfamily student-disciple of the Chen family, under the tutelage of Chen Chen Xing, who invented this Yang style eighty-eight posture *san shou* set.

Shortly after Yang Lu Chan's death in 1872, a controversy began over whether or not Yang's tai chi solo form was just a watered-down version of what he had learned at Chenjiagou (the Chen family village). Some people erroneously believe that he, for one reason or another, wanted to hide the true applications of tai chi chuan from the public at large. (All schools of tai chi chuan have been guilty of this, not simply Yang Lu Chan. Even now, students traveling to the Chen village complain that they are taught very little about application.) This is utter nonsense. Yang Lu Chan simply approached this problem differently. He was not as strict about teaching only family members as was the Chen family.

The doubts raised by the controversy serve only to give false credence to a school or teacher who claims his or her style is the original, or worse, the "secret" style of Yang Lu Chan. Most tai chi teachers, especially in America but also in Taiwan and China, fail to understand the specific events in the history of the Yang family itself when discussing their particular style of Yang tai chi.

Many students of the art consider Yang Lu Chan the "Mozart" of tai chi chuan. It is well documented that no one in the Chen village could defeat him. A formal banquet was held in his honor, and after his death, his body was brought back to the Chen village for burial. It is obvious from these acts that the Chen family honored and respected him. It is also safe to assume that his theories and skills at one point in his career surpassed those of his teachers and all

opponents he later challenged and defeated, which earned him the title of "Yang the Unbeatable" from martial artists of his day. It is only natural for his style to have developed differently from that of the Chen family, considering that he was also quite skilled in the Shaolin tradition of boxing before going to Chen village.

Yang Lu Chan created *san shou*, various *da lu* and *tui shou* exercises, along with other two-person weapon sets. He was indeed a genius, but this assessment is not meant to denigrate the genius of the Chen family. Each style of tai chi is influenced by the teacher and focuses on one or more of the important aspects of tai chi principles and energies. Where Chen might focus more on *fa-chin*, Yang style emphasizes interpreting and neutralizing energy. It would be futile as well as narrow-minded to try to discern which is the superior practice; it is the man that makes the art, not the art that makes the man.

Yang Lu Chan also showed his genius with his contribution to the creation of the *T'ai Chi Ch'uan Classics*. However, it is generally accepted that it was Yang Lu Chan's scholar-disciple, Wu Ho-ching, who actually put them in their present form. In typical Chinese tradition, they were attributed to the Sung dynasty Immortals Chang San-feng and Wang Tsung-yueh so that they would gain greater acceptance.

This history sets the stage for one of the major events of the Yang family. Yang Lu Chan taught his two sons, Ban-ho and Chien-ho, who also became teachers. Ban-ho had very few students. It is reported that his temperament was harsh, which made learning from him difficult. Since he had no children, the lineage continues through Chien-ho. Chien-ho had many disciples, along with a much milder nature. He also had a son, Cheng Fu, who resisted learning tai chi. In fact, he did not become serious about practice until after his father's death, at which time he was forced to learn from other family members and family notes.

After Chien-ho's death, the family dictated that all students of Chien-ho and Ban-ho become the disciples of Cheng-fu, so as not to belittle his rank (ah,

Chinese politics at its best). This infuriated many of Chien-ho's disciples. A few went along with the new order of things, but many did not. Those who did not complained that Cheng Fu's skills were no match for his father's, nor for those of many of his disciples. As a result, many practices do not appear in the repertoires of most disciples of Cheng Fu; presumably because he either did not know them or did not wish to teach them. It is also as likely that few students stayed long enough to learn *san shou* and weapon fencing sets. Even Master Liang's teacher, Cheng Man Ching, did not know *san shou*. Having spent only two years with Yang Cheng Fu, he did not have the opportunity to learn this or other sets.

Anyone who practices Yang style tai chi chuan must understand that *san shou* is the apex of the art. Yang Lu Chan watered-down nothing; rather he ingeniously improved the entire art of tai chi chuan. Those who practice only the solo form and *tui shou* are handicapped with possessing only half the art—more precisely, only half the program that Yang Lu Chan designed for attaining defensive skills. The solo form and *tui shou* are not enough to prepare the tai chi practitioner for free sparring in the ultimate sense because they do not develop the higher levels and energies of tai chi chuan. *San shou* practice takes one much further down the road in acquiring those skills.

Before tai chi practitioners who don't practice *san shou* start shouting accusations of arrogance or denigrating those masters who did not practice *san shou*, it must be interjected here that *san shou* is not the "miracle cure" for becoming a tai chi master, but rather an expedient in acquiring some of the genuine skills. Master Liang maintains that after studying with and observing the students of 15 prominent teachers, he discerned that those with *san shou* experience had acquired higher skills sooner than those with just *tui shou* experience. The reason, in all probability, is that *san shou* exposes the practitioner more readily and overtly to the energies of interpreting, receiving, neutralizing, and issuing. Because

the resource for these skills with just *tui shou* practice is much more limited, the development will be slower—not impossible, just slower.

The Secret of Lines

Besides the energies and the aspects of neutralize, seize, and attack, an equally important skill is incorporated into the *san shou* set by Master Liang, called lines. Coupled with the energies, especially intrinsic, lines will elevate one's skill level to that of what the *T'ai Chi Ch'uan Classics* call "removing a thousand pounds with only four ounces."

However, lines are probably the least known of all techniques and skills within tai chi chuan, equal in secrecy to that of "sticky energy." This is because unless one has some proficiency with the basic energies, lines won't be effective. One must not only study a long time with Master Liang, but also "curry much favor" to get him to discuss this aspect.

According to Master Liang, a line is the point on an opponent's body where his center of balance is most vulnerable. Attacking an opponent at the optimally effective angle and direction of a push, pull, or strike causes him to lose the ability to root and center himself. It is the knowledge of lines, and not some form of mystical *chi*, that makes a tai chi master's push look so effortless.

There are twenty-five basic lines. Each one takes into account a specific type of posture into which the opponent has positioned himself, whether he is rising or sinking, advancing or retreating, and also the insubstantial and substantial aspects of his body. For lines to be truly effective, it is imperative that there is some development of both interpreting and intrinsic energy. These are best developed through *san shou* practice.

To attempt a push, pull, or strike without the use of lines is what Master Liang calls "a blind man's bluff." Lines are, without question, the most expedient manner in which to counterattack an opponent.

The Precious Few

Within Master Liang's two-person dance set, one begins to understand how lines are applied in conjunction with neutralize, seize, and attack. Nevertheless, most tai chi practitioners do not understand, nor probably have ever heard of, these aspects. Master Liang himself claims that only a couple of his own teachers could clearly explain them—Cheng Man Ching and, to a greater extent, Master Hsiung Yang-ho.

Cheng, he says, could apply them to *tui shou*, but Hsiung also knew how they were incorporated into the *san shou* set. Some of Liang's other teachers also had similar knowledge, but it was Cheng and Hsiung who first taught him, so he gives them the credit. He notes that though he learned only ten lines from Cheng, Cheng claimed to know twenty-five. It wasn't until studying *san shou* with Hsiung that Liang learned their full extent and applications.

(For further information on the four cardinal directions, the four corners, and how these relate to tai chi chuan, see pages 22–23 of Master T. T. Liang's book *T'ai Chi Ch'uan for Health and Self-Defense*.)

Stuart Olson is a martial artist and freelance writer based in City of Industry, California. This material appeared in the August 1991 edition of Inside Kung-Fu *magazine.*

C. K. Chern's Vertical Axis Tai Chi

Sam Edwards

C. K. Chern's body posture and method of movement ensure greater relaxation and responsiveness in the body, while developing a stronger connection between the weighted foot and the ground.

Master C. K. Chern's unique vertical axis style is a modification of Cheng Man Ching's development of the classic Yang style tai chi chuan. Cheng Man Ching elevated the traditional low stances of the Yang style, simplified many of the movements, and emphasized momentum and softness.

Chern has raised and shortened the stance even more. All postures are single-weighted, and all rotations are made on the "bubbling well" (kidney one acupuncture point) of the weighted foot after the weight shift onto that foot is completed. Emphasis is on the weight's being low in the body, rather than the body's being low to the ground, with the upper body very loose and relaxed, the arms seldom rising above chest height.

Chern sees the body—erect and stabilized on one leg as an axis, with the other leg devoid of weight—like a spinning planet, the rotation increasing its subtle electromagnetic field, the momentum and centrifugal force "exciting" the *chi*.

Greater Relaxation

Chern's body posture and method of movement ensure greater relaxation and responsiveness in the body as well as developing a stronger connection between the weighted foot and the ground. With the addition of the earlier rotation about the single vertical axis of the weighted leg and the spine, practitioners quickly acquire a dynamic "root" that generally takes many years to develop in other tai chi chuan systems.

A unique moving-step push-hands arises naturally from this system, based on Chern's analogy of a spinning globe. The relaxed ability to rotate on the axis of the weighted foot promotes a natural, unstudied response to a partner that does not depend on trained technique. Push-hands can therefore be taught to students from the very beginning of their training as simply an extension and complement of the form.

Relaxation and body conditioning are promoted with *chi kung* exercises that, like Master Chern's other practices, emphasize simplicity and fundamental principles. In his workshops in the United States, Kyle Yu stressed that the bases of the system are both its foundation and its ultimate, most sophisticated aim. Gently falling backward against a wall, meditative walking, and a bear posture constitute the core of the energetic practice that master Chern directed Kyle to encourage in the U.S. outposts of vertical axis tai chi chuan.

Taking On the Wall

Falling against the wall is one of the core practices at Chern's school. Gently falling backward approximately one foot against a stable wall breaks up stagnant *chi* and encourages the free circulation of energy by resonance (not impact!) throughout the body. This exercise teaches the student to relax completely, as babies do—you can tap a baby on the foot and feel the resonance throughout its "open" body, even in parts of the skull.

The vibration and resonance also increase the body's internal substance and density. Allowing the energy of impact to travel freely down the body to the ground increases the student's connection to the earth or root.

A Single Sensation

Meditative walking is also deceptively simple: Stand with all the weight on one foot and release as much muscular tension as you can. It is particularly important to release the hip flexor muscles, resulting in a slight fold at the hip. Release the shoulders, too, letting them round forward slightly. Release the chest to allow the heart and lungs to relax. Release the buttocks. As you work on releasing unnecessary tension in the muscles of the body down to the foot, feel all the weight of the body in the foot. The idea is to encourage an energetically and physically lower center of gravity.

Walking takes on a new meaning when you maintain the feeling of release and relaxation. Shift the weight to the empty foot by gently pushing down on the ground with the weighted foot, maintaining a level pelvis, until you are again single weighted on the new leg. As the previously working leg empties of force and weight, there is a sensation of the remaining weight's becoming liquid and pouring to the other leg and on into the ground.

Turning on the Bubbling Well

Bear-posture *chi kung* adds rotation to the weight shifts involved in the walking exercise. Stand in the same relaxed posture, feet parallel and shoulders-width apart, all the weight on the left foot. Turn to the left to a 45-degree angle from your forward direction, allowing the arms to swing up to—at most—a 45-degree angle from the axis of the body, with the palms facing each other. Without changing the orientation of the body, shift the weight to the right foot by pushing off from the ground with the left foot. Then rotate the body on the weighted foot 90 degrees to the right (45 degrees away from the forward direction, but on the right side). Reverse the process and repeat.

The rotations of the bear posture exercise occur after the weight shift and, as Don Miller has written, are motivated by an imagined turning or spiraling on the bubbling well of the loaded foot rather than by a turn of the waist or spine.

One of Cheng Man Ching's distinctive training practices was to hold the postures of the tai chi form as static *chi kung* exercises. Students holding Master Chern's more upright posture and with greater relaxation in the arms and upper body find increased circulation of energy to the upper body.

Short—But Rewarding

The history of Chern's vertical axis tai chi in the United States has been short but richly rewarding. In 1990, Don Miller and I were part of the U.S. team competing in the Internationals held in Taiwan. The entire U.S. team was invited by Master Chern, coach of the winning Taiwanese team (the U.S. team was a close second), to travel as his guests to Chia-Yi for an informal match with his school (which had provided the majority of the players on Taiwan's national team).

Inspired by those amazing few days, Don and I returned the next year with Bruce Shapiro. All three of us had practiced martial arts for some years. Nevertheless, the notion that you can lower your center to your foot without physically lowering your body was a very difficult adjustment to make—even after experiencing how Master Chern could project any of the three across the room with ease, all the while standing erect and totally relaxed.

These short visits to Taiwan have already affected push-hands competition in the United States. Robert Macy, perennial super heavyweight champion, studies vertical axis tai chi (as well as Arthur Goodridge's unique combination of tai chi and I-chuan). Don Miller has won every heavyweight competition he has entered for years.

Spreading the Word

In early 1996, Kyle Yu first visited Los Angeles, where he demonstrated Master Chern's continuing innovations for Miller, Shapiro, and other experienced martial artists. Next he went to Mendocino, north of San Francisco, as a guest of the Redwood Coast T'ai Chi Association and the Sierra Nevada Internal Arts Association, both of which feature vertical axis tai chi.

Later in the year, Master Chern also sent Hou Li Hui, another senior instructor and push-hands champion, to work with the Redwood Coast and Sierra Nevada Associations on the form. The Redwood Coast T'ai Chi Association includes a number of practitioners with more than twenty years of experience in various martial arts such as tai chi chuan, jujitsu, *baguazhang,* and Choy Li Fut. All find that vertical axis tai chi chuan enhances rather than contradicts their other styles.

During his visit, Yu emphasized movement that is completely "let go"—almost in a drunken manner. In the weeks subsequent to Yu's visit, many members of the association experienced unlocking of habitual areas or tension patterns, particularly in the shoulders and pelvic girdle.

C. K. Chern is returning the practice of tai chi chuan to its underlying simplicity. Like Cheng Man Ching, he is clearing away the complications that it seems to be human nature to layer onto the simplest act. With the "drunken" relaxation, Master Chern's training methods enable even beginning students to grasp the qualities of *sung* (the Chinese word is generally translated as "relaxed" but carries many other connotations as well, most particularly that of "open" or "receptive"). Through his continuing rediscovery of simplicity, Master Chern has modified his training practices to enable us all to realize the elegant geometry and supreme relaxation that raised tai chi chuan to a "way."

Sam Edwards is the past coach of the Redwood Coast T'ai Chi Association and is currently coach of the Sierra Nevada Internal Arts Association. This material was published in the March 1997 edition of Inside Kung-Fu *magazine.*

16

Learn to Take Nothing for Granted

Lou Crockett

Most people who study tai chi chuan can give you good reasons for doing so: relaxation, nonstressful exercise, health, and so on. But how many students of the art really know what they are studying? How many have actually researched, explored, or even questioned the original motive or function of each movement?

Certainly enough practitioners of other martial arts are asking some very real questions about how tai chi chuan is often presented. Some of those questions need to be addressed: "When some tai chi chuan stylists 'do their thing,' why are their hands limp and held so close to the body, with the top hand only as high as the diaphragm?" "Why do some stare out into space like zombies, while moving around as if pulling their feet out of the mud?" "Why do they look drunk instead of alert and calm?" "Why is tai chi chuan called a martial art?" "Why do some people who do this look so powerful, and others just plain boring?"

These are legitimate questions, and if you are a student of tai chi chuan, regardless of the style, you should know the answers—the practical, functional, realistic reasons for every nuance of your solo tai chi chuan form.

Learn to Ask "Why?"

It is your *sifu*'s job to help you understand what you are doing, and why. Often, unfortunately, the responsibility is yours to politely ask. If the answers you get are not clear, don't assume your questions are dumb or complex.

Some defenders may argue, "It takes time to learn the art," and "Not everything is revealed until you are ready." Yes, it does take a while to learn the fundamental principles of tai chi chuan. One reason is that tai chi chuan's approach to everything is circuitous. And as with most activities, you won't really understand some aspects until you've reached the requisite level of experience or maturity.

Nevertheless, certain basic principles apply to tai chi chuan, just like every other martial art. You should know these right off the top. For everyone who has never asked "Why?" in a tai chi chuan class, here is a primer of questions and answers that apply to every legitimate style of tai chi chuan.

How About Those Elbows?

In tai chi chuan, as in any other boxing art, the hands must be held up, not hanging limply out and low in front of the body. The reason: could you deflect any kind of punch to your neck, face, or head without keeping your hands up and alert?

And how about those elbows: Are they down slightly to help protect those ribs, or are they floating up somewhere, or plastered to your sides? If they're floating up, you would be risking broken ribs or worse. Plastered to your sides, they could be jammed to your body as you are bounced off the nearest wall.

Heads Up

Do you carry your head up? Do you know why? Yes, one reason is to "raise the spirit" and increase awareness. It also helps protect the chin, along with maintaining visual awareness. Specifically, you lifted at the back of the head, stretching the cervical curve and spine, while automatically lowering the chin and providing a better peripheral view of your opponent's lower extremities.

Learn the Angles

When you step forward with your "empty" foot, do you turn it out at 45 degrees? Do you know that not all tai chi chuan styles do this? If your style does, then you should know why. You should also know

the potential danger to your legs and knees with this kind of "toes out" stepping. For one, the knee is probably the first target of an experienced fighter. No knees, no contest. Stepping out without a full understanding of why you are turning your toes out so far, or how to protect those knees when doing so, could eventually result in painful knee problems, even if you never get kicked.

Sticky Legs Practice

Most students of tai chi chuan hear the phrase "sticky hands" without probing its full connotation. It means to adhere to the opponent like glue—but not just with your hands. There is a similar expression in other Chinese martial arts: "sticky legs." Tai chi chuan utilizes this technique as well.

In fact, the Wu and Chen styles of tai chi chuan, which employ many throwing techniques, make great use of "sticky legs." The toes of the lead foot are angled slightly inward for hooking the opponent's foot or leg as he moves. Another reason for turning the toes in is to provide some protection for the knees. When you're kicked in the knee, if the foot is turned in, the knee tends to fold rather than snap because of the articulation of the foot, leg, and hip.

On the Ball

Why, in most styles of tai chi chuan, are students taught to "carry the ball"? The frequently cited image is to meant convey the concept of circling the arms to protect the upper and lower quadrants, or body zone targets, and your centerline. This formation of the arms and hands should be familiar to anyone who has ever watched a *chi sao* drill between exponents of Wing Chun kung fu. Of course, they are moving much faster than someone playing a slow tai chi chuan solo form. Nonetheless, the real purpose for "carry the ball" training is to teach you to keep your arms and hands in front of you to protect your centerline, upper quadrants (gates), and everything else from the waist up.

Lacking Punch?

If they were intended for fighting, why are there so few punches in Yang and Wu styles of tai chi chuan? You haven't been paying close enough attention. For one thing, there are a lot of punches! Of course, if they are not pointed out, you may not recognize them as such. For instance, take a familiar tai chi chuan movement such as "single whip." Depending on the system, the hooked hand is a type of fist. It can be used to strike with the bony protrusion of the forearm (ulna and radius) when the wrist is bent downward. Targets could be under the chin of an opponent, at the diaphragm, or under the triceps.

Using the second knuckle of the second and third fingers, reinforced by the thumb, a downward strike can be directed toward the bridge of the nose and/or mouth area, the sternum, or the clavicle, just for starters. Of course, if no one pointed it out, or if you never asked why, you may never have noticed that that particular hand configuration is quite common in Chinese fighting systems. Praying mantis kung fu uses a slight variation for hooking as well as striking. In other systems, it is called a "crane beak" fist. Some systems even accompany the fist with the "whooping" sound of a crane (one of Bruce Lee's favorite sounds).

All martial systems, including tai chi chuan, use the same fist with minor variations for hooking an opponent's wrist, elbow, knee joint, or ankle. As with all such techniques, the only limitation is that of the durability of the body, yours or your opponent's.

Speaking of durability, it should be noted that in most tai chi chuan styles, many offensive movements are performed with an open hand. Why? A good reason is to avoid personal injury. Since you train for sensitivity and flexibility in tai chi chuan, you quickly become aware that unless your fists and hands are conditioned to withstand enormous punishment, you can easily break them when hitting your opponents' head, knee, or elbow, or the wall behind them (if they duck).

An open-palm strike can be as devastating to an opponent as any penetrating punch. Tai chi chuan is almost all open-palm techniques. One reason is that it offers contact over a larger area. A shock effect occurs neurologically at the skin's surface and spreads to internal muscles, nerves, and nearby organs from an open-hand strike delivered with complete focus and body alignment. If the opponent is moving in the same direction as the blow's trajectory, it becomes a push or throw at the same time.

Work With, Not Against, Brute Force

Many external stylists, or "hard" stylists, have questioned tai chi chuan's distinct lack of clenched fists and its doctrine of "softness." A major reason for this approach is the relax, yield, stick, follow, and strike factor. In other words, the fighting system was designed to work with and not against brute force. The principles in tai chi chuan are very similar to the art of jujitsu.

In fact, it is no coincidence that tai chi chuan, Hsing I *chuan*, and *baguazhang*, the "internal" martial arts of China, have much in common with the Japanese "soft styles." Historically, there was a great deal of travel and exchange between the two cultures. Chinese merchants and officials traveled with highly skilled protection that was deliberately nonthreatening in appearance. Nothing will spoil a good trade deal faster than giving your hosts the impression you don't trust them.

The technique of "appear and disappear" in tai chi, Hsing I, and *baguazhang* combat training, for instance, is virtually identical to that of *nin-jutsu*, jujitsu, and aikido. The name of the technique is a literal description of how one moves around an opponent when "sticking and following" (which is why push-hands and *da lu*, or long pullback, are such an important part of the tai chi chuan training system).

Generally, the "internal" styles are designed for mid- to close-range work. They are structured to allow for little or no "telegraphing" of intention. Therefore, most tai chi chuan attacks are from an apparent and deliberately deceptive "unprepared-looking" stance. There is no posturing, no obvious confrontational stances, just open hands, and constant subtle movement until some action is initiated by either deliberate feint to cause the opponent to move, or actually waiting for an attack to be launched. Thus the constant training in tai chi chuan to absorb incoming force. That is also why there is padding on the walls of some of the traditional type tai chi chuan schools. When you have been pounded into the wall from across the room a few hundred times, you eventually learn to absorb force and not tense up under pressure.

Misunderstanding the Concept

By contrast, the frequently seen tai chi player with the limp hands and drunken appearance is, for the most part, the result of misunderstandings and/or misinterpretations of the concept of softness as it applies to the martial arts, and tai chi chuan in particular. Western concepts of "relaxation" are a world apart from the Chinese concept of "soft." Soft to the Chinese tai chi chuan player is more akin to "sensitive" or "calm," possibly even "quiet"—most certainly not limp or stuporlike.

There is an expression in Chinese fighting arts to "gaze like a tiger," meaning that every move you make requires your complete attention: all your vision, all your senses, all the time. This very sound technique is called *gazing*.

An instructor in the early 1970s introduced me to the concept of gazing. It was among the first of many lessons in humility. Since I was a beginner in tai chi chuan, the concept of "relaxed gaze" was a term in books that went unquestioned. I had never asked my *sifu* what it was or why it might be important. This instructor watched me "play my form" and asked why I was watching my hands and blinking. He then demonstrated why it is imperative to learn to relax the eyes, follow the movements of the limbs, and do it without blinking.

As I did my best "wave hands like clouds," watching every move of my hands, he hit me on the side of the head—twice. My pride hurt more than my ear. That is how he explained the concept of "look at the hands, look at the kicking foot, and watch everything around them with all of your vision," or gazing. Had I been watching "everything," I might have seen his attack coming and at least moved back.

The lesson: Don't blink, and don't just stare straight ahead. Look in the direction of the action. To do so takes self-control, but it can be done, even for extended periods of time. Watch what you are doing. Look in the *direction* of your hands or kicking foot. Watch what is going on all around you.

One other aspect involving the eyes that should be mentioned here is that if you look where you are making contact (striking), you are able to bring your entire being into focus to deliver the *jing* (power).

Toward Mutual Respect

If you do tai chi only for the exercise and ignore the martial applications, you will miss a lot of the discipline, skill, and technical expertise inherent in the entire art form. To be truly skilled in any art, you really do need to be familiar with all sides and aspects of that art. Then you can specialize, selecting the aspect that best suits you: meditation, exercise, therapy, martial skill—or all of it.

It is the tai chi chuan stylist who knows the why of the art who looks the most powerful (and is). The mutual respect generated when you can discuss techniques intelligently with senior practitioners of tai chi chuan is worth more than 10,000,000 words. When you ask your *sifu* why something is done, you are not being disrespectful. You are being curious. You are showing a genuine interest in your chosen art form. Of course, how you ask can make all the difference. Courtesy and respect will go a long way in helping you become the best you can be. Learn how to ask "Why?" and take nothing for granted.

This material appeared in the May 1994 edition of Inside Kung-Fu *magazine.*

17

How to Tell the Good from the Bad in Tai Chi Form

Featuring Bow-Sim Mark

If popularity is defined by the number of practitioners, the most popular martial art in the world is surely tai chi chuan. Along with hundreds of thousands of practitioners in North America and Europe, hundreds of millions in China practice the forms on a daily basis. (One hundred million people represents only about 10 percent of the total population of the People's Republic of China.)

These many practitioners comprise a cross section of the human population, with all the strengths and weaknesses common to human nature. Therefore, you'll find both superior tai chi masters and inferior tai chi masters, and all the degrees of competency in between.

The question, then, is how to tell a good tai chi instructor from an average one. This is a complex issue, because tai chi chuan is a subtle and sophisticated art. And since opinions differ on how the art should be used, and even on exactly what tai chi is, it is impossible to say that any person's opinion is "right" or "wrong." Given these caveats, the guidelines presented here can be used as a basis to judge practitioners as well as instructors. Regardless of the style of tai chi chuan, the basic requirements are the same.

Tai Chi Styles

Among the various styles of tai chi chuan are Sun style, Yang style, Chen style, and two separate styles that have names translated as "Wu" (the Chinese characters for the two Wu styles are completely different). These styles differ more in their place of origin, the size and amplitude of their movements, and the character of their tempo than in technique. All the styles share the same basic requirements and characteristics, although the teaching method may differ from instructor to instructor.

Most sources agree that tai chi chuan, properly performed, includes a well-balanced, centered posture, with light, even, and fluid movements. Emphasis is on flexibility and range of motion rather than on muscular power and rigidity. Breathing must be natural, in synch with the movements, and is normally not shallow. Nor is tai chi chuan limp and lifeless. The practitioner's mental attitude should project a certain vitality, a degree of interest and alertness.

It may not be necessary to go to China to become a good tai chi practitioner, since there are many good masters abroad, and since the Chinese have their own range of proficiency as well. It is true, however, that the country of origin of an art is likely to have more authentic masters of that art, especially when that country has the most practitioners.

Under the assumption that a person learning tai chi can benefit from study in the People's Republic, a few American practitioners have visited China for various lengths of time with the aim of perfecting their skills. One such person is Master Bow Sim Mark of Boston, who is president of the Chinese Wushu Research Institute there. Mark not only has trained with Chinese tai chi masters in her recent visits, but also began her training in China and has accumulated experience spanning three decades. One of her instructors, Master Fu Wing-fay, was a student of the famous general Lee King-lin, who was a master of the *wu-down wushu* system. This art includes Sun and Fu style tai chi chuan, *baguazhang*, Hsing I, and weapons—with special emphasis on the sword.

Sifu Mark migrated to Hong Kong in 1973, where she was chief instructor of the Women's Wushu Association. She did not arrive in Boston until 1975. Since then, she has trained a number of students and has delivered lectures on aspects of tai chi chuan at such institutions as Tufts University. Mark has also produced books on combined tai chi chuan (a standard set of forms developed about twenty years ago by a group of masters from mainland China), advanced sword technique, and basic *wushu* training methods. Her book *Combined T'ai Chi Ch'uan* provides more detailed guidance on how to tell a good tai chi practitioner from a poor one.

Judging Quality

Judging the quality of a tai chi form—your own or someone else's—includes the following principal aspects:

- the angles of the body, particularly the extremities, during movement
- the pacing of the form
- the "framework," or amplitude of motion

According to Sifu Mark, a person is considered to have reached a high level of perfection when he or she can carry out every movement with grace and precision.

In tai chi, the arms are never held against the body. At their lowest position, they are just far enough away that a fist can be placed under the armpit. The angle between the arms, once they have been separated, should be about 135 degrees. This occurs, for example, in the basic movement called "separation of hands," in which the hands are slowly separated to the sides. If the angle of the arms during this movement is more than 135 degrees, say as large as 180 degrees (in which the arms would form a straight line when viewed from above), the chest would be open. This violates an important tai chi requirement that one must "empty the chest and expand the upper back." Thus, opening the arms more than the prescribed 135 degrees would destroy the perfection of a person's tai chi chuan.

The lower extremities also have associated angles that are considered ideal. For example, one generally advances directly to the front (0 degrees); obliquely to the side (45 degrees); or directly to the side (90 degrees). When one retreats, it is usually directly to the rear. Also, the most the body is turned in any movement is 180 degrees.

The size of the performer's "framework" will affect the performance of the form. This term refers to the size of the steps and movements used in the form. A "small framework" involves higher stances with a relatively modest degree of bend at the knees in stepping. This range of motion is considered ideal for older people. The "medium framework" is associated with medium-height stances and a moderate degree of knee bend, so that the knee extends directly over the toes. In this framework, the feet are usually kept two feet apart. A "large framework" implies low stances and would be used by advanced students. Here the feet are generally positioned more than two feet apart, and whenever any leg is bent, the knee extends well over and ahead of the toes.

Common Faults in Tai Chi Chuan

The complexities and subtleties of tai chi chuan can make it difficult for a beginner to perform the movements correctly. Common faults occur in the areas of shoulders and overall posture, and in the waist and its coordination with the limbs.

For example, elevated or shrugged shoulders are sometimes seen in beginners as they attempt movements involving upward lifting of the arms. This prevents the shoulders from remaining loose, and the resulting posture lacks openness, elegance, and comfort. To correct this problem, one must relax and stretch the shoulder joints, empty the chest, sink the shoulders, and expand the upper back.

The interplay between softness and hardness is another revealing aspect of a person's form in tai chi. The art is characterized by a harmony between relaxation, or softness, and hardness. Softness does not mean limpness, and hardness does not mean rigidity. Rather, an elastic quality resulting from the merging of softness and hardness is the ideal.

Beginners also can suffer from confused motion. Tai chi teaches that "Whenever there is movement, the whole body moves." This saying refers to the fact that all movements are systematic, sequential, and based on a clear differentiation between yin and yang. Another common fault can be seen in the waist area. In tai chi, the waist must be used to control the motion of the entire body. When this is not done, the limbs and body move, but the waist does not, resulting in a stiff series of random movements. It is also necessary to keep the spine straight so that the waist is not crooked. When the spine is not straight, the entire manner in which the movements are executed is altered.

Instructor Basics and Beyond

Based on these guidelines, the student seeking a qualified instructor should look for someone whose form has a framework of constant size—ending in the same position in which the form began. This person should be able to perform the form at a particular pace every time, within a few seconds either way. The limbs should move in concert with the waist. The instructor's posture should be erect and balanced throughout the form. This means that the shoulders will not be shrugged or elevated, and the spine will be straight. And of course, every single movement should conform to a basic standard of technique.

These the aspects of form are fairly basic, and a practitioner who does not yet know how to stay within these rules should not be selected as a teacher. They are also fairly easy things for a beginner to spot, since it is possible to develop an eye for proper form in a number of movements simply by looking at photos. More difficult to discern are other, more advanced, qualities of proper tai chi chuan.

For example, a knowledgeable tai chi practitioner will demonstrate an internal motivation; every movement is motivated from the *dan tian*, the internal center point. "If you let the force flow through your arm," Sifu Mark explains, "that is tai chi. The force moves, not the muscles so much." Also, a knowledgeable instructor will be aware of applications for the movements, and be able to make the applications work in sparring. Further, a knowledgeable instructor would have a thorough understanding of the philosophy of yin and yang and be able to relate that to tai chi stances, techniques, and movements. Even more elusive is the proper mental attitude—the penetrating expression in the eyes of a great tai chi performer reflects an alert, aware attitude.

Raising the Standards

During a recent four-month stay in the cities of Beijing, Canton, and Hong Kong, Sifu Mark had the opportunity to reevaluate her skills and compare her technique with that of the tai chi masters of the People's Republic of China. One such master, Lee Tien-chi, was sufficiently impressed with Mark's technique to recommend her for admittance in the prestigious Beijing Institute of Physical Culture, which produces coaches for various sports teams, including *wushu* teams. In an exhibition of combined tai chi chuan during a *wushu* competition, she was rated very high by Chinese standards.

When asked about the difference between North American and Chinese practitioners, Mark noted that the Chinese have practitioners covering a range of proficiency, just as Americans do. However, because their training is more professional compared with American training, which is so far strictly amateur, their best performers conform to extremely high standards. Americans who have witnessed touring *wushu* teams from China can attest to this fact.

Much of the information in this discussion was excerpted from Bow Sim Mark's book Combined T'ai Chi Ch'uan *published by the Chinese Wushu Research Institute, 246 Harrison Avenue, Boston, MA 02111. Readers who are interested in studying tai chi chuan in greater depth are urged to consult the original volume. This material appeared in the May 1982 edition of* Inside Kung-Fu *magazine.*

PART III

Advanced Techniques

18

Meditation and Breathing Exercises

Doc-Fai Wong and Jane Hallander

Traditionally, there are thirteen tai chi meditations and martial arts stances, with several complementary breathing exercises. These meditation postures and special breathing exercises are sometimes referred to as *tai chi–chi kung* training

Meditations for Relaxation

Daily meditation is the best way to develop better internal power. The standing meditations used by the Yang family forced the body to relax. If students didn't relax during their one-hour meditation period, their shoulders and legs became tense and uncomfortable. Relief came through physical and mental relaxation. After their bodies relaxed into comfortable postures, their *chi* started moving freely throughout their bodies. That smoothly flowing *chi* provides body cells with far more energy-giving oxygen than is available to the average person.

Wu Chi Zhan Zhuang

The first *zhan zhuang*, or "standing meditation posture," practiced in traditional tai chi schools is called *wu chi*. While tai chi translates to "grand ultimate," *wu chi*, often considered the parent of tai chi, means "no ultimate." It is an emptiness or void and is the first step toward *chi* development.

Start the *wu chi* standing meditation with your feet parallel and at shoulders width. Bend your knees as much as possible while remaining comfortable. Keep your back straight and hips slightly tucked. When you place your hand on the small of your back, your lower back should be straight. Relax your shoulders and chest, making the chest slightly concave. Make sure your body is straight by mentally lining up your navel with your nose. Look straight ahead, focusing far into the distance. Let your arms hang naturally at your sides. Breathe calmly and quietly. Make sure your breathing remains natural.

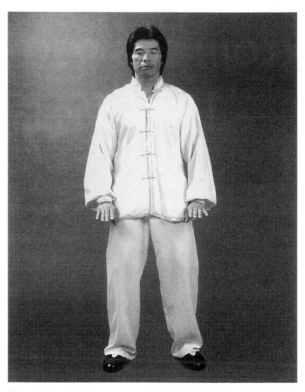

Wu chi zhan zhuang

Tai chi *zhan zhuang*

The middle finger of each hand should touch the center of your thigh where a pressure point called *feng shi* is located. The pressure point at the top of your head, called *bai hui*, should be in a straight line with the *hui yin* point, found directly in front of the anus. A straight line from the *hui yin* to the ground will be centered midway between the *yong quan* points located at the base of each foot pad. Now close your eyes.

Wu chi zhan zhuang provides relaxation before the more strenuous standing meditations. It is also the easiest standing meditation for beginners and older people. Because of its relaxing nature, *wu chi* is a good meditation with which to start.

Begin with five minutes of *wu chi* each day before performing other meditations or stances. Stand in the *wu chi* position for ten minutes the first day. Then gradually work up to one hour per day. When you can do the *wu chi* posture comfortably for one hour, move on to the next level in tai chi meditation.

Tai Chi Zhan Zhuang

The next level of tai chi meditation is known as tai chi standing meditation. It begins in much the same way as the tai chi form. With your knees slightly bent, raise both hands, palms facing downward, to shoulder level. Raise your arms only with your shoulder joints. Keep your shoulders relaxed while you raise your arms. Then lower your arms as if you were starting the tai chi form. Each hand is approximately one fist's distance in front and one fist's distance to the side of each thigh. Keep your palms facing down, with your elbows down and slightly bent, and your fingers pointing forward. As you lower your arms, bend your knees as far as possible.

Your eyes should look forward until you are ready for meditation. Then close both eyes. As with *wu chi zhan zhuang*, mentally line up your navel with your nose. Keep your head straight, as if someone were pulling it by a string from the top of your head.

Hun yuan zhan zhuang

Peng yue zhan zhuang

Keep your shoulders relaxed and chest slightly concave. Your hips should be tucked, with your pelvis pushed slightly forward. This prevents a swayed back. Keep your breathing quiet and natural. Tai chi standing meditation makes your *chi* breathing point drop lower into your abdomen. It is a comfortable meditation, because both hands point forward and the circulation flows into the fingers. This prevents the fingertips from getting numb. Bending the knees helps strengthen your leg muscles.

Hun Yuan Zhan Zhuang

The last in the tai chi standing meditation series is called *hun yuan*, or "universe meditation." Bend both knees and slowly bring your arms up to chest height. Your hands should be rounded, with the fingertips pointing toward each other. Keep your hands relaxed and about three to four inches apart.

As with the other *zhan zhuang* meditations, you keep your back straight, shoulders relaxed, and hips tucked. When everything is straight and relaxed, close your eyes. This particular meditation keeps your *chi* circulating and connected as it flows from the fingertips of one hand to the other hand and back in a circle. *Hun yuan* also helps strengthen the arms, developing *peng jing*, or ward-off energy.

Tai Chi Breathing Exercises

Tai chi breathing exercises can be done either before or after standing meditation to encourage better blood and *chi* circulation and calmer breathing patterns. They were developed as quiet combinations for external movements and natural breathing. The exercises described here were among the most popular with Yang family disciples.

Peng Yue Zhan Zhuang

Peng yue ("holding the moon") is an important tai chi breathing exercise. It balances the energy and creates harmony in what traditional Chinese medical experts call the "triple warmer."

"Triple warmer" is a Chinese medical term describing the body's three principal energy areas: the head, which controls upper-body energy; the torso, representing the body's central portions; and the legs, controlling the lower-body energy. You can actually feel when your triple-warmer energy is not balanced. Feeling light-headed, for instance, indicates not enough energy in that region. Another example is the stomach: if you feel full or empty, no matter how much you have eaten, your torso energy is probably unbalanced. Heavy or light feelings in your legs indicate that triple-warmer energy is not balanced in the lowest warmer region. The *peng yue* breathing exercise will help relieve these symptoms and balance the triple warmer.

Start in a standing position, with your feet parallel and spaced shoulders-width apart. Slightly bend your knees. Your back should be straight, with your buttocks tucked and your pelvis thrust slightly forward. Your shoulders must be relaxed and your chest slightly concave, with the chest muscles also relaxed. Do not slouch or round your shoulders too much. Your body should be relaxed. Focus your eyes straight ahead, mentally lining up your nose with your navel.

Starting with your hands at your sides, slowly raise your arms, palms scooping upward, in front of your torso. The fingertips of both hands should be pointed toward each other, keeping at least two inches of space between your hands. Raise your hands, palms still in the scooping position, until they are at navel level. Continue raising your hands, rotating slowly until they are pushing upward, with your palms facing the sky. Push as far up as you comfortably can. Then slowly pull your hands away from one another, as if you are pulling your fingertips.

Let your hands slowly swing back down in a smooth, even arc until they drop below your *dan tian* (three-fingers width below your navel). Now make a mental connection between the fingertips of both hands, bringing your hands to within two inches of one another. Repeat the process by starting another upward scooping motion.

The key to these tai chi breathing exercises is natural breathing. In the case of *peng yue*, each circle takes too long for an individual breathing cycle, so don't try to time your breathing to each circle. You should be concentrating on your total body connection during the exercise, feeling your internal energy move. Chinese refer to this as "listening to your inside energy."

Repeat each complete *peng yue* circle thirty-six times. *Peng yue* is excellent for beginning students, since most beginners use only the upper third of their total lung capacity.

Fen Yuan

One of the best *chi*-developing breathing exercises is *fen yuan*, or "parting the clouds." Start with one foot forward, with your weight resting on your rear leg. Slowly raise your arms, with the palms facing each other at navel height. Still moving slowly, bring your palms to within one inch of each other. Do not let them touch. Then slowly shift your weight forward. Simultaneously push both hands forward until the knee of your front leg lines up with the toe of the same foot. Your arms should be extended, with your elbows slightly bent, making the leg almost straight.

At this point, slowly turn your palms down outward and your thumbs downward. With your hands back-to-back, slowly pull them apart until your arms are at 45-degree angles to your body. Now shift your weight over the rear leg. Keep your back straight, with your shoulders relaxed and chest slightly concave throughout this exercise. When you have shifted your weight directly over your rear leg, slowly turn

Fen yuan sequence

your palms inward so that they are facing. Bring your arms and hands back to the starting position.

Repeat the exercise thirty-six times. Throughout the *fen yuan* exercise, look into the distance. Do not focus on anything.

Ye Ma Fen Zhong

"Part the wild horse's mane," or *ye ma fen zhong*, is a breathing exercise that closely resembles the tai chi form technique bearing the same name. The difference is that when you practice the breathing exercise, you remain stationary.

Start *ye ma fen zhong* with one foot forward and your weight directly over the rear leg. Hold one arm below your navel, with the palm facing up. The other arm is at midchest height, with the palm facing down, as if you were holding a beach ball. The movement starts with the bottom hand angling upward to the same hand position as the upper hand in "part

the wild horse's mane" in the tai chi form. The top hand simultaneously pushes down as if it were doing the form technique. Then the forward hand moves back in a circle to become the top hand. The other hand, which started on the top, makes a circle back, becoming the lower hand. Shift your weight forward and back with each opening of the rounded hands. Look straight ahead, keeping your back straight and body relaxed. Repeat this exercise thirty-six times.

Dao Juan Gong

Dao juan gong translates to "reverse turning arms." Like its cousin, *ye ma fen zhong*, *dao juan gong* is similar to techniques in the tai chi form "repulse the monkey" and "brush knee." Start with one foot forward in a brush-knee position, with your weight on your back leg. If your left leg is the forward leg, your left hand should be pushing forward. Your right hand will be scooped upward in a "repulse the monkey"

Ye me fen zhong **sequence**

position next to your right leg. Bring your right hand up in a circle next to your right ear and continue forward to the brush-knee pushing position. Now turn that same hand, palm upward, as if you were doing "repulse the monkey," and pull it back to your body—as in the same tai chi form. At the same time, the opposite hand moves forward to a brush-knee pushing position.

Repeat thirty-six times, breathing quietly and naturally.

With each complete change in hand position, shift your body weight forward and back.

One Hundred Days to *Chi* Development

With all of the breathing exercises, you can change your leg position halfway through the exercise. Remember to look straight ahead.

If you practice at least one of the meditations one hour a day for 100 days, and supplement these with breathing exercises, you should start feeling *chi* development. Assuming you are a relatively relaxed person, you should feel heat in the *lao gong* pressure point in the center of your palms. You may also feel tingling in your fingertips. Some individuals even feel the pulse pumping into their hands and into the *yong quan* pressure point at the bottom of the feet. At this time, all four pressure points (both hands and feet) are connected by an uninterrupted flow of *chi*.

Dao juan gong sequence

19

The Four Skills of Tai Chi Chuan

Howard Choy

"How can I improve my tai chi?" is a question often asked by my students. It is also a question I have been grappling with for as long as I can remember. I once posed the same question to my teacher, the late grand master Yang Sau Chung, and he tersely replied, "By practicing the form correctly!"

"But how?" you may ask.

A good teacher helps, but a teacher can't be there correcting all the time. Wu Tu-Nan, a well-known tai chi master from China, proposed that there are four kinds of tai chi skills (kung), and if you practice the form (or push-hands or weapons, for that matter) with these skills in mind, then it will be correctly performed, and you will gradually improve your tai chi. They are: function, relaxation, jin, and chi.

The Skill of Function

Tai chi is a martial art: each movement has a practical function. These functions must be understood. For example, when we execute the movement "step up, deflect downward, parry, and punch," do we understand how these moves are used in a self-defense situation? How to step forward, how to deflect downward, how to parry, how to punch? Not only do we need to visualize our own movement, but we also must visualize the distance and posture of the opponent when performing the form.

Understanding the practical use of a move will help you correctly execute that move. The direction of the body, the coordination of the limbs, the breathing, and the chi flow are related to the use. The more you practice visualizing the actual use and imagining yourself boxing with an opponent, the better you will be in executing the form. The function corrects the move because it has a job to do; you will gradually remove all superfluous and useless "bad habits" and reach the stage of proper tai chi.

The Skill of Relaxation

A distinction must be made here between being relaxed and being floppy and sluggish. A relaxed body is one without friction in the joints or tension in the muscles. The mind is alert and the body sunk (low center of gravity). A floppy body is in negative tension. It is equally as detrimental to your progress as a tensed body. Being floppy or being tense makes you sluggish. It blocks the flow of the vital energy (*chi*), and we lose the resilient, springy, sensitive quality associated with soft and relaxed muscles.

Correct posture also helps relaxation. The body is held vertical at all times while performing the form. In this way, the muscles designed to keep our body upright are functioning properly.

The Skill of *Jin*

What is *jin*? Although the source of *jin* lies in strength, it is not the same as strength. Strength is static force, while *jin* is dynamic. When the body is relaxed and sunk, the *jin* is gathered and concentrated by the mind and can be released at will in various forms to a particular part of the body. *Jin* can be fast or slow, hard or soft, tight or loose, stiff or springy, delayed or explosive. The powerhouse of *jin* lies in the *dan tian*, released through the waist. Its energy is permeated throughout the body by the free flow of the *chi*. Hence the *jin* is intimately related to the breath and *chi* flow.

As a dynamic force, *jin* is governed by the laws of Newtonian physics. Take the equation $F = md/t$, for example. *Jin* as a dynamic force (F) can be increased by a corresponding increase in the mass (m), distance (d), and speed (t) of delivery. Although the weight of your body is finite, the mass can be concentrated by lowering the center of gravity at the point of execution. Distance can be increased without pulling back by executing your movement in a circular and/or screw action. Also, speed can be increased by proper means of breathing and relaxing and tensing the muscles at the appropriate time with correct posture.

Each of the eight tai chi basic movements—*peng* (ward-off), *lu* (rollback), *ji* (press), *an* (push), *cai* (grab), *lie* (break or control elbow), *zhou* (elbow), and kao (shoulder)—has a particular *jin* associated with it. Chen style tai chi has special emphasis on "screw action" *jin* and "cannon" *jin*. Alone with pushhands, four main *jins* also are involved: they are "listening" *jin*, "understanding" *jin*, "neutralizing" *jin*, and "expressing " (explosive) *jin*.

The Skill of *Chi*

Tai chi is a form of moving *chi kung* (breathing exercise). The *Classics* make numerous references to *chi*. There are two main types of *chi* skill in tai chi: *chi* circulation and *chi* utilization. The amount of *chi* in a person at a given movement is determined by both hereditary background, which is finite and unchangeable, and diet and environment (including methods used to maximize the intake of oxygen and exhalation of carbon dioxide), which are infinite and changeable.

Circulation begins with the *dan tian*, where *chi* is stored. *Chi* is activated by the mind and flows along the meridian channels to their ends at the extremity of our limbs and then returns to the *dan tian*. Proper *chi* circulation is important to your health. This is where the benefits of tai chi really shine.

Chi utilization refers to the control and use of the great energy in one's body. The internal *chi* cultivated and circulated in the body can be expressed through the mind and applied externally to another person through correct postures and breathing.

The four tai chi skills discussed here are interrelated and essential to all tai chi exercises—from push-hands and *da lu* to *san shou* and weapons. Success in tai chi lies in understanding these four skills and then correctly practicing them with patience and perseverance.

Howard Choy has been practicing tai chi for more than twenty years under various masters in Australia and Asia. He spent two years in Hong Kong with the late grand master Yang Sau Chung, the last keeper of the Yang style tai chi chuan. This material was published in the September 1988 edition of Inside Kung-Fu *magazine.*

20

Master Chen Xiaowang's Five Levels of Skill in Tai Chi Training

Howard Choy and Ahtee Chia

Since the publication of our interview with Master Chen Xiaowang (see "Chen Xiaowang: Keeper of the Tai Chi Secrets" in Part Four of this book), many readers have requested more information about Chen family tai chi. Most people want to know what they can do to improve their tai chi training. I posed this question to Master Chen, and he replied that just as we learn to crawl before we walk and walk before we run, tai chi training is done in a progressive way.

He emphasizes that initial training in the basic principles provides the foundation on which more advanced skills are built. You must be patient and master one level before attempting the next. Progress in tai chi does not depend on how many forms you have learned, but rather on how well you are able to absorb and integrate the principles in your form. It does not matter which style of tai chi you practice or whether your stance is high or low. What is important is that you are able to harness your *chi* and circulate it to all parts of your body. Your move-

ments will then look soft yet powerful, your demeanor relaxed yet alert.

According to Master Chen, there are five levels of proficiency in tai chi training, as described here, and each has its own aims and training methods. Knowing these can help you assess your own level of achievement and what you need to work on to make progress.

Level One: Form and Posture

Correct posture forms the foundation of tai chi chuan. This is necessary before the *chi* can flow properly. To adopt the correct posture, keep the body vertical, the head held as if suspended from above, the shoulders and chest relaxed, the waist supple, the knees bent, and the groin open. Let your intrinsic *chi* settle and sink to the *dan tian*, or lower abdomen. You may not be able to do this straight away, but aim for gradual correctness in relation to direction, angle, position, and movement of the limbs to attain the right postures.

Do not aim for perfection. Your tai chi form will be angular and disconnected. This is normal for a beginner. With diligent and proper practice, after six months you should be able to master the shape of the form. You will also start to feel the *chi* in your body. At this stage, you are using the movement to generate the *chi*. As you become more familiar with the form, you will begin to understand the intrinsic *jin,* or dynamic energy. However, you will start to feel some movements of the *chi* even though you cannot get it to flow smoothly and join them up.

This stage is said to be one yin and nine yang. It is like a pole that is poked into the ground. Being shallow and lacking a proper base, it is easily pushed over. At this stage, there is too much yang and not enough yin. Sparring and push-hands are not recommended.

Level Two: *Chi* Flow

At this level, you will begin to feel the movement of the intrinsic *chi*. Keep practicing the form to gain more fluidity and smoothness of movement. Do not bob up and down. Keep an even height of posture throughout. Although you are now able to feel the intrinsic *chi*, you are not yet able to direct it. There are two reasons for this.

First, your *chi* is uncoordinated and your posture is not quite right. You still do not understand the subtler details. For example, in trying to hollow the chest, you collapse it too much, or in trying to keep the waist supple, you make it too loose. Or you may stick your buttocks out too far and push your chest forward. Your posture will need to be adjusted in order for you to gain proper coordination of the body and eliminate all contradictions of purpose, to gain unity of the internal with the external.

Internal harmony means that the heart unites with the mind, the *chi* with the strength, and the sinews with the bones. External harmony means that the hand is coordinated with the feet, the elbow with the knee, and the shoulder with the hips. It is only then that the external is unified with the internal, where the open exists within the closed, and the closed exists within the open.

The second reason is that you may be doing the form either too fast, so that you lose the smoothness of the movement, or too slowly, so that your movements become disjointed.

At this stage, the "reeling silk" exercise is very important, and you should use the technique in your movements. The *Classics* say, "In 'reeling silk' the *chi* originates from the waist, permeates everywhere, and is ever present."

To do "reeling silk" properly, first relax the shoulders, sink the elbows, hollow the chest, drop the waist, open the groin, and bend the knees. Start with the hand at the *dan tian*. The hand leads the elbow, the elbow leads the shoulder, the shoulder leads the waist. On the return cycle, the waist activates the shoulder, the shoulder activates the elbow, and the elbow activates the hand. On the upper half of the body, the wrist is coordinated with the trunk, and on the lower half, the ankles turn the legs. The body is like a tree—the roots represent the legs, the tree trunk the body, and the branches and leaves the arms and fingers. The *chi* circulates from the roots to the trunk and then to the leaves and then retraces its path to the roots again.

During the first level, you will feel that you are making rapid progress. However, at the transition from the first to the second level, you will feel that you are not making progress at all. Your *chi* flows sometimes and not at other times. When you express energy (*fa jing*) in a punch, you may make a snapping sound, but when you try to do the same in push-hands, nothing seems to work.

At this stage, it is easy to feel discouraged and frustrated, and you may even give up. A strong determination and persistence is required. What you need to do is reexamine your form; go back to the basic principles. Correct your posture, and move the whole body as a unit. When one part of the body moves, the whole body moves. There is no excess or deficiency; flow with the changes, and rotate and move naturally.

Everybody has the potential to achieve success in tai chi with proper training. This level usually takes four years to complete. Your *chi* will start to flow, and you will understand how to use it. Your confidence will increase, and your tai chi will start to become more interesting.

Push-hands and form practice require the same skills. Any problems or gains that you acquired in your push-hands practice will also manifest in your form, and vice versa. Pay attention to the basic movements of *peng* (ward-off), *lu* (rollback), *ji* (press), and *an* (push). If your upper and lower body are coordinated, you are not easily defeated: you will be able to use four ounces to deflect a thousand pounds.

The problem at this level is that you may find it difficult to attain perfect coordination; your opponent can use this weakness to defeat you. An opponent can also lead you into a weak position and then defeat you. You may use too much or too little force. You may not sink your energy enough. Because you still cannot deflect your opponent's energy, you tend to use force against force. You may need to step back, you may lose your balance easily or may hang on to your opponent when pushed. Generally your movements are not crisp and clean.

This level is two yin and eight yang—still incomplete and uncoordinated.

Level Three: Moving from a Large Circle to a Medium Circle

"Circle" implies not just the movement of the hands and feet, but also the internal *chi* movement. To improve your tai chi, you must progressively decrease the circle—from large to medium to small,

and finally to no circle. You start with the big circle to make it easier to feel your *chi*, but as you progress, your sensibility and control is more subtle and you can decrease the circle.

Third-level training is the transition from big circle to medium circle. The *Classics* say "Where the mind goes, the *chi* goes and the body follows."

Once at this level, you need to learn to use your mind. During the first level, you concentrated on learning the shape and postures of the form. At the second level, you worked on eliminating the contradictions of body movement and *chi* flow and learned to correct your posture so that your intrinsic *chi* flows freely. At level three, you have a good understanding of the *chi* flow, you are beginning to use your mind and not just brute force, your movements are light but not floating, and you can sink your *chi* without being stiff. You try to make the external look soft and the internal strong. There is softness within the hardness. Your whole body is coordinated, and you have eliminated most of the bad habits.

At this stage, you must not just concentrate on the *chi* flow and neglect the external movements. There must be a synthesis of body and mind; otherwise the *chi* will not flow freely. During the second level, your breathing may be too shallow or too deep because you are not relaxed or your movement is not coordinated with your breathing. Pay attention to your breathing—let it be natural and coordinated with your movement, especially where the movement is complicated or requires speed and subtlety.

Work on gaining a better understanding of the martial application of the movements. Do more push-hands training, fine-tune your posture, understand how to express your *jin*, how to deflect and change your energy flow and increase your intrinsic *chi*. By working on the practical application, you gain a better understanding of correct posture. In addition, you will become stronger and can start practicing the tai chi weapons forms such as the broadsword, double-edged sword, spear, and staff.

You will also be able to practice the explosive movements on their own. Your confidence will increase, and after about two years you should progress to the fourth level.

In summary, at the third level, you gain a basic understanding of the coordination of the internal *chi* flow with the external movement. You are able to correct yourself if necessary, your movements are natural, and your internal *chi* is full. However, your intrinsic *chi* is still relatively weak, and your body-mind coordination is not yet perfect. When you push hands with someone of lesser skill than yourself, you can use technique to overcome him. However, if you do it with someone more advanced, you will feel that you don't have enough *pengji*, or ward-off energy, and your *chi* is easily penetrated. You will lose your balance and your body-mind coordination, and your energy is easily read.

This level is said to be three yin and seven yang. Your skills are still not altogether proper.

Level Four: Moving from a Medium Circle to a Small Circle

At this level, you progress from the medium circle to the small circle. This is quite an advanced level. You are very close to ultimate success. The martial application is even more important at this stage. Work on circulating your *chi*, and pay attention to coordinating your breathing, the movement, and the martial application. All your movements must be continuous, without weakness in any part of your body, and the intrinsic *chi* will permeate your whole body.

When you practice the form, imagine that you are surrounded by attacks, but when you fight, imagine that there is no one around so that your movements are swift and natural and you will maintain your composure. The training method for this level is the same as for the third level, except that the circle is smaller. Your internal *jin* will be strong, and

you will be able to attack and defend with the same movement. Your *chi* and your mind will be coordinated. Your *chi* will circulate wherever you direct it.

Your posture is now stable, and you are not easily defeated in push-hands. You can deflect the other's energy with subtle body movements and can change direction and energy in rhythm with the changes in direction and energy of your opponent. Your internal *chi* is completely coordinated with your external movement, and you can sense what your opponent is going to do before he moves. Your *fa jing,* or expressed energy, is cleaner, and your attack is accurate. You can easily find your opponent's weakness.

This stage is said to be four yin and six yang—you are now an accomplished martial artist. This level takes about three years.

Level Five: Moving from a Small Circle to No Circle

From form to the formless. Your movements are now alive and coordinated, your internal *jin* is full, and you seek excellence within excellence. A day's work is a day's achievement. You can change endlessly, and your energy is invisible. Internally, there is movement between the substantial and the insubstantial, but externally no movement or change is visible.

From a fighting point of view, the hard and soft become one, and you are relaxed and alert. Full of springy energy, you can defend and attack at will. You can express *chi* with any part of your body. Your whole body is sensitive and alive. In other words, you can use any part of your body like a fist and strike anywhere at will.

This level is said to be five yin and five yang—perfect balance. Your yin and yang is continuous without end; when you move, it is in harmony with the tai chi principles, so everything is possible. You have gained mastery of the body and the mind. Your mind is tranquil and calm, and even when you are attacked suddenly, your equipoise is undisturbed. There is no limit to your tai chi development, and the ultimate goal seems attainable.

Although the tai chi journey is one without an end, at least now you can find out where you are and roughly how you can achieve your goal.

Now You Have the Road Map

Master Chen explains that the five levels of proficiency in tai chi training can be likened to a road map. If you are lost and want to get to your destination, you must first find out where you are at present and in which direction you should be heading.

Howard Choy and Ahtee Chia are both architects studying Chen family tai chi chuan with Master Chen Xiaowang in Sydney, Australia. This material appeared in the May 1992 edition of Inside Kung-Fu *magazine.*

21

The Five Stages of Chen Tai Chi Combat Training

Stephan Jacob Berwick

Until recently, combat training in tai chi chuan either was not known or was highly misunderstood. Over the past decade, however, especially with the increased popularity of tai chi's founding style—the Chen family system—tai chi's original self-defense training has been revealed throughout the world.

This popularization notwithstanding, the complete traditional fighting curriculum has never been explained and summarized for most contemporary tai chi enthusiasts. Given these facts, the classical training inherited by nineteenth-generation Grand Master Chen Xiaowang, and passed to his senior disciple, New York's Master Ren Guang Yi, holds important lessons for tai chi enthusiasts of any style seeking to deepen their understanding and practice of tai chi chuan usage.

"Free-pushing," the widely practiced type of sparring common in most tai chi chuan schools, is usually heralded as the epitome of tai chi usage. Complete combat training for self-defense and full-contact assault is all too often not achieved by most practitioners. Unfortunately, such training in tai chi is still rare.

For most practitioners, the enormous health benefits of tai chi chuan practice are adequate. But for the combat trainee, classical tai chi chuan's ultimate goal—as embodied by the Chen style—is self-defense. The battle-hardened, seventeenth-century general, Chen Wang Ting, created tai chi chuan to train warriors in a healthful, well-rounded manner.

Combat training is taught at five stages, according to the traditional standard passed to Master Ren Guang Yi. Progression of these stages bridges the gaps between forms, *tui shou* (pushing hands), and free-fighting. Time tested, the classic fighting techniques of Chen tai chi are taught and mastered at these sequential stages. Each stage corresponds to a proficiency with foundation skills that are the core of Chen style technical usage.

Although combat training in classical Chen tai chi chuan is arduous and painful, it is progressive.

According to the traditional methodology, successful completion of five discernible stages of combat training develops the Chen practitioner into a complete fighter. The first two stages teach the actual technique, while the latter train for usage and free fighting in systematic sequence.

Stage One: Learn and Perfect the Five Levels of *Tui Shou,* or Push-Hands

Tui shou introduces technical usage and the combat and health benefits of sensitivity training. Working in pairs, practitioners perfect the basic requirements of sunken relaxation and correct stance usage with the single-arm, horizontally circular *dan tui shoo,* or "single-hand pushing." At this novice level, sunk shoulders, harmony with the partner, and stance control are the goals. Thereafter, the five levels of push-hands utilize the arms and footwork.

Master Ren Guang Yi offers the following advice: "Push-hands practice for fighters must emphasize the building of endurance and leg strength. All five levels should be practiced at least one hour per session to derive the whole-body training that is important in tai chi chuan combat."

He adds, "Regardless of which style of tai chi one practices, the health and toughening aspects of concerted push-hands practice build the unique combination of leg strength, sensitivity, and overall fitness that is the hallmark of advanced tai chi chuan.

"It is important to remember and adhere to five basic requirements to derive the advanced benefits of push-hands practice. The first is to keep the upper body (shoulders) relaxed and sunken. This not only is healthier for the heart, but also forces the legs to control the movement and flow of force. It is harder on the legs, but the goal is to strengthen your base. Second, keep your eyes on the chest of your partner. In Chen tai chi, watching the chest is considered better than watching the eyes, because the eyes can

deceive. Third, work to build low but not overly wide stances. Although Chen stylists are renowned for their low stances, the top practitioners have stances that are not too wide. In fact, the stances usually look like square (and occasionally rectangular) boxes that can easily lean side-to-side.

"Fourth, keep the arms relaxed yet firm. This is often misunderstood. Relaxed pressure that is springlike in sensation should be applied to your partner's limbs. This builds sensitivity for redirecting and neutralization skill. And finally, maintain as upright a posture as possible. The health benefits of good posture are always important, but in push-hands practice, it teaches proper alignment, which forces the legs to do most of the work. This is one of the secrets of tai chi chuan, especially when you're using the art for self-defense."

These traditional requirements can serve as important training tips to help trainees advance their skill. Most important, concerted push-hands training will build *chan szu chin,* or "silk-reeling power," beyond levels that can be developed in forms practice. Chen style's unique coiling of the joints with proper *chan szu* is fueled by powerful, correct stances and relaxed, upright posture. Initiated by the legs and directed by the torso, this powerful coiling of the joints is crucial for *chin na,* or "joint locking," and overall neutralization skill.

Master Ren notes, "Without *chan szu chin,* the coiling necessary for advanced *chin na* and body strikes becomes difficult, if not impossible to achieve. But to get there, focused, correct push-hands practice increases the trainee's *chan szu chin.*"

The Five Levels of Push–Hands

Huang Kua. The first level of push-hands, *huang kua* or "reeling flowers," utilizes the shoulders to open and close the arms in three vertical directions while maintaining fluid contact with both the arms and stance. This stationary pushing builds a greater awareness of posture, leg usage, sensitivity, and torso-focused technical application. The health benefits unique to *tui shou* are revealed at this level when improved leg strength, correct posture, relaxation, and increased motor skills emerge.

Ding bu. Level two increases the physical contact between trainees with smaller circular movements that engage both partners' hands to cover the forearms and elbows. Called *ding bu*, or "fixed stance," and most common to the public, this technique reveals the uniquely fluid *chin na* that is highly developed in Chen tai chi. Moving the arms in vertical circles on a plane directly facing the practitioners, the repetitive shift of weight in this stepless pushing is crucial to the introduction of stepping in level four.

Hua bu. Moving back and forth with one step, *hua bu*, or "moving step," further trains practitioners in sensitivity and *chin na*. Beginning with the unique movement of stage two, the arm is dragged down and sideward with a rear step. As the arm is dragged by one practitioner, the other—whose arm is being held and dragged—steps forward. This important pushing technique introduces sinking, stepping, and arm coiling, which are health-giving and crucial to combat application.

Da lu. The fourth level, "large-frame rollback," is a demanding technique that trains both sides of a double circular push and single drag in a stance with one step. Called *da lu*, this rare technique conditions the legs and accustoms the boxer to pushing and locking with both the legs and arms to train rootedness in application. The health benefits of vigorous leg training are obvious, but the importance of *da lu* to combat is enormous. In Master Ren's class, his emphasis on this often physically painful level of push-hands has built a generation of American tai chi stylists with unprecedented leg strength, relaxed body power, and powerful stances.

Ren says, "Level-four push-hands is the best conditioning tool for advanced tai chi training. Your leg and torso power are strengthened in tandem. This type of high-pressure yet relaxed strength and endurance training builds attributes that can help any tai chi stylist." After the student has perfected this difficult level of *tui shou*, techniques two to four combine in level five.

Huang jiao bu. In *huang jiao bu*, or "free-flowing step," multiple stepping in varied directions is combined with the covering and dragging of early *tui shou* technique. Utilizing specific movements in freely expressed patterns bridges the gap between application practice and free-fighting in Chen tai chi. At this level, the practitioners are free to move in rapidly changing techniques that involve sensitivity, complex stepping, dragging, locking, and finally, neutralization. Upon mastery of this level, the combat-oriented stylist is ready for usage—he is ready to enter stage two of combat training.

Stage Two: Assimilate the Eight Skills or "Powers"

In translation, the descriptions of these skills or "powers" are self-explanatory. They are, in fact, quite easy to understand but difficult to master. Although formally introduced at stage two, practice of these crucial tai chi chuan skills—sometimes referred to as "directions"—actually begins with concerted *tui shou* practice. And their perfection is a constant goal of the advanced practitioner.

1. *Peng*—To expand and adhere with a rising force that is defensive.
2. *Lu*—To divert, hold, and pull.
3. *Ji*—To follow and push.
4. *An*—To cover the hand and elbow with both hands and push.
5. *Cai*—To hold and twist with vehemence.

6. *Lie*—To step in and throw from behind, or "split."
7. *Zhou*—To grab and strike with the elbow.
8. *Kao*—To "lean" or strike with the shoulder, knee, or hip.

In general, most practitioners are quite familiar with the first four skills. The first, *peng*, is particularly well noted by most advanced practitioners as the major transition technique that connects the other skills in free-fighting. As such, a concerted focus on *peng* is often highly regarded by many tai chi stylists.

Though less familiar, the next four skills are also important to basic Chen training. The throwing and striking skills upon which Chen style is famed are summarized in skills five through eight. Unlike the first four, the latter are typically instilled when the student begins practicing at higher speeds and with more force. Compared with other styles of tai chi, Chen style's perfect balance of yin and yang can be represented by the eight skills. The first four are indicative of yin force, while the last four are yang in nature.

Master Ren advises, "Students should seek to understand these skills before actually perfecting them. Their mastery will occur over the course of overall training, but it is important to see the skills early in one's tai chi career to establish the high standard and particular goals of Chen tai chi practice."

Stage Three: Train Techniques Slowly for Technical Mastery and Sensitivity

When the eight skills are understood, application training for combat begins. Chen stylists commence free-fighting training from the base of push-hands practice. This induces a fluid use of *chin na*, neutralizing throws, and shoulder strikes. This stage can therefore be considered the most important for tai chi combat training. Application training (with techniques from *tui shou* and the forms) is introduced with a slow, gradual, and rehearsed practice of usage for technical familiarity and sensitivity.

At stage three, the deadly hand, foot, knee, and elbow strikes are practiced repetitively with a partner. Technical combinations from the forms are isolated and performed at slower but varied speeds to build responsiveness and internalize the style's unique applications.

Master Ren recommends, "Students must work together on gradual practice of rehearsed applications." He points out that a student's basic push-hands skill is utilized in the practice of technical usage training. This most important stage links the contact practice of push-hands with the technical usage contained in the forms and the five levels of *tui shou*.

"With the right coaching," Ren adds, "this type of rehearsed practice seems gradual but actually teaches plenty of technique in a short time. Students should emphasize heavy repetition of just single applications first and then progress to combination practice largely derived from the forms." Of course, the standard five requirements introduced in push-hands practice must be maintained to build correct usage ability.

When a trainee can perform a variety of applications competently at high speed, technique practice should not be overrehearsed. Master Ren explains, "The goal of stage three is to build a vocabulary of applications that will form the basis of a student's future arsenal."

Stage Four: Build Neutralization Skill with the Practice of Controlled Technique in Free Combinations

At this level of training, usage practice seeks to build neutralization skill. The introduction of neutralization is instilled with controlled application practice in free-form combinations. Sparring, therefore, begins at this stage. The goal is to build opponent control and neutralization skill. Practice at this stage is similar to the free push-hands training common in most tai chi schools and competitions.

According to Master Ren, "What is most important at this stage is learning how to be physically relaxed but aggressive and calm while free-pushing. When novices begin free-pushing, they are usually too physically tense or overaggressive. So, the balance between physical relaxation and calm, mental aggressiveness is the goal of this stage."

Master Ren also recommends that one's stance while free-pushing should never get too wide. "With a more natural stance, preferably no larger than a meter wide, the body will remain relaxed and thus more responsive to the opponent."

Practicing in pairs, Chen pupils work to maintain firm rootedness while training to adhere and be sensitive to the opponent's movements and intentions. While maintaining constant limb and body contact at close range, the trainees attempt to dislodge, throw, lock, and shoulder-strike each other with relaxed power. This type of sparring builds the neutralization technique and rooted stances vital to tai chi usage. In fact, the Chen stylist's firm stance deemphasizes muscular strength and permits Chen tai chi's natural, relaxed power to emerge.

The techniques are then integrated in push-hands and, of course, sparring and free-fighting. With such training, the goals of Chen tai chi combat emerge: sensitivity, fluidity, coiling, and relaxed, explosive power with neutralizing techniques.

Stage Five: Train Applications from Slow to Fast and Free-Fight with Full Speed and Power

At this stage, Chen stylists practice free-fighting from the base of free push-hands practice. Applications from the forms are repetitively practiced from slow to fast to increase the trainee's technical vocabulary and deepen usage skill. As applications knowledge is enriched, full-contact sparring begins.

Such sparring expands the base of free-pushing with *chin na*, shoulder and knee strikes, kicks, and brutal throws. Because of the danger of this type of practice, it is the final stage of combat development, which builds the complete arsenal of the Chen tai chi chuan boxer.

Because free-sparring is the focus of this advanced stage, supplementary equipment can be utilized, including protective equipment such as body armor and gloves. Also, heavy bag training is useful. Training with heavy bags is effective practice in particular for the subtle shoulder, hip, and knee strikes typical to Chen tai chi.

Master Ren cautions: "Too much bag training should be avoided. You should use this type of training only to build relaxed striking power. If you rely too much on bag training, you may lose some of the necessary relaxation, and it may not be healthy internally—especially when you get stronger. When your chi is directed to striking, relaxation—and not overtraining—is the key to health and proper power development.

Chin na practice is also emphasized in this stage. Since advanced joint locking in Chen tai chi is dependent on well-forged *chan szu chin*, mastery of *chin na* usually begins in this stage (with *chin na*'s high importance in Chen tai chi, students are actually introduced to its practice when push-hands training commences).

The Training Matrix

Perfection of the crucial eight skills occurs over the course of a student's advancement through the five stages. As mentioned earlier, stage three is of particular importance. It is a crucial transition point for the combat trainee and should not be underestimated.

The standard training progression of traditional, combat-oriented tai chi is as follows (average time frames represent total cumulative training time, not training time per stage):

Stage One

Peng, Li, Ji, An—at one year

Stage Two

Peng, Li, Ji, An, Cai, Lie, Zhou, Kao—at 1.5 years

Stage Three

An, Cai, Lie, Zhou, Kao—at 2.5 years

Stage Four

Peng, Li, Ji, An, Cai, Lie, Zhou, Kao—at 4 years

Stage Five

Peng, Li, Ji, An, Cai, Lie, Zhou, Kao—at 5+ years

Although the eight skills are taught by stage two, perfection of the skills is not accomplished until the student is deep into stage five. The five levels of *tui shou* particularly build the first four skills. Thus, by stage three, the last four skills should be the focus. This progression provides adequate preparation for the free-fighting practice introduced in stage four and advanced in stage five.

The estimated total training times in the matrix are based on consistent training in the traditional manner. Master Ren says, "It should take just over five to six years for the serious practitioner to become quite strong and possess fairly good combat skill." He adds, "When I first came to the United States, I was surprised at how many people were taught that at least ten years of training will get a practitioner only past the intermediate level. This is ludicrous! Even in this modern age, consistent, correct training should get the student past the intermediate level in about six years."

He emphasizes that even with full-time training, progress should not be rushed. "With a good teacher

and hard training, the Chen stylist is kept quite busy throughout the five stages. "Without rushing through the stages, a student will be really surprised at what he will accomplish," Master Ren asserts. Thus, for the combat trainee, the matrix can be a guide or template for measuring progress and planning suitable training programs.

Results of Training: Iron Wrapped in Cotton

The fluidity and flexibility of this training, indicative of ancient methods, is easily displayed by long-term practitioners. During an interview over lunch in New York's Chinatown, Master Ren Guang Yi held the attention of the waiters and fellow diners with his physical demonstrations of the eight skills between bites of food. Although the performance was fun for the informal audience, most striking was Ren's ability to deliver the techniques at random, with full speed and at any angle, while seated.

Even intermediate students will exhibit certain indications of combat skill or power. For example, the famous concept of "iron wrapped in cotton" is accurate. As the practitioner advances through the five stages, the body's musculature will exhibit a density or hardness. Also, one's gait may seem stronger, almost heavier. And typical of Chen stylists, the thighs increase dramatically in size. Correct practice will build the legs in ways not even bodybuilders can mimic. The muscle around the upper, inner kneecap thickens, and the feet strengthen. In practice, dedicated, well-taught students will notice a heaviness to their limbs, not powered by raw muscular strength. This heaviness is a relaxed power typified by quality Chen stylists. Opponents will notice this sensation, in particular. This condition is healthful and serves the student well in the development of usage and combat skill.

Master Ren warns, "Be careful! You may not realize how much strength you will build if you progress through the five stages. I still occasionally remind myself to not smack someone's back too hard or twist too firmly with a friendly handshake. It's funny sometimes, but when a student hits the intermediate level (usually at stage three), he should start to take note of his newfound strength. It will help him control it and therefore increase it."

Even more dramatic is the skill demonstrated by Chen Grand Master Chen Xiaowang. "My power does not match that of my teacher," insists Master Ren, his senior student. Master Ren's now legendary ability with full-contact tai chi chuan usage hints at the might of Chen Xiaowang. He concludes: "Fighting practice with Grand Master Chen brought me to tears at times. It was quite painful. But his ability to know and control his power represents the highest level of skill."

Stephan Berwick is one of only five senior disciples of master Ren Guang Yi. His background in Chinese martial arts spans almost twenty-five years. He is currently serving as a foreign service officer in the U.S. Department of State. This material appeared in the October 1997 edition of Inside Kung-Fu.

22

Tai Chi's Internal Secrets

Doc-Fai Wong and Jane Hallander

In ancient times, students were not taught tai chi forms until their *chi* was sufficiently developed. Today, everyone first learns the tai chi form before moving to push-hands or maybe token meditation practice. That's not the way the Yang family intended its martial art to be taught.

Progress Begins with *Chi*

The earliest Yang family tai chi teachers didn't start with the form. Students practiced special standing meditation postures and breathing exercises before learning anything else. Each training session began with an hour of standing meditation to build up *chi* (often written *qi*).

Only when their *chi* was sufficiently developed did they start learning tai chi's martial arts stances. As they progressed, they eventually combined their training sessions to include meditation, breathing; and martial arts stances. This lasted for two to three years before commencement of tai chi form position work. Every three months, they changed to a different martial arts stance, until all thirteen positions had been practiced. Some exchanged their tai chi knowledge with *xingyiquan* (Hsing I) and *baguazhang* (paqua) teachers, adding to the original list of thirteen. Each posture developed *jing* (energy) in different parts of the body, while externally strengthening their arms and legs.

After several years, they were taught the tai chi form. However, this was not the connected moving form we know today. First they had to stand and hold each technique in the form for twenty breaths. Then they changed to another form posture, repeating the same twenty-breath position for each posture throughout the set.

By practicing the form this way, students learned only one movement at a time. Naturally, it took a long time to finish the entire form. Because tai chi students didn't learn to connect form movements until after they had finished memorizing all the postures and their applications, it took several years just to learn the tai chi form. It might have taken even longer, except that the Yang long form contains a number of repeat movements.

Students of Yang family teachers such as Yang Cheng Fu also spent time practicing *tui shou* (push-hands). Their push-hands practice included single-hand, double-hand, and something called *ba zhen tui shou* (eight-front push-hands) that positioned practitioners in stances similar to today's Chen style push-hands. *Ba zhen* eventually became today's Yang style *da lu*, sometimes called *si zhen si yi* (four front and four corners).

Choice of Speeds

After training for four to five years, Yang stylists put their tai chi form into continuous movement. Today, most people practice their form at a very low speed. That wasn't the case in tai chi's early days. Back then, there were two ways to practice the tai chi form. The easiest and most popular was called *zhuo jia*, or "walking the form." The method practiced by serious students was known as *xing gong*, or "developing the form." *Zhuo jia* is done faster than *xing gong*. It's more like a warm-up form, compared with the *chi*-developing *xing gong* method which puts concentration, focus, and intention into a slow, precise form practice. Although it takes longer and requires more work, *xing gong* practice brings greater internal development to tai chi students than the faster, easier *zhuo jia* method.

At this stage, Yang style tai chi students also practiced actual freestyle sparring with students who attacked with conventional kicks and punches. It took approximately eight years for Yang family tai chi disciples to complete their training. They learned moving forms and weapons, such as the straight sword, saber, and spear techniques, as the last part of their training. Then they practiced on their own.

In later years, Yang Cheng Fu found that tai chi would never be popular with the general public when taught the old-fashioned way. Most people simply didn't want to devote eight years to what they considered boring training. To keep students interested, Yang opened his teaching with the moving form. Only when students became close practitioners or disciples did they learn the internal side of tai chi training.

Of course, just because Yang Cheng Fu taught the public tai chi in reverse didn't mean the rest of his family did. His brother, Yang Shou Hou, and a few other classmates of Yang Cheng Fu still began with the old way of standing meditation. There were more, however, who studied tai chi for its health benefits. This created two branches of Yang tai chi for health. One branch consisted of many of Yang Cheng Fu's students, who learned the form only for health purposes and called it *tai chi chuan*. The other group learned only the meditation and breathing part of Yang tai chi, but no tai chi form or push-hands. They called their branch *tai chi–chi kung*, now known as *chi kung* (also spelled *qi gong*).

Among those who practiced tai chi only for health reasons, some liked the variety and relaxation of practicing the form. Those were Yang Cheng Fu's everyday students. Others liked the simplicity and lack of need for extra space that the meditations and stance training provided. Hence the two ways to practice Yang tai chi for health. Only those students who mastered tai chi for both health and martial arts had everything.

The Keys to *Chi* Development

What makes tai chi so beneficial for chi development? The answer lies in tai chi's most important principles—relaxation and calmness. These are the keys to *chi* development. Since tai chi is done slowly, smoothly and evenly, the result is relaxation. Calmness comes from concentrating on timing, sequence, and correct form.

Chi kung is not tai chi. However, it is necessary for mastering *tai chi*. *Chi kung* means "*chi* development" and is as simple as meditation and breathing exercises. Meditation requires no movement. It is standing in one place while using a variety of arm positions. *Chi kung* meditation requires the body to be totally relaxed *without* external movement. Standing meditations are initially uncomfortable for most students, forcing them to physically relax tense muscles over the one-hour meditation period. Students learn to relax their minds and breathe evenly. Blood circulation also starts flowing evenly. This corresponds with the tai chi theory that silence produces action.

The other facet of *chi kung* is its breathing exercises. These include the tai chi form, where the body moves slowly. Proper breathing is a must for relaxation, just as relaxation is critical for good breathing practice. If your breathing isn't even, you won't be relaxed while practicing the tai chi form.

Most people don't realize that under tension or stress, they exhale longer than they inhale. If they are not relaxed while practicing tai chi, their shoulders tense and their breathing rises, throwing off the timing and smoothness of their form. Tai chi breathing exercises teach students to inhale and exhale at the same rate.

Each breathing exercise and meditation posture benefits specific parts of the body, for both health and martial arts. For example, one is good for lowering blood pressure while simultaneously strengthening the upper arms and shoulders. Another brings the three primary areas of body energy into harmony as it develops *peng jing*, or "ward-off fighting energy."

Correct tai chi practice requires both meditation and movement. Standing meditation causes relaxation and develops *chi*. Movement, including breathing exercises, activates the *chi*. For instance, the *peng yue* ("carry the moon") breathing exercise stirs and balances internal energy. Through its circular pattern, it actually directs energy into the correct parts of the body by creating a magnetic field from the body movements. After the internal energy is balanced through the *peng yue* breathing exercise, the meditation that follows is calm and pure, naturally lowering the body's *chi* breathing point.

Comprehensive tai chi study must include some internal (*chi*) training. Without *chi* development, tai chi would be just another external martial art or exercise. *Chi* development comes from passive meditation and stance training. It must also include *chi* and physical activity, gained from forms practice and breathing exercises.

If you practice tai chi as a martial art, you must also have push-hands practice, which requires a partner. You practice forms technique on another person. Tai chi, the martial art, is impossible without two-person practice.

Doc Fai Wong is a contributing editor of Inside Kung-Fu. *Jane Hallander is a longtime martial arts writer and well-known internal stylist. This material appeared in the October 1991 edition of* Inside Kung-Fu.

Tai Chi Free-Fighting

J. Justin Meehan

Tai chi chuan will always be a martial art. The Chinese term *chuan*, which means "fist," qualifies tai chi as a fighting art, rather than solely a philosophical concept. Those who practice tai chi chuan for health alone therefore limit their understanding and progress, because they have not examined its martial applications.

As a martial art, tai chi chuan is a complete system which leads the student through a step-by-step process: form, applications, two person exercises, two-person routines, and the ultimate test, free-fighting. While many practitioners are content merely to sample the wares, the ultimate enjoyment, test, and reward for years of dedicated pursuit should be meeting another martial artist or partner in the "supreme ultimate" freedom of ever-changing reality. Painting by the numbers may be important and useful for the beginner, but there should come a time when the student attempts to create perfection from the emptiness of a blank canvas.

Free-fighting is opposed to the use of force against force. Furthermore, free-fighting should be served like dessert, at the end of a meal. Beginning too early may result in the imprinting of bad habits which later would have to be dismantled. As a corollary, it is preferable to have an experienced master on hand to aid in corrections and refinement. The student is also well advised to work with a trusted friend or accomplished partner with no ego problems.

Fulfillment of Tai Chi Principles

At the outset, it must be understood that every aspect of tai chi free-fighting is a fulfillment of the tai chi principles as handed down by noted and recognized master teachers and recorded in the so-called *T'ai Chi Classics*. In truth, it is almost impossible to understand the *Classics* without familiarity with martial application. The way a tai chi chuan practitioner fights should be qualitatively different from the way a Western boxer or wrestler, Chinese Hung Gar, praying mantis, or Wing Chun practitioner spars. Otherwise, what would be the use of studying your art for so many years?

We begin by understanding the tai chi diagram. The outer circle represents the natural boundaries of all reality. It is composed of yin (soft) and yang (hard) in a dynamic circular or spiral configuration. A tai chi practitioner does not just exchange kicks, punches, and blocks as is the case in most kung-fu movies. He must seek contact with his opponent and manipulate that meeting to his advantage to blend hard against soft and soft against hard in a circular fashion. His goal is not merely to counter technique with technique, but to completely overwhelm, smother, mislead, and take advantage of his opponent's momentum, energy and mind.

A Blend of Hard and Soft

While this approach may seem clear at the outset, it is a direct challenge to those who have practiced only the soft style. There can be no tai chi, or reality, without soft and hard. In tai chi chuan, the hard is different from the rigid strength of other arts, because it must contain elements of yin and be ready to transform into yin. As a corollary, the yin must contain yang and be prepared to change into yang. Merely practicing a form with a hollow emptiness will aid only in relaxation. Even for health benefits, there must be an interchange of hard and soft.

So, regardless of the practitioner's style or form of tai chi, the individual must ask himself, "Does my practice include both yin and yang?" For most practitioners, the answer will be no. Their goal, therefore, must be the balancing of their practice by including the yang so that they will truly be practicing the combined art of yin and yang, or tai chi chuan. The tai chi chuan curriculum is like our educational system: a student who goes into a higher class or level without completing the fundamental lower level will be forever doomed to return to the lower level before he can make progress or graduate.

The Foundation of Tai Chi Free-Fighting

The approach to free-fighting described here is useful, practical, and instructive. Called tai chi free-fighting, it is a training method, rather than fighting itself. While most tai chi practitioners are morally opposed to injuring or destroying another human being, they follow the example of fencing and have a level of interaction and/or competition that allows one to practice the art to the fullest without risking injury and setbacks to oneself or others. The centuries-old practice of push-hands is a perfect example of the interaction and competition needed in tai chi chuan. It can be said that such an interest is in the true tai chi spirit. To assume that a tai chi chuan practitioner could defeat an opponent in an actual fighting encounter without realistic training is illogical.

The type of free-fighting discussed here requires no special protective gear. Free-fighting should first be practiced between teacher and student, then between friends who have similar ability. Once the foundation has been laid, there is no reason, except the increased threat of injury, why practitioners of different styles cannot spar.

Necessary Background and Attributes

Free-fighting requires a thorough understanding of at least one form, as well as push-hands, *da lu*, and, ultimately, the tai chi chuan two-man form. The form gives us our techniques. The push-hands and *da lu* help blend our major techniques with a partner. The two-man form shows us proper distance, timing, and the essential applications for the eighty-eight continuous movements of the Yang form.

In the beginning, just as in learning the form, both partners agree to move in slow motion. This gives each person a turn to attack, intercept, blend, and counter. The slow pace results in no loss of control and allows each partner to relax and formulate a response from the form. A laboratory-type atmosphere allows each partner to experiment with the form's varied techniques and applications. In fact, until fluidity, adaptability, and relaxation set in, this should be the initial goal of sparring. Practice should take a minimum of ten to twenty minutes so that the partners can relax, if only as a result of exhaustion. Relaxation must be achieved before any progress can be made.

Once relaxation sets in, the speed and level of contact can increase. As the body and mind relax, reaction time and timing speed up. Though the partners feel that they are working at a controlled, manageable, fluid pace, an outsider may perceive things differently. It's just a matter of relativity. The pace and intensity will change according to the energy of the participants. The greater energy of one can boost the energy of the partner. However, if one's energy sinks, it may also give the partner an opportunity to drop an energy level.

At the lower energy level, one can best work on the tactile manipulation of the partner's stability, movement, and momentum. As the pace quickens, strikes and kicks punctuate the tempo with greater frequency. Drawing and building on each other's energy level, the partners meet and engage fast and slow, high and low, and hard and soft.

By agreement, the early strikes are like light touches. If your opponent can touch you, you know you could have been hit in that area. Since a touch is not a strike, it is still incumbent upon the practitioner to supplement his training with bag, glove, and dummy practice, as well as fighting with equipment, to ensure that he does not mistake the importance of delivering power.

The practice of touch results in an ever more elusive, quicker, lighter, and faster punching action, which ultimately results in increased power. As the Wing Chun maxim explains, if one exerts force early, the force will be in the arm; if one releases force at the end, the force will be (preferably) in the punch itself. The emphasis should be to involve as much of the body as possible in the most effective line of flow, without losing the ability to change, blend, fold, or follow up.

It is extremely important to maintain contact with your opponent; otherwise, what's the use of studying tai chi? From touch comes energy manipulation. As the opponent increases his effectiveness in manipulation, we upset his concentration and "listening" ability by changing into a striking pattern. This forces the opponent to alter his technique and concentration. At that moment, we reengage and concentrate on mastering our opponent's weight, momentum, techniques, and motion. To disengage is to acknowledge retreat and seek a new beginning.

If the range of space is confined, the participant is forced to develop contact and proper stepping. Thus, there should be room only for three steps forward and backward.

The energy exchange becomes more intense and the interchange of technique is livelier depending on the space. We learn to circle our partner, to step in at indirect angles, to replace our opponent's space, and, perhaps, to uproot him as a finishing technique. Although intensity increases, the level of relaxation continues to sink, enabling the practitioner to carry the offensive until he meets obstruction, and then to change into softness to reroute, neutralize, and mislead all obstacles in his path.

Can This Be Tai Chi?

The variations are limitless: decreased lighting to increase tactile sensitivity; fighting on a two-by-four plank to challenge balance; or wearing equipment.

The potential is infinite, and yet at all times, especially when opponents are locked into force-on-force or brute struggling, it must be asked, in the immortal words of Yang Lu Chan, "Can this be tai chi?" Investing in loss, we begin again. Maybe this time we will allow only two techniques, such as push and pull, until we regain our sense of purpose, and then intuitively return to full freedom with a new sense of purpose and dedication.

As time goes on, our bodies may soak with sweat, and breathing may become labored. Rather than stop, we must continue and drop into deeper relaxation. We sink our mind and breath to the *dan tian* and recapture our respiration so that breath and movement are reunited. In controlling our breathing, we relax again. Rather than stop to rest, we break through the level of tenseness. We reach a level where time slows and reaction time outstrips the need to think out each response.

We become natural. And, as in the best practice of our form, our channels begin to open: the muscles relax, the joints open, the blood flows, and the life force concentrates, wells up, and rises to the top. The eyes, the windows to the soul, glow with spirit. Our *chi* now leads our movement and protects our body. We can even reach a level of sheer ecstasy. Who among us wishes to avoid or deny this level? Finally, in overcoming the most primeval struggle for ego and self-protection, we free ourselves to pursue with greater energy the higher levels.

J. Justin Meehan is a freelance writer and martial artist in St. Louis. This material was published in the December 1986 edition of Inside Kung-Fu *magazine.*

24

Push-Hands Power
How to Tell if Your Opponent Has It

Nan Lu
As told to Robert H. Feldman, M.D.

After studying tai chi chuan for a few months, many beginners want to learn push-hands. However, push-hands is not simply an exercise or drill that follows the study of the tai chi chuan form. It is a higher manifestation or mirror of the practitioner's skill in doing the form. When tai chi push-hands is not done correctly, the Chinese characterize it as having *ding jing*, which means "external" or "forceful energy," as opposed to internal power.

Jing, commonly described as power, or energy, can be a product of either muscular energy or *chi* energy. Muscular energy is more specifically defined as *li,* while *chi* energy manifests itself as *jing* in internal martial arts. *Jing* may be classified in many different categories of hard or soft, offensive or defensive, passive or sensing, and active or neutralizing. Here, we are primarily discussing sensing *jing,* perceiving the energy of the opponent.

In push-hands, this is predominantly done by a touch through the skin. This *jing* is called *tien jing*. It has many different levels and is important in the development of internal martial arts. In general, when students practice push-hands with a variety of opponents, they will sense a great variation in the opponent's ability and skill. This depends, of course, on many factors, including the depth of understanding of tai chi, personal disposition and physical makeup, the extent and length of practice, and what one has been taught.

The Four Perceptible Qualities

The Chinese *Classics* state there are four qualities one may sense in push-hands:

Mu

Mu may be translated as "numb" or "dull." It is best ascribed to individuals with a low level of skill in push-hands, whose movements are too slow and jerky. Often these individuals will hold, block, resist, or pressure their opponents. They use brute power to push or pull the other person and will take advantage of an opponent's lower level of skill. This quality of *jing* is contrary to the laws of tai chi in that one's opponents can usually sense the type of attack but are not skilled enough to neutralize it. Unfortunately, this is the most common type of opponent that one encounters.

Tai chi push-hands can be characterized according to a simple principle: "People do not know me, yet I know them." This concept is manifested in the more highly skilled practitioners. The following three qualities apply to individuals who have obtained a superior or higher skill in tai chi:

Zong

Zong may be translated as "heavy" or "weighted." Its quality is not that of a hard or rigid power. However, when pushed by an individual having this quality, one experiences a dull, heavy force. The force may be characterized as soft on the outside yet hard on the inside. This is not external force, but rather internal power. It comes from a balanced posture and application of an internal focus of tai chi *jing*. Often individuals having this quality feature a large, heavy build.

Qing

Qing may be translated as "light." When one is pushed by such an opponent, the force may be characterized as light or floating and simultaneously powerful. It is as if one is lifted off the ground. This force is soft yet explosive and can cause one to be pushed a considerable distance.

Cui

Cui may be translated as "fragile." An individual who manifests this power will leave you "dumbfounded." The force is sharp and disorienting. It can be compared to the shattering of glass. With this type of opponent, it is hard to keep your concentration because of his lightning power and speed. You cannot sense the direction of the force and are completely disarmed and overwhelmed before you realize what has happened.

The latter three qualities are signs of a highly evolved tai chi chuan practitioner. The force comes suddenly and without warning, and the opponent cannot tell from where or how he is pushed. To learn this skill requires the good fortune of having studied under a true master. Such individuals are often difficult to find and harder to persuade to teach. What is most important, however, is that the practitioner have a sound tai chi form that adheres to the principles set forth in the *T'ai Chi Classics*. If the form is poorly done, one cannot really attain internal tai chi power.

Nan Lu is founder and chief instructor of the New York T'ai Chi Ch'uan Academy. He also is a former All-South China wushu champion. Dr. Robert Feldman has studied traditional Chinese martial arts and Chinese medicine for twenty years. This material appeared in the May 1990 edition of Inside Kung-Fu *magazine.*

25

The Tai Chi Sword
Ancient China's Ultimate Weapon

Jane Hallander

When the "swallow returns to the nest," the opponent's knee is penetrated by a straight thrust, in one example of the advanced techniques in the Yang tai chi sword form, a weapon descended from Taoist priests.

Of all Chinese weapons, perhaps the most sophisticated is the double-edged straight sword. There are no hacking, slashing attacks with this weapon; 90 percent of all techniques are subtle wrist cuts and slices, based on the premise that the opponent always has a similar sword —so he must first be disarmed before he can be killed. In China, the straight sword was the gentleman's dueling weapon.

A Wu Dang Mountain Tradition

One of the top tai chi sword form experts in the United States is San Francisco's Doc Fai Wong. Wong learned his sword technique and forms from Hong Kong's Hu Yuen Chou, a direct student of both Yang Cheng Fu (grandson of the founder of Yang family tai

chi) and China's greatest contemporary Wu Dang swordsman, General Li Jin Ling.

Although well known for his other Chinese martial art of Choy Li Fut, Wong actually started learning tai chi before learning Choy Li Fut, at about age fifteen. He always admired straight sword techniques; however, his first Wu style tai chi instructor didn't teach the tai chi sword. That is one reason he began studying Yang style tai chi with Hu Yuen Chou, both a Wu Dang and tai chi sword expert.

"While the tai chi hand form originally comes from the Chen family, the tai chi sword is not a Chen family weapon. It isn't even an original tai chi weapon. Yang Ban-ho, son of the founder of Yang family tai chi, learned the straight sword from a Taoist priest from the Wu Dang Mountain," explains Wong. Some of China's best straight double-edged swordsmanship came from Wu Dang Mountain Taoist priests.

Development Comes in Stages

There are thirteen basic techniques in the Wu Dang sword system. The Yang tai chi sword form uses the same thirteen techniques. Despite the Wu Dang pedigree, the stages of training for developing sword expertise more closely resemble tai chi training than the faster Wu Dang style of training. Initially, after memorizing the form sequence, you practice in a relaxed, continuous, and slow mode. Wong explains that the form is practiced slowly to develop accurate footwork and sword techniques while connecting the body and mind together as a unit. "The sword is an extension of your hand," he says. "However, this form is more advanced than hand forms, because you have to connect an extra joint—the sword itself—with the rest of your body."

Key Exercises

Tai chi sword form training itself follows the same basic training principles that apply to Wu Dang swordsmanship. There are wrist-circling exercises with sword in hand that connect the waist and hip power with the rest of the body and the sword. The most important Wu Dang sword exercise is a horizontal circle, performed with the palm up, in both clockwise and counterclockwise directions. This one develops slicing power, once used to cut the opponent's sword-bearing hand or wrist.

Another important hand and sword workout is a vertical lifting and dropping exercise. This exercise helps bring out the dynamic power needed to chop through wrist and leg tendons—again rendering an opponent helpless.

The third wrist exercise is a horizontal slicing action, with the palm up and the sword blade flat,

that slices left and right. As with the straight sword forms inherent in all Chinese martial arts, the left hand forms a *jian que* (sword symbol) position, with the index and middle fingers straight and joined together. The rest of the fingers are bent down and held by the thumb.

This sword-finger position has several meanings. In Asian religious practice, *jian que* represents a spiritual sword, which fells ghosts by its magical cutting abilities. For martial arts training, *jian que* is used to balance the empty hand, putting out the same amount of energy as the sword. Imagined *jian que* energy equals the sword's extra weight and length. Chinese broadsword practice uses the same principle, with the left hand balancing the weight and energy of the broadsword. The sword finger was also used for pressure-point strikes and grabbing the opponent's sword arm.

Jing Follows *Jian*

The first stage of tai chi swordsmanship emphasizes relaxation and flowing movement—like the tai chi form. As noted, martial arts development doesn't start until the second stage—after the student learns the sequence and flowing movement of the *jian* techniques. The second stage adds *jing* (essence of power) to certain techniques.

Two types of *jing* are applied to straight sword techniques. One is a passive, slicing power, used to cut wrists horizontally and thrust forward into targets on the opponent's torso. The other type of sword *jing* is dynamic and whiplike. This *jing* uses a loose, relaxed, hip motion to propel the sword tip into strikes to the temple, taps to the top or bottom of the wrist, or tendon-cutting strikes to the opponent's legs.

All dynamic sword techniques have their action powered by the hip and a flexible, relaxed waist. The tai chi sword practitioner's wrist straightens from a relaxed position with a slight, quick tensing of the fingers, causing the sword tip to act like a whip—penetrating the target and snapping or rebounding with quick speed.

Penetrate the Target

Straight, thrusting motions also use hip and waist action to smoothly penetrate their targets. Targets and techniques include a diagonal poke downward to the opponent's knee, called "swallow returns to the nest." There is also a diagonal upward thrust to the opponent's chin, named "night bird returns to the forest," and a forward solar-plexus thrust, appropriately named "pointing like a compass needle." Another thrusting technique turns the wrist upward to thrust straight through the body. It is named "pushing the canoe down the stream."

Dynamic striking techniques include downward strikes with the sword tip striking the top of the opponent's wrist. This is done by snapping downward toward the target with a powerful wrist action, controlling the strike well enough to stop with only an inch penetration of the target wrist. The application is attacking from above or below the opponent's wrist, making him drop his weapon. These wrist-striking techniques bear names such as "meteor chasing the moon" and "celestial horse walking in the sky."

Ninety percent of all *jian* techniques are directed to the wrist: since the opponent always had his own sword, it was necessary to disarm him before killing him. A popular Wu Dang sword technique was a snapping action of the sword tip upward to the bottom of the wrist or groin area, called "phoenix raises his head." Another—"white tiger wags his tail"—was a dynamic strike to the wrist, armpit, or chin.

The sword could be used either with the edge up or with the blade flat. An example of the sword blade with the flat side up is "phoenix opens both wings," a diagonal strike to the opponent's side or wrist. It was also targeted to the jugular vein or tem-

ple. A diagonal downward strike to the opposition's ankle, severing the ankle tendons, was called "netting the moon from the sea bottom."

Falling Flowers, Coiling Snakes

Passive slicing sword techniques do not show outward power but are equally as effective as their dynamic cousins. "Lion shakes his head" and "left and right falling flowers" are examples of slices under the opponent's sword-bearing wrist. The sword tip is angled upward, with the palm facing downward. The sword blade angles diagonally across the swordsman's body, keeping the opponent from reaching the defender's wrist with his own sword. "Left and right falling flowers" gradually cuts lower—like flowers falling slowly in a breeze.

Other passive slicing techniques include an upward motion that cuts the inside of an opponent's wrist, called "large and small dipper stars." Similar techniques known as "lifting the curtain" and "black dragon coils around the pillar" are designed to cut the armpit.

Slicing the top of the wrist has the sword tip pointed downward, with the sword-gripping hand raised above the sword blade to prevent being cut by the opponent's blade. In the tai chi form these techniques are called "spreading the grass to search for snakes" and "black dragon wiggles his tail."

Although Chinese straight-sword techniques contain no sword-against-sword blocking techniques, there are several connecting techniques in which one sword parries the forward thrust of the opponent's blade or presses down on the blade to trap it. There is no striking of metal against metal with either sword.

Contact Techniques

Any contact techniques are called sticky-sword techniques. The technique named "green dragon comes up from the sea" is an example of a sticky-sword motion. The tai chi stylist circles over the top of the opponent's sword blade, then presses down, disarming the opponent. A finishing thrust to the throat ends the sequence.

Parrying an opponent's sword from its intended target involves some sticky contact, but not hard metal-against-metal hitting. One such parry is called "waiting to catch a fish." The tai chi stylist pushes the opponent's sword to the side, then immediately comes back to attack the opponent's open body. A similar parry movement is "left and right cartwheel sword."

Wong emphasizes that all techniques that do not use *yang jing* (fast, dynamic power) must use plenty of waist and hip movement, called *yin jing* by some (soft, passive power) and "hidden internal power" by others. There are also three jumping techniques in the tai chi sword form—"agile cat catches the rat,"

"wild horse jumps over the canyon," and "carp jumps over the dragon gate." These jumping techniques are designed to cover distance quickly, leaping over any natural obstacles in the swordsman's path.

Although many people perform all of their jumps in an identical manner, each jump should be different. The "agile cat catches the rat" jump should be light and low, since the cat must be agile and light to catch a rat. "Wild horse jumps over the canyon" is a long-distance jump, with the horse jumping far because the canyon is wide. "Carp jumps over the dragon gate" is a high jump, as you envision a large carp springing from the water to leap the dam's gate.

The Yang tai chi sword form will teach martial artists the essentials of Chinese straight sword fighting, plus develop internal power and strength.

Jane Hallander is a frequent contributor to Inside Kung-Fu *magazine. This material appeared in the November 1993 edition.*

The Tai Chi Whip
Whirling Internal Fury

By Robert Dreeben

Of all tai chi weapons forms, the whip form is perhaps the least known and the most secretive. Most tai chi practitioners are familiar with the straight sword, saber form, spear and staff form, and even the tai chi cane.

For years, the whip form was taught only to family members or close high-level students; thus, only a few students know the weapon. Yet, the form's dynamics, expression, and structure embody tai chi theory, internal emphasis, and combat application. If more students had access to the form, it would no doubt be as popular today as the tai chi straight sword.

The Weapon

The "whip" consists of a flexible piece of semihard wood, usually rattan, but sometimes Chinese wax wood is also used. The thickness is approximately one and a quarter inches round; the length is tailor-measured for each practitioner. The proper length is determined by standing at attention with the whip vertically touching the ground in front of you. The distance from the floor up to your eyebrow is the correct length for the weapon.

The whip is a Yang family weapon, and because of the secretiveness of the form, its history is not widely known. One of the first public demonstrations of the whip was given in New York City's Chinatown for the New Year's celebration in 1988 by Sifu Matthew Leung. While there are instructors of the whip form in Hong Kong and Taiwan, there are only a handful in United States.

To the novice, it may seem that employing rattan rather than a hardwood would be only moderately effective. Even in the Filipino arts, rattan is usually used for training in stick fighting, while hardwoods such as oak, maple, cocobolo, lignum vitae (the hardest wood known), and purpleheart are reserved for the "real" heavy artillery. However, flexibility is what sets the whip form apart from the external, heavy Shaolin-style staff set. While the heavy staff intrinsically possesses stopping power by sheer virtue of its weight, the whip achieves this by use of high-speed torsion and internal energy.

Form

The whip form in action looks like anything but tai chi. The movements are fast, snappy, and vicious. Yet, after closer observation through practice, one can see the emergence of all the classic tai chi principles of yielding, energy redirection, and power release.

The form comprises two sections, both extremely long. Though some *sifu* teach part one as a separate form, then part two as an advanced form, in tai chi truth, basic and advanced are one in the same. The limits of your mind and body are what dictate basic and advanced. The execution level is always full speed, although certain transitional postures are done at half speed.

Combatively, the whip form is a complete tactical package. The form contains close, medium, and long-range blocks, strikes, and deflections. Included also are a wide array of locks, throws, and weapon-retention techniques. There are even one-arm techniques.

The essence of the whip is actually three different weapons: the spear, the staff, and the pure whip. However, by dissecting the form, you can see that it's much more than a staff technique here and a spear technique there. The whip is the ultimate expression of power release that the human body can transmit through a long, flexible wooden weapon. Once the form is learned and mastered, almost any physical movement that can be performed with the stick can also be used with limitless variation against any type of attack. Thus, form becomes formless.

Technique

Instructors of the whip compare its "spirit" to a leopard, as opposed to a tiger. The saying is that "The spirit of the heavy Shaolin staff is like that of a tiger: each blow is a fully committed finishing strike; the spirit of the whip is like that of a leopard: ferocious and relentless, each strike becomes another in a relentless barrage of attacking fury."

The analogy illustrates one of the many positive aspects of using a lighter weapon. While heavy staffs are always good, their weight makes it tougher to launch continual successive blows in any direction at a high rate of speed.

The whip is an internal weapon and therefore uses the body's *jing* along with coordinated physical movements that coincide with tai chi principles. Many strikes and deflections have parts of the whip in contact with the upper and lower *dan tian*, combined with waist turning and arm twisting and sliding. Here's an example of how many bodily energies are employed in a typical whip strike: First, the forward momentum from the stepping footwork, followed by rotation of the trunk (waist and shoulders synchronized), then a twisting of the arm and a sharp sliding of the hand and arm down the length of the whip. All this culminates in a high-velocity strike that causes the stick to radically bend on or before impact, like a leather whip. The name "whip" was given to the weapon because of this similarity.

If you have a weak staff, the high-speed, torsion-filled strikes can cause the whip to break at the bend. Therefore, the whip wood must be extremely strong to withstand transmission of energy as well as impact with the opponent. On certain strikes, the whip will actually bend around the enemy's weapon and hit him in the head. On an external level, the whip form ranks with any staff or spear system. Once the form is worked to a high internal level, continual practice will develop the *wei chi*, the body's protective layer of *chi* that circulates just below the skin. This is a spillover benefit that will enhance your empty-hand technique.

Learning the Whip Form

The whip is not easy to learn. When you train in any internal weapon form, you must concentrate on inner and outer body linkages and varied energy dispersion. Can you learn the whip form if you're not a tai chi practitioner? Most *sifu* would say no. However, this response can be interpreted as traditional bias rather than a fair assessment. Even today, there is plenty of politics and even holding back of information in the martial arts world. Some traditional Chinese *sifu* will not teach everything to outsiders. There is no objective reason that a practitioner from another system, whether or not internal, cannot learn the whip or any other internal weapon form. A student who doesn't know tai chi theories and principles can learn them as they relate to the whip form.

The whip is an extremely long form. In fact, it is the longest weapon form most students will ever witness. Once you've completed the set, all the time, patience, and practice you've put into it will have paid off, leaving you with one of the best staff-type forms in existence.

Robert Dreeben is a kung-fu instructor, freelance writer, and police officer in New York state. This material appeared in the July 1992 edition of Inside Kung-Fu magazine.

27

The Four Emotions of Tai Chi Chuan

Eliot Z. Cohen

The setting: Hong Kong. The time: more than thirty-five years ago. The event: a celebration commemorating the traditional birthday of Cheung Salm Fung (Chang San-feng in Mandarin), the legendary thirteenth-century founder of tai chi chuan. The format of the event includes an exhibition by masters of tai chi, preceded by a panel discussion.

Among the masters on stage is a man of about ninety. During the discussion, he declares that most of those who are recognized as masters of tai chi chuan do not really have a complete understanding of that art. He insists that one cannot truly master tai chi chuan until he has learned the method of concentration known as the "four emotions of tai chi chuan."

The old man then gives a brief explanation of this technique, since it is clear that most of those present, on stage as well as in the audience, are hearing of it for the first time. He begins by identifying the four emotions:

- *Hei* (happiness)
- *Noh* (anger, indignation)
- *Oi* (sadness, depression)
- *Lok* (enjoyment)

He explains that most of the movements of the tai chi form correspond to one or more of these four emotions. When these emotions are correctly expressed by the practitioner, they serve as a means toward the proper focusing of the mind, thus enhancing the smooth execution of the form.

When it comes time for the exhibition, he is the first to perform. He demonstrates the fast form from the Ng Gar (Wu) system of tai chi. Present in the audience is a teenager who already has some years of training under his sash. His name is Shum Leung, now Sifu Shum Leung, of New York. Even now, more than a generation later, Sifu Shum looks back on that performance as the best demonstration of the tai chi form he has ever seen.

Movement Reflects *Yi*

As mentioned, the end of the technique is the proper focus of the mind, or *yi* in Cantonese, long considered to be paramount for the mastery of tai chi chuan. A passage in the *T'ai Chi Classics*, attributed to Wang Chung Yuch of the Ming dynasty, says: "The mind gives the command; the breath (*chi*) goes forth as the banner, and the waist executes the command."*

The *yi* activates the *chi*, which stirs the muscles, which propel the waist, which sets in motion the hands and feet. Clear, unencumbered *yi* is thus reflected in smooth and unencumbered movement, just as cluttered and obstructed *yi* is reflected in cluttered and obstructed movement.

As with any art, proper concentration helps one attain the level of *yi* necessary for the proper execution of the tai chi form. However, concentration is one of the most difficult techniques to learn. What many people believe to be concentration is merely the act of thinking about concentration. A student who is told to concentrate probably will instinctively express a serious countenance and then proceed to reflect on the need to concentrate.

For many martial arts students, an aggressive countenance appears to be the expression of preference. The exception is tai chi chuan, during the practice of which many practitioners tend to force an overly serene or spaced-out expression. The method of the four emotions is based on the premise that neither extreme is conducive to the practice of tai chi chuan. Nor, for that matter, are any contrived and artificial expressions.

One reason why the four emotions technique is not widely known is that while it is applicable to any tai chi chuan style, it cannot be applied to the slow form synonymous with the study of tai chi. The slow form is, in fact, the heart and soul of tai chi practice; but in a system that does not already contain a fast form, the form must be speeded up if the four emotions technique is to be employed. (In the *Ng Gar* system taught by Sifu Shum, the fast form is similar to the slow; but its moves are more connected and it is performed about six times faster than the ideal speed of the slow form.)

Applying the Four Emotions Technique

The four emotions are paired into two sets of opposites—*hei-noh* and *oi-lok*. Note that although *hei* (happiness) and *lok* (enjoyment) are sometimes interchangeable in conversational use, there is a difference in meaning between them. For example, money can buy *lok* (various luxuries and other pleasures), but having a lot of money to spend is *hei*. Thus, *lok* connotes enjoyments such as a good movie, a scrumptious meal, or a comfortable chair or bed. Having the means to enjoy these things is *hei*. Also, if one were having a good time at a friend's wedding, that would be *lok*; but for the person getting married, *hei* would apply.

When learning the technique, it is helpful to consider its applications. For example, when moving forward with striking techniques, or performing moves involving punches or kicks, the practitioner would express the emotion of *noh*. These moves are comparatively direct, aggressive methods for obliterating an opponent. This emotion is considered to be the opposite of *hei*, which is expressed in a sequence such as "wave hands like clouds." Such movements involve more sidestepping and less head-on attack, and thus are more conducive to the tranquil mood of *hei*.

Lok includes moves calling for more than normal eye concentration. An example is the recurrent movement known as "single whip," in which the practitioner appears to be savoring the action. This expression is considered to be the opposite of *oi*, which is applied to moves performed while one is

*The translation is by Sifu Shum in his book on tai chi chuan.

retreating from an opponent. An example of *oi* is the sequence of "brush knee, twist step," performed while moving backward. When this same sequence is performed while advancing, it is included among the movements of *noh*.

The pacing of the form is based, in part, on the use of the four emotions. Consequently, whereas the slow form is evenly paced, some movements of the fast form are performed faster than others. When the four emotions technique is applied, the movements of each emotion are done at the same speed as those of its opposite. Thus, the more circular, indirect moves of *hei* are performed at the same speed as the more direct attacking moves of *noh*; and both are performed faster than the savoring moves of *lok*, or the melancholy retreating moves of *oi*.

The most important of the four emotions is *hei*. It is the foundation of the technique; only when the mind is calm and relaxed can the other emotions be properly channeled. If the mind is encumbered with unchanneled anger, concentration is greatly impaired, and practice could actually be counterproductive.

The Secret of Spontaneity

The difficulty of the four emotions method is not so much in knowing which mood to express with which movement, but rather in knowing how to express that mood. It does not take much "expression" to pass the point of exaggeration. Even the skilled observer who knows what to look for should barely detect the changes of expression on the face of the performer. It must be emphasized that this technique of emotional expression is only for the "internal" use of the practitioner.

The "secret" of the four emotions technique can be summed up in a single word: spontaneity. The master does not force the emotions, but instead allows them to unfold naturally. Instead of trying to perpetuate them, he witnesses them. He doesn't *control*; he *experiences*. He is guided by the principle that what is natural need not be forced, just as what is unnatural should not be forced.

For the martial arts student, this concept of spontaneity is the definition of the properly focused mind. The idea neither began with tai chi chuan nor is exclusive to Chinese culture. Yet, it pervades the doctrines of the ancient Taoists and, in that context, has greatly influenced the evolution of Chinese martial arts. An example is the time-honored Taoist concept of *wu-wei*, which is generally translated as "inaction." As it is put forth in the writings attributed to Chang-tzu, *wu-wei* can be explained as "nonagitation," "effort in action," or "spontaneous action." Chang-tzu gives several examples of men who had attained such skill in various arts or crafts that they no longer needed to analyze, scrutinize, or intellectualize what they were doing. They had achieved such a high level of spontaneity that they were said to have "forgotten" the techniques and forms of their arts.

However it is attained, the properly focused, spontaneous mind is the strongest weapon of the wisdom-warrior; and is that which turns form into art and art into illumination. This separates the ordinary "experts," whose skills decrease as their years increase, from the true master who has triumphed over the encumbrances of old age. Only by aspiring to the *yi* of such masters can one begin to understand the meaning of tai chi chuan.

Eliot Cohen has studied tai chi chuan since 1977 under Master Shum Leung in New York City. This was his first contribution to Inside Kung-Fu *magazine and was published in the January 1988 edition.*

28

The Twelve Keys to Tai Chi Standardization

Jean Lukitsh

Tai chi is rapidly growing in popularity around the world. Supported by recent scientific studies, the medical profession has even begun to prescribe tai chi practice as treatment for a number of ills. It is now time for tai chi enthusiasts everywhere to define the essential elements that make their art so special and unique.

Tai chi is truly rich in content and varied in expression. Even the so-called standardized forms, such as the twenty-four-movement form, may show minor changes from practitioner to practitioner. Yet, tai chi remains recognizable in all its permutations. Obviously, certain basic principles are common to all types of tai chi. Furthermore, advancement in the art of tai chi could be said to depend on the fuller expression of these essential elements. Although the body of historical and philosophical texts on the practice of tai chi is well known to any serious student, many of these texts are couched in esoteric language or are easily subject to misinterpretation, especially by beginning students. What is needed,

therefore, is a simple, concise "ruler," or set of standard principles, that can be of benefit to any tai chi student, from beginner to expert.

The development of a standard of practice for tai chi is an awesome undertaking. Only a recognized master of the art, with decades of practice and teaching experience, could attempt it. Fortunately, there is such an expert with the requisite knowledge and experience. Master Bow Sim Mark, an internationally recognized authority on tai chi chuan, has devoted her life to popularizing tai chi in the United States and abroad.

In addition to the classes she has offered for more than twenty years at her Boston-based Chinese Wushu Research Institute, she has produced numerous books and videos on tai chi and related arts. Two years ago, she founded the Bow Sim Mark T'ai Chi Arts Association in Boston. The Association now has branches around the country, as well as in Europe and Asia. The purpose of the Association is to research and promote the practice of tai chi in a manner that exemplifies the art's essential characteristics and requirements.

Tai chi did not develop in a vacuum. It is the culmination of a historical process, with deep roots in traditional Chinese culture. Tai chi is, first and foremost, a martial art. From its inception, it drew on older fighting styles and techniques. The very name (often translated as "grand ultimate") indicates that the combat techniques have been refined to a high level. Over the centuries, a number of styles of tai chi have developed, and many incorporate concepts from Taoist philosophy and traditional Chinese health exercises, although never at the expense of the martial arts character. Despite the variances, tai chi remains unique among fighting systems and spiritual exercises. It is always recognizable and unmistakable.

Furthermore, tai chi is an internal martial art, meaning that muscular strength is less important for correct practice than balance, relaxation, and flexibility. At advanced levels, the practitioner strives to allow the *chi*, or energy, to flow freely through the body. But how can these goals be accomplished?

The unique character of tai chi derives from certain basic characteristics and requirements. By checking their movements against these guidelines, tai chi students can refine and advance their practice. There are six characteristics, which describe the quality of the movement, and six requirements, which have to do with posture and alignment of the body.

Characteristics

• **Circularity**—Tai chi is circular in all aspects. The limbs are curved, the shapes formed in the space around the practitioner follow curves and spirals, and the joints move in circles. The waist turns from side to side, creating a columnar volume of space. The circles are not always immediately obvious but can be felt over time by the experienced practitioner. Behind this element of tai chi lies the philosophical basis of tai chi as self-defense: anything moving toward me is rotated away, and my center (the mass of my body, containing vital organs and controlling my balance) is continually shifting in relation to any external threat.

• **Relaxation**—To be relaxed in tai chi is not to be limp or weak; rather, muscle tension is used efficiently and as sparingly as possible. Everyone understands the concept of relaxation in theory, but it is difficult to remain relaxed under any circumstance. After first learning to dissipate any extraneous muscle tension beyond the bare minimum needed to execute a movement, the experienced tai chi practitioner uses natural body alignment, gravity, and even the force generated by an opponent to do as much of the moving work as possible.

• **Calmness**—As also exemplified by circularity and relaxation, calmness in tai chi is about efficiency in movement. It means paring the movement down to essentials, avoiding exaggeration, moving only as much as is necessary to execute the form. Common examples of "overexcited" movement in tai chi are bobbing up and down during weight shifts and using too much arm movement instead of letting the waist control the direction of move.

• **Continuity**—Tai chi should not be choppy, with sudden starts and stops or abrupt changes in direction. After much practice, the tai chi student should be able to feel one movement flowing effortlessly into the next. As the form progresses, the constant changing of right to left, up and down, opening and closing, becomes an expression of the harmony of yin and yang.

• **Intent**—Tai chi is a form of meditation, but it is a physical meditation, with mind and body working together. While some mental disciplines teach the practitioner to ignore physical discomfort, the student of tai chi seeks to optimize both mental and physical function. Mind and body are another manifestation of yin and yang, neither inferior to the other. To pay attention to body alignment, muscle tension, and changes in balance while practicing a tai chi form, the student must learn to avoid distraction and dispel boredom. The form is practiced slowly, so the hyperactivity that characterizes much of our daily thought processes must also slow down. The mind and the movement eventually work as one.

• **Focusing of Energy**—The concept of energy focusing has no easy equivalent in Western thought or biological science. In Chinese culture, it has been long accepted that various studies, tai chi practice being only one, will lead to awareness of, and mastery over, a type of innate energy that flows through the body. These studies are collectively known as *chi kung* (or *qigong*). Some styles of tai chi include techniques for concentrating the *chi* and directing it to various parts of the body. Advanced practitioners in these systems are able to produce an explosive or vibratory sensation in opponents by focusing energy in this way.

The ability to express these characteristics through the tai chi form develops over time and through practice. However, simply repeating the movements over and over, without also identifying and correcting mistakes and misalignments, will not advance the student's ability. The physical requirements underlying the tai chi movements provide the framework necessary to achieve fluid expression of the characteristics.

Requirements

• **Head, Neck, and Spine Straight**—The desired posture for tai chi is "naturally" straight. A useful exercise is to imagine an invisible string attached to the top of the head, holding one upright like a marionette. This stretch should not produce a rigid posture, but rather train the spine to be erect yet relaxed at all times.

• **Shoulders and Elbows Down**—When you're practicing tai chi, the shoulders should remain in a relaxed, "downward" position, even when the arms move up. This stretches the joint, resulting in increased range of motion, and also makes it more difficult for an opponent to trap or lock the arm. The elbow is also angled downward, both to allow the natural pull of gravity to help relax the arm and to guard against grappling or twisting techniques.

• **Keep Yin and Yang Clear in the Lower Body**—When moving through the tai chi form, practitioners should always be aware of their center of gravity and feel how it is in balance over either one leg or the other. The weighted leg is yang, and the unweighted, or empty, leg is yin. The yin foot can move, stepping forward or back, or changing angles, while the yang foot keeps us stable. The base of support should be neither too narrow nor too wide. An ideal stance has the feet about shoulders-width apart. The heels should not be on a straight line but rather have an inch or two of space between them. The knees are bent and turned out in the direction of the toes. The interplay between yin and yang results in a fluid but strong base.

• **Chest Empty**—This requirement continues the circle formed by the arms through the practitioner's trunk. A slight inward curve of the chest is combined with a slight outward expansion of the upper back to create a structural alignment of the upper body that maximizes power while minimizing target area. Forcing this alignment into place defeats its purpose, and so it is best addressed by advanced students.

• **Movement Originates in the Waist**—The arms do not move independently in tai chi. Rather, the direction of a movement is determined by turning the waist. If the arms are circular and relaxed, only a very little effort is then needed to execute the movement. This type of movement is also more powerful, since the strength of the entire upper body comes into play instead of just a single limb.

• **Lower Back Naturally Straight**—The angle of the lower spine and the pelvis is an important determinant of postural stability. When you're practicing tai chi, the lower back should be relaxed, stretched, and naturally straight; tilted neither up nor down. You must also keep the center of gravity as low as possible. The hips, like the shoulders, should not angle up and down with the leg movement.

While each individual element of tai chi practice is relatively simple, the concentration and body awareness required to transform ordinary movement into a more transcendent exercise demonstrates the value of tai chi as a life-enhancing art. Advanced practice of tai chi is within reach of anyone who has the desire and patience to research the movements and individualize them in accordance with these basic concepts.

No two tai chi practitioners will move in exactly the same way, and the forms themselves can change and be adapted to a variety of circumstances. As long as the characteristics and requirements form the basis of the movement, the result will be recognizably tai chi.

Jean Lukitsh has been a student of Bow Sim Mark since 1978. This material appeared in the August 1998 edition of Inside Kung-Fu *magazine.*

29

Correct Practice of the Tai Chi Form

Doc-Fai Wong and Jane Hallander

Tai chi is a scientific martial art. If you don't follow the principles, the result is poor tai chi. Each principle is structured around precise body actions, incorporating different angles and directions. There is no question that good tai chi comes through hard work and correct practice. If you do not correctly practice the form, you will never reach your full potential in tai chi push-hands practice.

Keep the Five Body Parts Down

The external appearance—how you position your arms and legs when you move—of tai chi form techniques, postures, and footwork must be correct. As a rule, correct form is also nice-looking form, but with tai chi there's more to it than just beauty. Once you learn the form and memorize its sequence, you must work on keeping five parts of your body down. From top to bottom, those five areas are the shoulders, chest, elbows, hips, and back heel.

Shoulders

In tai chi chuan practice, your shoulders are always down and relaxed. If your shoulders are raised, they cause your chest muscles to tense, making your breathing rise in the chest cavity.

For martial arts purposes, people with tense, raised shoulders are easily thrown off balance, because their bodies are too stiff. When your shoulders are tense, your striking energy is broken at the shoulder joint, which seriously restricts your power and force. This is illustrated through accounts of old tai chi masters in China throwing people across a room with no apparent effort.

Shoulders raised—Incorrect

Shoulders relaxed and dropped—Correct

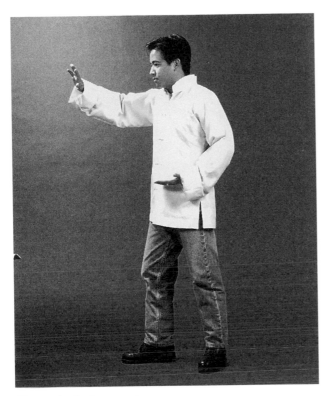

Chest raised—Incorrect

Chest relaxed—Correct

Chest

Don't stand in any tai chi posture with your chest sticking out, as though you were a soldier standing at attention. Your chest should always be relaxed and slightly concave.

Correct breathing is another reason for keeping your chest muscles relaxed. Most people use only one-third of their lung capacity when they breathe. The goal for both martial arts and health is to use your full lung capacity and breathe deeply into the lower abdomen. You cannot have tense chest muscles and expect to breathe with your entire lung capacity.

A relaxed chest is important to martial artists, because if your chest sticks out, your back is swayed. This means your back lacks strength because it's no longer connected. If your chest is relaxed, it is easier for your breathing and *chi* to move down into your *dan tian*. Why is this important for martial artists? When you breathe only in the upper part of your chest, your upper body is too heavy and your lower extremities are too light, which may throw you off balance. Also, breathing too high in the chest causes the heel of your back foot to come off the ground. This makes it easy for people to pull or push you off balance.

Elbows

Keep your elbows down. If the elbows are raised sideways, any striking or defending arm leverage is weak. In close-range grappling situations, raised elbows make it easy for someone to put you into an arm or shoulder lock. By raising your elbow sideways, you've already accomplished half the joint lock, making it easy for your opponent to finish the task. Raised elbows also make your shoulders stiff and chest muscles tense, causing you to breathe high in the chest.

Elbows raised—Incorrect

Elbows dropped—Correct

One way to check your elbow position is to raise your hands in front with your palms facing you as if you were holding a mirror in each palm. Keep your elbows straight down. Then turn your palms outward into a pushing position, without moving the elbows. Your elbow position is now correct.

Hips and Waist

No matter what style of tai chi you practice, your hips should always be tucked, with your pelvis turned upward. If your hips stick out to the rear, your back is swayed and there is no body connection. This leads to little power and balance.

Any martial artist should take full advantage of the *ming men*—the pressure point directly opposite the navel—and its resulting lower-back energy. Chinese traditional medical practitioners believe that the *ming men* is as important as the *dan tian* energy source, located three fingers below the navel. A look at an anatomy chart shows a large mass of nerves—

serving the lower back, abdominal organs, and the lower extremities—surrounding the *ming men*. This is a critical nerve mass, especially regarding strength coming from the hips and back. For maximum strength and health benefits, you should curve your tailbone inward, thereby straightening, instead of swaying, your lower back.

Your waist should be relaxed and flexible; a flexible waist makes your lower-body foundation stronger by letting you set your feet in their strongest natural position. It also makes it easier to control and maximize the weight distribution over your center of gravity. Waist action, combined with a straight back, determines the connection between upper and lower body.

Back Foot

When you're practicing tai chi, your back foot and heel must remain flat on the ground. A common mistake with tai chi practitioners is turning the back

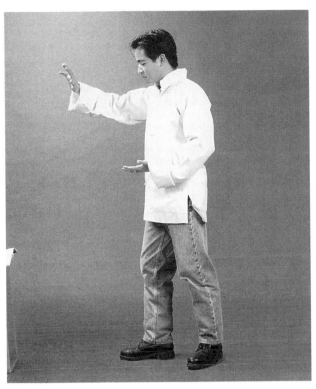

Waist too tense, with hip joint pushed forward—Incorrect

Waist and hip joint relaxed—Correct

foot's heel or pulling the side of the foot off the ground. Your feet must be flat before they are rooted and stable.

Whenever any part of your back foot is off the ground, it is easy to mistakenly turn your knee inward. It's also easier for you to lean too far forward, pushing the knee of your front leg well over your toe. When your energy is carried down the side of your back ankle, your foot will stay flat.

Perfecting the Form

Now that you know the five parts of your body to keep down, here are a few more pointers on correct tai chi forms.

• **Position your head as if it is suspended from a thread attached at the top.** Always look straight at your imaginary target. Holding your head upright and looking straight ahead keeps your energy

moving forward and helps *chi* flow and visual focus. Yang Cheng Fu wrote:

Your intention is to slightly push your head upward. However, do not use too much concentration and strength. If you do, your neck becomes stiff. Your head position should be natural, using only a small amount of intention. If you don't hold your head correctly, your spirit is not alert.

• **Keep your back straight, with your weight directly over your center of gravity for correct balance.** Don't make the mistake of judging someone's or your own back position by the illusion created by loose clothing. You should feel whether your back is straight by the line from neck to tailbone.

• **Don't let your shoulder blades protrude.** Your shoulders should be slightly rounded but not stooped. With your shoulders relaxed and rounded,

Back straight with hips tucked forward—Correct

Buttocks stick out, lower back swayed—Incorrect

Leaning too far forward—Incorrect

place your *chi* intention along the length of your back. Imagine you are pushing your internal energy into your back. If you do this, your strength and energy will come from your back, rather than just your arms and shoulders. Yesterday's tai chi masters all said that real strength comes primarily from the spine.

• **When your hand extends forward in a pushing position, your arm should appear straight but not straight.** In other words, there is a very slight bend to your elbow that makes it look bent but not bent. Don't push with a straight arm and locked elbow joint. If you actually push or hit something, you will injure your elbow joint. Keep your upper arm away from your rib cage, bringing it in close only when punching forward. If you keep it an inch or two away from your ribs, you have better resistance against a push to that arm. You have little resistance when your arm is positioned against your body.

• **Always make sure that your elbows stay down.** The wrist joins your hand to your arm. If your wrist has no intention in its positioning, your palm will drop down like a dead rose. The neck of a rose without water droops; add water, and it comes back to life. When your wrist hangs like a drooping rose, it's because you have no intention in your hand and wrist action. In an actual fighting situation, a person could easily break your wrist if you have no energy in the hand. However, if you bend the wrist too much, it will stop the circulation of energy and strength into the palm. Correct wrist position should be the same as holding your hands against a wall, elbows down, without tensing the wrists. Try this, then step back and check your hand position. This principle applies to the "push," "single whip," "fair lady," "brush knee," and "repulse the monkey" tai chi techniques.

• **When you move, use intention, not physical strength, for power.** In an actual fighting situation, power comes from a combination of body mass times speed of movement. Therefore, when you practice tai chi, your body must be loose and relaxed. Use absolutely no tense force. Once your muscles tense, even slightly, your *chi* circulation gets stuck in those muscles.

But, you might ask, "If you don't use any strength, how can you develop force?" In the body, *chi* meridians might be compared to a drainage system: if the drain isn't blocked, water will flow. It's the same with our bodies: when the *chi* meridians are not blocked, *chi* will move. If your body is tense with stiff strength, your *chi* and blood circulation are disturbed and blocked. When muscles are tense, movements are slower. Without speed behind your body mass, there's little power. Your best speed is produced by relaxed muscles.

When you use just intention-directing movement, your *chi* is directed by your intention, and your blood directed by your *chi*. That leads to proper body circulation. Practice relaxation and intention long enough, and you will develop real inner energy. One old tai chi chuan book says if you can reach extremely soft practice, you will later produce extremely hard techniques. The book also says that good tai chi practitioners have arms that are like cotton wrapped around steel—soft but very heavy.

• **Both palms should stay relaxed, with your fingers naturally spread.** Another must for correct tai chi practice is palm energy. Don't let your fingers curl. Too limp or too stiff also is not correct. Correct palm and finger position is similar to putting your hand out and asking for something.

• **Your eyes should look straight in the direction of your imaginary target.** Eye position is a critical part of correct tai chi practice. Tai chi is a martial art. Don't practice it with a mindless, unfocused gaze. Your eyes follow your hand's direction but should never directly look at the hand. Looking at the hand is a common mistake. Your eyes should look at the attacking hand's direction.

• **Keep your body level when moving from posture to posture.** What Chinese call *shen* (spirit) also is very important. Think of your *shen* as the general and your body as the soldier. If you have a strong spirit, then your body moves are light and lively. *Shen* directs the body. Don't bob up and down. Bobbing leads to weak balance and foundation. You cannot deliver power if your body is moving up and down as much as forward.

The only technique that drops the body lower than its usual position is the "snake creeps down" posture. Likewise, in our Yang style, the "stork spreads its wings" position is an upright posture, standing slightly taller than the other techniques. All other movements should stay at the same level throughout the form.

• **On a martial arts level, timing is essential; if your reaction time is off, you'll likely miss your target.** Although tai chi is practiced slowly, timing is developed into a subconscious habit by keeping everything even and at the same speed. Consider all tai chi movements like pulling a silk thread from a cocoon—soft and even—being careful not to break the thread with jerky movements.

• **Your weight and center of gravity should completely shift from one foot to the other before you initiate another movement.** Your footwork is closely related to timing. Old tai chi masters refer to correct footwork as being "empty and full," rather than "double weighted." As your weight shifts from one foot to another, one becomes full and the other empty. Being double weighted, where both feet carry almost equal amounts of body weight, is an undesirable situation. From a double-weighted position, it is difficult to move and quickly change directions. People moving while double weighted have their center of gravity split into two uneven divisions. This reduces their stability. They are stiff, heavy, and awkward. When you understand the theory of empty and full footwork, you can quickly shift in all directions with lively, well-balanced form.

If correctly done, your moving steps are similar to a cat's. A cat steps so lightly that it doesn't make a sound. When you move the same way—light and relaxed—you advance and retreat easily and quickly in fighting situations.

Motion Starts from the Feet

Moving isn't everything in tai chi. Equally as important are the stationary stances. An example of a correct tai chi stance is the common "bow and arrow" stance. Your forward knee should not extend beyond the toe of the same foot. If it does, you are putting too much stress on your knee and will probably develop sore knees. Your toe should turn 15 degrees inward for stability. The knee of your back leg should be slightly bent, helping your back remain straight. If the knee of your back leg is bent too much, your knee will turn inward and the back of your foot may come off the ground. Keep 60 percent of your weight over the front foot and the remainder over the back foot. Before moving, shift your weight over your stationary foot, preventing double weightedness.

While still in the "bow and arrow" stance, slightly open your legs and concentrate on expanding your energy in all directions. According to the ancient *T'ai Chi Ch'uan Classics*, your upper and lower body follow each other. In other words, motion starts from the feet. Energy is first released through the legs, controlled by the waist, and manifested through the fingers. All motion from the feet to the leg to the waist simultaneously acts together, leading to the old tai chi saying "All motion starts at the same time and finishes at the same time." When your hand moves, your waist and foot also move. Even your eyes move with the rest of the motion. When this is done, your upper and lower body automatically connect. If one body part isn't in action with the others, your power connection and flow is broken.

The Tai Chi Advantage

Tai chi differs from other, more external martial arts in that its movement is continuous and unbroken. Other martial arts use strength that is basically physical action with a stop-and-go type of energy; the disadvantage comes when your opponent catches you at the point in your timing when the old strength is finished and the new strength hasn't started its cycle. That's the time when he easily throws you off guard and off balance. In tai chi, we use *yi* (intention) and even timing, combined with relaxed physical strength. From beginning to end, there is a cycle of continuous recirculated energy and movement.

Since many martial artists from other systems use only broken physical strength, they find themselves puffing and out of breath after a sparring match or long form. Good tai chi practitioners know to take their time and relax, especially when fighting external stylists. They wait until the external martial artist is tired, then get him with relaxed tai chi principles. This was called "calm waiting for action" by ancient tai chi experts. When practicing tai chi forms, do them slowly and evenly. Then your breathing goes deep and low in your abdomen, taking your *chi* down with it. The ancients called this action "seeking calm." Practice the form to learn relaxation and calmness. When you fight, you are calmer and more relaxed than your opponent. This helps conserve energy.

The tai chi form itself is based on "empty and full" and "open and close." "Empty and full" was explained in the footwork discussion.

Open is exemplified in the technique "part the wild horse's mane." In that posture, not only do your hands and legs spread open, but also your mind and intention should push *chi* outward. The opposite, close, is a closing movement, such as in "cross hands." It also is the result of your mind and intention's bringing *chi* closer to your body. In terms of sheer strength, *chi* gives you expanding energy when you push or punch. This is "open" energy. Chi also gives you extra contracting energy when you need to pull your opponent closer. That is "closing" energy.

Some portions of tai chi practice defy conventional explanations. You'll find the meaning only after you've practiced correct basics over a long time. Here are a few translations from the *T'ai Chi Classics* that you must experience before you understand:

- Using power is not right. No strength is also not right. Soft carrying hard is right.
- Losing contact is not right. Forcing is not right. Not losing, not tensing is right.
- Adhesive is not right. Not adhesive is not right. Not leaving and not forcing is right.
- Light is not right. Heavy is not right. Loose and heavy is right.
- Too much aggressiveness is not right. No aggressiveness is not right. Courage carrying caution is right.
- Hitting people is not right. Not hitting people is not right. Having their respect is right (use a technique that doesn't hurt them but shows your power).

These are the secrets to advanced *tui shou*. You must understand the tai chi form before you understand these principles.

PART IV

Profiles and Personalities

30

Tai Chi Catches on with the NFL

Jane Hallander

Like many other athletes, professional football players often cross-train in sports that complement their occupation. Since football is a hard contact sport, it only makes sense that football players would enjoy certain types of martial arts.

External Chinese martial arts have been tried by players and teams with varying success. However, rarely do professional football players take up the internal art of tai chi chuan. Quinn Early, a wide receiver for the Buffalo Bills, is an exception. He's been with the Bills for two years and is entering his eleventh NFL season. Having started his career with the San Diego Chargers, Early has been practicing tai chi since 1990 with San Diego-based Yang tai chi instructor Sean Kyle.

Kyle is a student of Nathan Fisher, who runs several White Dragon Martial Art Centers in the San Diego area. Fisher was a gold-medal winner at the Republic of China's International Push-Hands tournament in Taiwan several years ago and was all-around push-hands champion at A Taste of China.

He has also trained many winners in tai chi forms and push-hands competitions.

Plenty to Offer

Tai chi actually has a lot to offer professional football players. The art teaches people to react naturally whether in self-defense or evading an oncoming lineman. Tai chi applications look exactly like the form movements, making responses to attackers automatic and natural. Tai chi is practiced slowly for good reasons. Moving slowly creates muscle memory and reactions that happen smoothly and evenly. Any sport that requires strength and agility can benefit from internal martial arts practice.

Oxygen delivery through correct breathing patterns, combined with good body mechanics and correct joint alignment during tai chi practice, help keep athletes from injuries. Early notes that his tai chi training helps him stay relaxed and able to absorb an opposing player's blow. This, in turn, allows him to gain more yardage after the initial hit.

He says that he discovered when he started tai chi training that his muscles didn't tense, as often happens when other sports are combined with martial arts training. This gives him better speed, since relaxation is essential for explosiveness. Also, tai chi emphasizes "empty and full" footwork, in which most of the body's weight is on one foot (full), balanced over the center of gravity, before the tai chi stylist moves the other leg (empty). Empty and full footwork principles also create good body movement habits that help keep an athlete injury free.

Early finds that the natural position of the lower (lumbar region) back taught in tai chi both strengthens his back and abdominal muscles and protects him from aggressive hits from opposing tackles by naturally rooting his body and letting him absorb the blow and without falling or injuring himself. "Before I studied tai chi, if I got hit, I'd usually go down from the initial contact. Now I can absorb the blow and twist my body, turning and diving forward to gain more yards. My yardage gained has gone up dramatically, as has the number of passes caught. I have gone from catching thirty to forty passes the year before my martial arts training to now, where I'm averaging sixty to eighty caught passes a year," Early explains.

A Leg Up

Since tai chi movements are practiced slowly, the tai chi practitioner's weight is carried slowly from one leg to the other, a form of resistance training that strengthens the legs. Another tai chi principle says that the elbows should be pointed downward, toward the ground. This helps Early keep his balance and not be uprooted by a body block or tackle. He credits tai chi with teaching him the ability to move quickly without tension or stiffness, resulting in better responsiveness and acceleration, while also enabling him to conserve energy and increase his endurance during a game.

Because of the relaxation and timing of each movement, breathing patterns are even and deep in tai chi. That makes mental concentration high, since more oxygen is available to the brain, and the athlete's muscles don't tire as easily because they are also receiving more oxygen. Staying calm amid apparent chaos develops better concentration and decision making under pressure. Early's own breathing patterns improved dramatically. During collisions in the course of a game, he used to find himself straining, grunting, and exhaling more than he was inhaling. Now, he says, he's relaxed and breathes more deeply and evenly, which means he burns less energy. This all adds up to a fourth quarter in which he has more energy and stays fresh, compared with other players who are starting to drag.

Tai chi has also contributed to the longevity of his football career, he maintains. "Once you turn thirty in professional football, when team owners and coaches look at you, little red flags go up in their minds," he notes. He adds, "You have to bring something a little extra to prove you still have the ability to stay on top of the game. In 1990, when I had just started martial arts training, I had tendonitis in both knees badly enough that it was difficult to walk up and down stairs. The tendonitis disappeared within a year or so after I started tai chi and Choy Li Fut. I haven't been bothered with it since. I now have greater flexibility and stamina during games. My muscles are not fatigued and I don't worry so much about injuries. I haven't missed a game in six years."

The Push-Hands Advantage

Quinn Early often uses the sticking principle of tai chi's *nian jing* (adhering energy) to stay with a charging defenseman until the right moment arises. He then redirects the opponent's oncoming force and evades the tackle, heading for open territory. It is the defensive back's job to keep the wide receiver from getting to the ball. When the back tries to grab him, Early takes him off balance by using sticking and redirecting energy, then gains the advantage.

He describes the effects of tai chi push-hands talents on the practice field: "When I played for the (New Orleans) Saints, those offensive linemen weigh in at around 300 pounds. They practice on lines made of bright orange strips laid out on the field, where they try to throw each other off balance on the orange strip. One day, I was watching this game, when one of the linemen asked if I wanted to try it. I said sure and decided to apply tai chi push-hands principles. I pushed my teammate off the strip pretty easily. Of course, then everyone lined up in a row, and I found myself pushing them off the colored strip, one by one, down the line of players. One of them asked me what my secret was, so I told him it's just simple tai chi basics."

Early adds, "Everything I do in football is hard physical training." I've found that tai chi is necessary to balance that hard, forceful training. I find that tai chi is relaxing, and meditation is like a good night's sleep. It makes you feel so much better than if you just practice hard, external training. It's a balance to that hard side of my life. When I first started studying martial arts, I did it for flexibility and to gain some stamina. Now it is an everyday thing and way of life."

Spreading the Word

With martial arts at his side, Quinn Early plans to play football productively for at least a few more years. When he does retire, he's thinking about teaching martial arts, especially tai chi. He's even considering creating a special program for interested professional football teams. After all, if it can do for others what it has done for Early, tai chi could be the biggest fad to hit the NFL since the helmet.

Jane Hallander is a former Inside Kung-Fu *"Writer of the Year." This material appeared in the September 1998 edition of* Inside Kung-Fu *magazine.*

31

A Tale of Two Chengs

Craig Vorhees

The tai chi of the late professor Cheng Man Ching is, perhaps, the most popular of any single teacher in the United States today. This popularity is due chiefly to the publicity given to the style by writer Robert W. Smith, and to the unflagging effort of two of professor Cheng's students, Ben Lo of San Francisco and William C. C. Chen of New York City.

Students of professor Cheng's style are often, then, confused when they see differences in the two men's training methods, especially since both men say their tai chi is a true representation of Cheng Man Ching's teaching. Both men conduct seminars around the country and, among students living outside San Francisco or New York, have fostered quite a bit of discussion on the relative merits of each method. Having participated in workshops given by both William C. C. Chen and Ben Lo, I have the benefit of firsthand experience with their respective teaching methods.

Basic Differences

The basic difference in Lo's and Chen's approaches to training reflects the central trade-off in all arts between structure and flow. No artist can escape this trade-off; painters, musicians, and dancers all confront this problem in their choice of training techniques.

Ben Lo's Method

Ben Lo's method is very structured. He insists on a perfectly vertical body as the student moves through the postures. He also has people stop and hold postures for several seconds, occasionally with all the weight on one foot. This works the thigh muscles intensely. Also, he makes his students keep their feet flat on the floor while fully turning the hips from side to side. This produces tension in the hip joint while it is being stretched.

Both holding postures and keeping the feet flat on the floor while turning produce pain while stretching and strengthening the body. "Later on, you can enjoy it. For the beginner, it is suffering," Lo explains. The pain and frustration at not finding quick progress can be difficult for some people.

I am reminded of the Wyeth family which produced three generations of American painters. The elder Wyeth was so rigorous and demanding that the younger Wyeth complained that the training would kill his talent. The older Wyeth replied, "If it does, it should." He felt that if talent couldn't stand up to hard training, it wasn't real in the first place. And, by implication, the sooner you found out, the better.

Lo's standards are very high, and his method calls for frequent stops to check balance, weight placement, and verticalness of posture. This checkpoint method has vast potential for developing balance and strength and is enlightening for people like me who have no idea of where their hip is. Lo maintains that professor Cheng trained him extensively in holding postures and that he saw professor Cheng do the linking form all the way through only four or five times in all the years they trained together.

In Lo's method, the postures are broken down and then put back together. As he takes his students through this process, he asks a lot of effort from them. This increases the dropout rate, but those who stick with it end up with a very good tai chi body.

William C. C. Chen's Method

William C. C. Chen's training program is much easier and simpler. He does not require both feet flat on the ground while moving the hips. This allows the student to rotate easily and fully without tension. His stances are higher and narrower and, therefore, more mobile. Thus, his students are more relaxed as they go through their exercises, and this makes for more elastic movements. Because they do not often stop in each movement, they can develop a good sense of flow and are in a better position to detect the natural momentum of the body parts.

These more-comfortable postures are easier to maintain on a daily basis for Chen's students, and at the workshop they don't have to feel disadvantaged because they can't get down as low as the young ones.

At a workshop, I once asked Lo which way I should do a posture. He said, "This way, because it is more difficult." And here we learn their respective positions on the structure-versus-flow trade-off. Chen thinks the easy way is better. When Lo came for a seminar, there were always a couple of people who couldn't finish because their legs were too tired. The rest would leave the workshop with very low stances and then gradually get higher and higher over time, until the next workshop, when he would get everyone down low again. Chen and Lo seem to be addressing the same problem—people's natural tendency to avoid low, painful stances—from differing viewpoints on what constitutes good training.

Besides stance work, both Chen and Lo also have a different way of shifting weight in their postures. This is the heart of stylistic differences. The size of the stance and the order of the postures in the sequence are secondary to the way energy flows through the movements. The difference is subtle, and I must exaggerate it slightly to describe it.

A Weighty Issue

When Lo does his form, he pauses for a moment at 70/30 weight distribution (70 percent of the weight on the forward leg) before moving on forward to 100 percent of the weight on the front leg.

Chen, on the other hand, breezes right on through to 100 percent forward weight distribution with hardly a wave at 70/30. Actually, the pace of Chen's form is slower than Lo's, but Lo's idea is more 70/30-oriented, while Chen has a more weight-forward tendency.

Both Lo and Chen include hand pushing as a major part of their curriculum. Lo favors a structured hand-pushing program with fairly complicated hand techniques drawn from the "grasp the sparrow's tail" sequence of the form. He stresses fixed-steps hand pushing, with weight shifts within the stance hovering around 70/30. Chen prefers more generalized hand actions and concentrates first on flow and balance rather than specific technique. He likes push-hands involving moving steps with their built-in 100/0 weight distribution and favors freestyle hand pushing early in the training.

Most Americans who studied with the professor have a training program more like Lo's but with higher, less painful stances. Although they do take steps when hand pushing, their primary focus is on fixed-step training. Most of these teachers studied under Cheng Man Ching during the last ten years of his life. Chen, in contrast, studied under the professor at an early period and then went out on his own. Perhaps this explains some of the difference. Regardless, most of the teachers in this country lean toward Ben Lo's approach.

Since Chen's methods are in the minority among American schools, it is sometimes difficult to avoid the impression that he is an innovator. In fact, I have heard fellow students refer to "professor Cheng's tai chi" and "William's tai chi" as if they were two separate entities. This is especially true when discussing "body upright." Chen leans forward slightly as he moves forward in his stance until he passes the 70/30 point and brings his torso straight up only as he moves to the 100/0 weight distribution. Chen always said that this way of doing it came straight from the professor and he didn't modify it.

Here in Kansas, I have friends who have either studied under or attended workshops featuring both Chen and Lo. Therefore, I was already somewhat familiar with both views when I went to Colorado to study under an American and a Filipino student of professor Cheng. Since their training methods were closer to Ben Lo's, I often found myself saying, "What about William?" (This was reversed when I went to William's workshop and naturally said, "What about Ben?")

The Body of Evidence

At Jane and Bataan Faigo's school, I saw several films of Cheng Man Ching practicing push-hands. As I watched, I looked closely to see whether he would keep his feet flat on the ground with his weight in about the middle of his stance or if he would step his front foot forward and then jump all of his weight onto it as he pushed. To my surprise, he did it first one way and then the other. Photographic evidence thus exists today that definitely shows Cheng Man Ching moving both ways.

Pages 36 and 53 of Robert W. Smith's book *Chinese Boxing* show Professor Cheng and tai chi master Wang Yen-nien demonstrating William Chen's uprooting exercise just as it is taught at his workshops. You can see their bodies leaning forward as they pass through 70/30 and straightening up as their weight continues over the front leg. The central dynamic of Chen's form is a pantomime of this action. Instead of an innovator, in William Chen we find a traditionalist.

Ever since the middle of the last century when the Yang family went public with the art, people have been saying that tai chi is declining. But if the Yangs hadn't de-emphasized the fast form and eliminated jumping kicks in the interest of old people, thereby making it possible for everyone to practice it, none of us would have it today. It has long been a tai chi tradition to simplify and make easier. In fact, all martial arts have been subject to this trend since the modernization of Oriental armies in the nineteenth century. After hearing Lo talk about the grueling, almost brutal training that Professor Cheng put him through, we may confidently conclude that he, too, has made things a lot easier for us.

William Chen's brilliance lies in his streamlined teaching program, so well suited to Americans. After all, he started teaching here on his own at a fairly early age. Ben Lo shines for me most in the refined level of his kung fu. Throwing a punch at Ben Lo is like walking along at night and falling into a hole: one moment you are strolling aimlessly without a care in the world and the next moment you're on the ground. You don't know what happened or how you got there.

Ben Lo and William C. C. Chen have both spent years on the road promoting tai chi in America, and their full impact on the development of Chinese martial arts may not be fully felt for years to come.

Author Craig Vorhees is an internal stylist based in Kansas. This material appeared in the August 1993 edition of Inside Kung-Fu.

32

William C. C. Chen
Tai Chi's Fighting Force

Scott M. Rodell

William C. C. Chen believes the best way to learn tai chi's self-defense aspects is through free-fighting. However, many instructors don't agree.

Chen's self-defense skills have made him the best-known senior student of the late Cheng Man Ching. Chen enjoyed the rare opportunity to train closely with Cheng. Taking up the art while still a teenager, he lived and trained with Cheng for three years. During this time, Chen helped Cheng refine his internal energy. Despite his skills, Chen remains a soft-spoken man with a small New York City studio. And that's just the way he likes it.

Though few martial artists doubt Chen's level of mastery, he remains humble and concerned that his training beliefs might be too strong and contradict other teachers. He stresses that while his manner of teaching has proved successful in the past, not all teachers may agree that the self-defense aspects of tai chi must be taught: "As far as my knowledge, I don't know how to do (tai chi) without fighting. But

that doesn't mean that someone else won't have a different way of teaching self-defense without fighting. That would be great."

In the following interview, Chen explains how he's able to hold his ground, whether the opposition is an armed attacker, a motorcycle, or the frustrations of tai chi mastery.

INSIDE KUNG FU: Now that tai chi is becoming popular in the United States and throughout China, there are many old-timers who aren't very hopeful for the art. They feel the quality is decreasing. Yet, you are always very optimistic. What do you think tai chi is going to be like in the future?

WILLIAM C. C. CHEN: I think there are more people doing it today. And that is because tai chi today is normally limited to those people who study for health reasons. But anyone now who really studies also for self-defense has more potential: there is more to gain. When tai chi was taught as a martial art, many people became frustrated: so many years of study, and still they do not know how to apply the movements for self-defense. In a little while, they start to be disappointed. And yet, they know tai chi chuan is good for self-defense. If someone could just find a way of explaining tai chi chuan that is easy for them to understand, there is a potentially large group of students there.

IKF: Do you think it's going to keep growing?

WC: Yes, especially now. I'm happy about it. I've wondered how tai chi works for self-defense, wondered for ten to fifteen years, or maybe more. That's why I went to tournaments and got beat up. During the past ten years, I have developed a principle, and it is working: the right words for me are "body mechanics." Every movement we do, we use body mechanics. I've been trying out these theories on myself and my students and other martial artists. They seem very reasonable and they're working.

IKF: What kind of changes do you perceive in your students after they study with you—say a beginner who continues learning over a period of time?

WC: The student becomes more relaxed, more balanced, and begins to have more understanding about tai chi not only for health, but also for self-defense.

Are the Martial Arts Obsolete?

IKF: Of course, a lot of people today say that martial arts are obsolete, because no matter how good your skill, there is always someone who has a gun, and no one can beat a gun. So, why is it useful to study martial arts?

WC: Martial artists just have an option. If you are a martial artist and your attacker is not—and he has a gun and you have a gun—you have a better chance. If you know the martial arts and somebody has a gun, at least you might have a chance to get out of the way or run away, or be more calm or relaxed. You'll know how to solve the situation. With a martial arts background, you have more ability to take the gun away. If you don't have that, and they have a gun, you can't do anything about it. If you know the martial arts, and they have a gun and you have a gun, you have the upper hand.

ikf: Many tai chi schools these days don't have free-fighting practice, but they do have push-hands. How can someone who knows only push-hands apply this training to self-defense?

WC: In my experience, I really can't put them together. Maybe somebody else could. If someone comes to me and learns only the movements and push-hands, I don't think I could teach him to fight unless he's in the fighting class. He has to have practical training. The reason we put on gloves and mouthpieces is to create more reality with less injury. It's done to show the art more, and the students don't kill each other.

ikf: People who really want to learn self-defense ought to put on the gloves and do it, they can't learn just through push-hands?

WC: I can't teach a person to defend himself unless he is in reality fighting. Push-hands to me is push-hands. Can anyone practicing push-hands fight? If the person already knows how to fight and does a little push-hands, then he can fight; but if not, push-hands and fighting are different.

IKF: **How important is push-hands, then? What should you learn from push-hands that is used in your boxing?**

WC: Push-hands is learning how to keep the balance and neutralizing incoming force, all without getting hurt, because push-hands doesn't involve hitting. This way, students have more time to practice. You can't practice fighting too long because you get hurt. You're always able to do push-hands with your friends. Also, because you never get hurt, you won't lose your friends—you won't hurt anybody, and nobody will hurt you. That's why people like push hands!

IKF: **Then, push-hands is an important first step in training?**

WC: Yes, it's an important first step. You gain balance and sensitivity, and you learn calmness and how to neutralize. After push-hands, fighting should be much easier.

IKF: **Can students go from form directly to fighting?**

WC: They can; push-hands is not required. But if they do push-hands, they improve much faster. I'll give you an example: Suppose there is someone who is pretty smart in high school and goes right into business. Being smart doesn't mean he's going to be successful. If he goes to college and has some advisers, trains first, that would prove more beneficial.

IKF: **Some people think that if you do a lot of boxing, you will lose the meditative aspect of tai chi chuan. Is that true?**

WC: That's true. A lot of people have a big problem. They go too fast. They don't have knowledge of the basic training. They don't understand what the slow-motion forms are doing. They go right into fighting, and fighting gets you tense. So, you're losing the knowledge of how to keep balance, neutralization, sensitivity, and the like. You lose the inside coordination, so training through push-hands is an advantage.

IKF: **People who want to learn boxing should proceed slowly?**

WC: One of the characteristics of tai chi is the development of accurate coordination because of the slow motion, slow and calm. I especially emphasize in my fighting class slow and gentle. The coordination will remain the same as you speed up.

IKF: **So, first you start boxing in slow motion?**

WC: Slowly and gently, so everybody stays relaxed. That's why we put on the gloves. Without the gloves, you wouldn't even make contact—you don't want to hurt your friends. Then you have no reality and get lost.

IKF: **Did Professor Cheng ever talk about these points? How did he say a tai chi fighter should react?**

WC: His idea is pretty much that if you do it enough, you'll know how to apply it. He talked about it, but he never held fighting practice.

IKF: **There are always different stories about masters. Did you ever see Professor Cheng in a match or someone challenge him?**

WC: Not during my period of stay with him. I talked to his son Patrick—he's wondering, too. He said, "Gee, I never saw my father do anything to anybody." But I saw him push somebody away; that's all I saw.

IKF: **You always hear those stories, and you never know what's true.**

WC: Right, right. That's why I tell only what I know. Normally when people came to Professor

Cheng's class, they would try to do some push-hands. I was always there, so I was the one who people always tried out. I'm sure a lot of people did come to challenge, but I just didn't get to see them. Also, Patrick, the professor's son, wondered why all these good fighters were convinced by Professor Cheng's techniques after coming to see him. They were very easy to convince, especially those people who studied martial arts for a long time and had a lot of knowledge.

No Tricks to Training

IKF: What sort of training or daily routine do you think is useful?

WC: I encourage students to train with one or two movements at a time. Become proficient with those one or two movements, and be able to apply them for self-defense. When you can speed them up, move on to the next movement. Practicing only the movements of the form a few times a day, you never get into the habit; so, when you want to use it, it doesn't come. You have to condition yourself.

IKF: You think a student should do one movement hundreds of times a day until it is perfect?

WC: Yes. Pick up a few movements, and do them hundreds of times until the coordination becomes very good, before you speed it up.

IKF: Do you still do this?

WC: Nowadays I'm not training as much as I used to. Mostly I just do the movements for circulation purposes. In class, I'm teaching and learning at the same time, so I do enough anyway.

IKF: There is a funny clip at the beginning of your sword form film in which you lie down

and a motorcycle runs over you. Of course, there are people who say, "Aw, that's some trick." How do you do it?

WC: Actually, this is not a trick, but it's not that fantastic. I can do it, and a lot of other people can do it. But if you want to try it, you have to have good training. My body is pretty strong, so I can absorb a lot of punches. Also, the weight of a motorcycle is not that much. I did it because people wanted to see it. Also, the mayor wanted to give a speech . . . so I gave the demonstration to hold an audience for him. But it's not a trick; you do need a little training. In other words, you can't just go under there. Then you get hurt.

Use the Mind to Lead the Energy

IKF: Does this strength come from just doing the form for years, or do you have to do something else, too?

WC: The form is really the key. And another key is how to lead the energy. You have to have special knowledge to do so. Nothing comes by doing just one thing.

IKF: So, you have to do more than just the form?

WC: The form is the main training. The form gives you the energy. The form circulates the energy. It will give you flexibility, or inside looseness. Then you use the mind to lead the energy to where you want it to go. I think you could say the form clears the path.

IKF: Then you'll have that strength?

WC: Yes. Then you could look at the *chi*, as I did with the Taoist training with Professor Cheng. He had been doing tai chi for a long time but didn't get to the internal part, like absorbing the opponent's punch, till later. That's the time I was there . . . I was the one who helped him in training.

IKF: Did you learn the technique for receiving energy from doing it with Professor Cheng?

WC: Right, then I tried it out myself. And it works. And that helps my sparring techniques.

IKF: Do you use your mind to circulate energy when you do the form, or do you just keep your mind on the *dan tian*?

WC: You keep your mind on the *dan tian*. Then you loosen up your body and start to circulate. Then you have to use your mind to focus. You have to use the mind to practice with. You're not just doing tai chi relaxed, not thinking about anything. To me, that doesn't help, especially with the self-defense part. You have to know where to focus the energy. First you get into the *dan tian*; that's the base. Afterward you have to lead the energy where you want it to go.

IKF: When you are doing circulation, do you move your mind through the whole circuit?

WC: No, the inside circulation is there, but then you have to know where to focus. If you know what that movement is for, the application, then it will help you to know where to focus. You think about what that movement is for.

IKF: Part of the mind is on the *dan tian*, and part is with your hand?

WC: Yes. In other words, the *dan tian* is a compressor. The body has what I call "multiple pistons." You might kick with your legs or punch with the arm or the elbow. If you know only the application for elbows, you cannot focus your mind somewhere else. But if you know all the applications, you are able to focus and know where the energy is supposed to go. The compressor increases the pressure in the piston, and where is it going to come out? If you are using the left hand as a push, the compressor can activate it, and that is where the mind has to be. Otherwise there is no force. That is what they call internal coordination.

IKF: So, you coordinate that with your *dan tian*?

WC: With the *dan tian*. If you're thinking, "That's a push," where are you going to push? If you're going to push with the shoulder, then the mind has to be in the shoulder. If you're going to push with the hand, the mind has to be in the hand. The mind leads the energy. If you're thinking about fighting, you know that's going to be a punch, so the mind has to be in the fist. The mind has to go with the compressor and lead the energy, connect the roots to the other end. Push to the palm, punch to the hand, or attack with the fingers. Your mind has to be there: that's called focus.

IKF: Your mind leads all the way from the bubbling well to your hand?

WC: Right. The reason is that the compressor is in your *dan tian*. You have to let the compression settle in the ground, "ground" meaning floor or foot. You have to place your hydraulics into the ground before the piston comes out. If you say "bubbling well," it means ground. "Hydraulics" means you have to place it solidly in the ground first. Whenever you pump out energy, the first thing is to go to the ground.

IKF: You first push down, then you bring the energy out?

WC: Right.

IKF: How does this idea relate to *fa jing* (releasing energy)?

WC: *Fa jing* is how to activate the explosion. The pushing out of the body is explosive, and the punching is explosive. In 1950, Jack Dempsey called his punch the "knockout punch." Explosive punch is the same thing.

IKF: This happens so quickly, how do you focus your mind for *fa jing*?

WC: In *fa jing*, your mind has to be focused on how to explode your hydraulic system. The hydraulic system is normally slowly expanding.

Putting Principles to Work

IKF: You said earlier that you don't train as much as you used to when you started. How much did you train?

WC: By myself, at least three or four hours. That's only the training by myself. Now I don't emphasize the training for punches and certain techniques. As you said, tai chi is getting popular. I feel that now that I have developed my body mechanics theory, it's not just talking; it's working—it works for me, and it's also very easy for people to understand. Enrollment in my workshops has doubled from last year to this year. People are practicing tai chi and want to learn self-defense. Actually, I look at fighting as an art. I enjoy it like a piece of art instead of learning how to fight with people.

IKF: Do you see tai chi as a different type of martial art?

WC: A different kind of art. In other words, how you generate more power, use less energy: that

seems like a piece of art. Don't think about it in terms of violence. In the case of the guy with the knife and you have a knife, you will have more energy. Martial artists would never say that no one can touch them; there is always the possibility of being touched. You might get hurt a little bit. There is a Chinese phrase: "If you want to get a little tiger cub, you have to get into the cave." You risk your life to get the cub. Not everything comes easy.

IKF: Have you ever had to use tai chi chuan to defend yourself on the street?

WC: Several times.

IKF: What went through your mind?

WC: You just have to do it. You don't get mad; it's just part of the practice. When I fought with someone, I didn't really get mad; so, that's the way you have to do it.

IKF: It just happens?

WC: It just happens. You don't really want to kill the guy. It was a practice.

IKF: You say that with a laugh, but if someone attacks you on the street, can you really think of it like practice?

WC: It's not, really, but I feel that it's just part of the training. When I'm training, that's the way it is. There wasn't that much difference.

IKF: It's been ten years since Professor Cheng died. What is the most important thing you learned from him?

WC: The principles, ideas. I lived at his house, so I knew him, and he had no magic power; he was just

another human being. That made me more comfortable with study. Before, I thought he was super-
natural. Because of that, I thought, "I'll never get
it." Then I saw that he's just another human being
and looked for why he's good. So, I put in all these
years trying to find out. Then I try to find simple
ways to teach it.

*Scott Rodell is director of the Great River Taoist Cen-
ter in Washington, D.C., where he teaches tai chi
chuan and* nei gong. *His interview with William C.
C. Chen appeared in the December 1988 edition of*
Inside Kung-Fu *magazine.*

33

A Visit with Chen Xiaowang

Nineteenth-Generation Heir of Chen Style Tai Chi

J. Mackenzie Stewart

In December 1981, the All-China Sports Federation invited an eight-man delegation, sponsored by the National Chinese Wushu Association of America, to visit the People's Republic of China for the purpose of studying Chen style tai chi chuan, the oldest authenticated style of tai chi in existence. The delegation, led by Anthony Chan, studied in the capital city of Beijing under Professor Feng Zhi Qiang and Ge Chunyan. In addition to their studies, the group visited the 1500-year-old Shaolin temple in Henan Province. The highlight was December 19, when a group of "surprise guests" shared their warmth and wisdom with us.

Professor Feng Zhi Qiang is twenty minutes late for class today. His students practice their individual warm-up routines in silence, eagerly awaiting his appearance. The "practice hall" is the back of the sixth-floor cinema in the Xuan Wu Men Hotel, Beijing, China. The Xuan Wu Men, located about two miles southwest of Tien An Men Square, is primarily a hotel for overseas tourists, and is also the American delegation's home during their stay.

The air is dry this cold December day, and the steaming thermoses of water which the hotel provides daily are rapidly being drained by parched tai chi players. Bryant Fong, Anthony Chan's assistant, appears in the doorway and says to the class, "Why don't you all come down to our room? Mr. Feng is

there, and he has some friends with him that he would like us all to meet."

In the living room of Anthony and Bryant's suite, Anthony, Professor Feng, and Ge Chunyan (the delegation's assistant instructor and a member of the Beijing Wushu Team) greet us, and the strangers stand up to meet us. Anthony Chan makes the introductions: "These people are friends of Mr. Feng. They are members of the Chen family and have come from Chenjiagou Village to see us. They are very interested in what we are doing here and would like to sit in on our class today."

For a few moments, the American group members are too stunned and excited to speak. This is the first meeting of non-Chinese Westerners with members of the Chen family, and certainly an important moment in tai chi chuan history. Anthony continues, "This is Chen Jiang Hat, and the gentleman next to her is her husband. She is Master Chen Fa Ke's daughter; her father was Mr. Feng's teacher." Then, indicating a robust-looking young man standing in the center of the group, Anthony says, "This is Chen Xiaowang. He is also a relative of Chen Fa Ke, and I hear his tai chi is very good." With the introductions completed, everyone heads to the "practice hall."

After almost three weeks of intensive daily practice, the group has finished learning the first form in the Chen style, a form called "Old Style Number One." The Chen family village representatives sit down and watch as Professor Feng leads us through our class. After several repetitions, we stop to rest, and Professor Feng then invites our distinguished guests to demonstrate their tai chi chuan.

Chen Xiaowang is the first to do so. One can tell even before he moves that his level of skill is very high. Standing in the *wu-chi*, or "preparation stance," Chen Xiaowang is the picture of *wu-wei*, or "effortlessness," alert relaxation. Yet, one senses that this profound poise could explode in an instant into powerful response were any person foolish enough to challenge him. As with Professor Feng, there is a noticeable glow in his eyes as he moves through his form with masterful power and precision. Never had any of us seen a form performance such as this.

Xiaowang's level of concentration is uncanny. He moves with fluid grace through intricate and difficult maneuvers, all the while looking as if he is in some far-away zone of time and space, his mind's eye turned inward. "It reminded me of someone in a voodoo trance," one of the delegation members later commented. Chen's transitions from the softest soft movements, moving as if he has no bones, into explosive, fast, hard corkscrew punches and breaks are done as easily as if he were scratching his head.

Chen finishes his form with an air of peace and stillness, and then casually strolls around for a few minutes to cool down before sitting to watch as his aunt demonstrates Chen routine number two, *pao chui*, or "cannon fist." Chen Jiang Hat's performance is impressive, even though she is in her seventies and tells us that she has not practiced regularly for thirty years!

Chen Xiaowang is gently resting the backs of his hands on his thighs as he sits in what looks like a Taoist meditation posture. When queried about this posture, Chen smiles and says, "Feel my palms." His palms feel soft and relaxed and are hot in the center. "My hands are always hot, no matter what I do," he says, still smiling warmly. He agrees to an impromptu interview, a translation of which follows.

INSIDE KUNG FU: What is the *chan szu chin*?

CHEN XIAOWANG: What do you think it is?

IKF: Well, I've heard that it's called the "corkscrew strength" or "spiraling energy," and that if the foot is really rooted into the ground, the push or movement starts from the foot. All of the momentum of the force starts twisting up from the foot, through the leg, the hips, the back, and the arm, and is finally expressed in the hand. The whole body is relaxed so that all the energy is focused, and the entire motion is combined with mind intent. That's all I understand about it.

CXW: This corkscrew strength does not initiate from the foot. It initiates from the trunk of the body; it initiates from the waist, from the kidney area. It transfers down toward the foot, and then it rebounds from the foot back up and on through the body. Don't forget, everything initiates from the waist; it then goes down to the foot and bounces back up from the foot. Otherwise, if you are just using the strength of the foot, it will not be as powerful. When the power is really coming through, its expression is not limited to the hands; it could be in the elbow; in your hip; in your knee;

in your thigh. In Chen style, whenever there is movement—not necessarily a striking move, but whenever you have movement—you have this *chan szu chin*.

Basically the strength itself is soft. This thread is like the silk cocoon. The term itself has nothing to do with tai chi chuan: The two characters *chan szu* do not refer to the corkscrew strength itself. *Chan szu* means the "weaving" of the cocoon. But this itself does not really relate to tai chi. For example, movements like "cloud hands," the hands move in circular motions, sort of like a silkworm weaving a cocoon. So, the term *chan szu* is used to describe the action of tai chi. If you want to be really technical, *chan szu* is the threading of a cocoon, and the corkscrew strength is different. *Chan szu* is the big circular movement. The corkscrew strength is something else; it is a twisting strength.

Sometimes these terms can be interrelated; they can even describe the same thing. For example, in the movements that I was demonstrating, my hands look as if they are weaving a cocoon, but my waist is almost turning on an axis, so that is more like a corkscrew. To give another example, sometimes as they are making the circle in the weaving of the cocoon, the hands are simultaneously turning on their own axis, so you can have corkscrew within the weaving of the cocoon. But no matter how one tries to describe it, we are only using adjectives. It is more important to use the energy appropriately than to try to put it in if it is not comfortable. The most important thing is that these motions do not obstruct the flow of *chi* to all the limbs.

IKF: Can we get anywhere just by practicing what little we've had a chance to learn? Will some of these things that you've been speaking about become clear to us after we practice for a while?

cxw: It is only natural that you cannot yet feel these theories applied to you when you are going through the forms. Basically you can divide tai chi into five levels.

The first level is just learning the external movements, trying to make it look like tai chi, knowing the requirements of the physical action, and at the same time knowing the theory, knowing what should be right. You complete the first level when your movements are precisely the way they should be.

You move into the second level when you can feel some sort of inner strength building up, mostly in the form of heat throughout your body. At the first level, you try to make the movements precise. By the second level, you know the movements so well that you don't consciously think about it. Then you start to work on the contradictions. For example, you could be doing a movement that looks very correct on the outside, but on the inside, you feel almost as if you are having a cramp. In other words, your muscles are still stiff in the wrong places. At the second level, you have to work on the internal smoothness in combination with the external precision.

When you smooth out all the contradictions, when the internal is in good coordination with the external, when you feel your flow of energy throughout your body—the day you get to that point, you are in the third level. In terms of fighting applications, in the first stage, even if you are learning the techniques, your body is not yet ready to use them for fighting. It is like something that is top heavy: you can easily be toppled. At the second level, you know the techniques; you know how to use them. But usually, the internal is still not really in coordination with the external. At that stage, when you start to push hands with people, or actually start fighting, a lot of the techniques cannot come out; they do not flow smoothly.

So, when you get to the third stage, when your internal is in good coordination with the external, at times you feel that you can execute these techniques. You may often be able to effectively defend yourself or topple your opponent, but you may end up injuring yourself in the process because your internal energy is not yet strong enough. By the third level, you should be able to handle and smoothly perform the technique itself, and the applications. During this level, we require players to thoroughly know the applications and methods. The reason is that at this stage you are beginning to cultivate the *chi* inside. However, if you do not know the technique well enough, when you try to execute it you may either overuse your *chi* or underuse your internal strength.

The fourth level is when you know your movements very well; you don't even have to think about them. There is no contradiction between inner and outer. When you are performing your movements, even when you are doing the set by yourself, you imagine that you are fighting an opponent in every move that you make. It seems as if you are actually applying techniques as you go along through the form. In other words, even when you are practicing, without an opponent, it seems as if there are enemies all around you. However, when you really face an enemy, you can handle yourself; it seems like you are handling these enemies as if they are not there.

When you get up to the fourth stage, that is when you start to work on learning the weapons forms. Prior to that, it will not be useful to work on the weapons. In the first three levels, all the movements are big. You perform the movements in an expanded, almost exaggerated way in order to understand them, so that it can begin to feel like a real and effective technique. However, when you reach the fourth level, these big circles can be refined into medium-size circles, and you will still be able to feel the strength and flavor fully in each technique.

The important point in fighting an opponent is that first you have to touch him. Without touching him, you cannot do anything to him. As soon as you touch him, the requirement is that you use just enough strength to conquer him; you don't overpower your opponent using unnecessary strength. You issue just enough to put him off his feet, to unbalance him.

To summarize, at the first level, you have 10 percent yin and 90 percent yang. At the second level, you have 20 percent yin and 80 percent yang. Third level, you have 30 percent yin and 70 percent yang. Fourth level, you have 40 percent yin and 60 percent yang.

Then when you reach the fifth level, you have 50 percent yin and 50 percent yang; they are totally balanced. Also, the medium-sized circles get even smaller; they become small circles. This yin and yang is softness and hardness. So, in the first level, you have 90 percent hard things and 10 percent soft things. As you reach the ultimate, the fifth level, when it becomes good, you have 50 percent soft and 50 percent hard; totally balanced.

IKF: In the *T'ai chi Ch'uan Classics*, I think one of the Chen family, Chen Xin, wrote about this, and called it something like "wonderful hand."

CXW: Right. The "wonderful hand" means that as soon as it moves, there is a combination of yin and yang, softness and hardness in it, neither too much softness nor too much hardness. Whenever it moves, there is total balance between hardness and softness. When you get to that totally balanced stage—and then not only when you are practicing martial arts; it could be when you are walking, or when you are sleeping, or when you are driving—at that point, it doesn't matter which way your opponent comes. You should be able to handle yourself and still apply this "wonderful hand." It becomes totally natural, an instinctive kind of reaction. At that point, all of your body is open and coordinated; whichever part of your body requires strength, it can be exerted to that spot.

However, even when you reach five yin and five yang, it is still no big thing; it does not mean that you have reached the top. Martial arts practice has no limits.

At this point, the lesson is over for the day, and

the Chen representatives have to leave. In the short span of an afternoon class, the mutual love and respect for Chen tai chi chuan has drawn the entire group together with a spirit of closeness. The feeling is like that of a family gathering. As we escort our guests to the door, Chen Xiaowang seems to exude the very qualities of tai chi chuan's "wonderful hand": a deep humility combined with self-assurance, gentleness, and grace, blended harmoniously with the impression of tremendous power in reserve.

The writer expresses his gratitude to Anthony Chan for his interpretation and translation of the interview, and for his wonderful spirit which made the delegation's China visit a great success.

J. Mackenzie Stewart is a veteran tai chi player who recently traveled to China to study the art. He makes his home in Rochester, New York.

34

Chen Xiaowang
Keeper of the Tai Chi Secrets

Howard Choy

Chen Xiaowang, grandson of the famous Chen Fake, is recognized as the present-day keeper of Chen style tai chi chuan. In this rare interview, Master Chen reveals the true history of his family's style.

It is not very often one comes across a genuine kung-fu master. In my twenty years of searching the world (especially in China) for a true teacher, I have not met more than six martial artists who I consider a "master" in the true sense. So, it was with great fortune that I welcomed Master Chen Xiaowang as a guest in my home and am able to study with him daily during his stay in Australia.

Master Chen is the son of Chen Zhaoxu, the eldest son of the Chen family tai chi master Chen Fake. As such, he is recognized as the present-day (nineteenth-generation) keeper of the Chen style tai chi chuan. Master Chen was born in 1945 in Chenjiagou Village, Henan Province. He began the study of his family art of tai chi at the age of seven by his father and his uncles Zhaokui and especially Zhaopi. Master Chen was awarded the tai chi chuan gold medal at three consecutive National Wushu Tournaments from 1980 to 1982 and was again crowned the tai chi chuan Champion at the First International Wushu Competition held in Xi'an in 1985.

Before he left China, Master Chen was chairperson of the Henan Province Chen Push Hand T'ai Chi Ch'uan Association; deputy head of the Wushu Academy of Henan Province; and technical adviser and official assessor for the standardized competition routines for the Chen, Yang, Wu, and Sun styles of tai chi chuan. Since 1988, he has been a senior *wushu* instructor (equivalent to a university associate professor) in China. Apart from his martial prowess, Master Chen is also a calligrapher and a noted author. He has written three books on tai chi chuan and is a member of the Society of Chinese Calligraphy and Literature. Since 1985, Chen has traveled to teach in Japan, Singapore, Malaysia, and the United States as well as Australia, his current port.

Our interview was conducted in Mandarin. I translated and edited the conversation with the help of Master Chen's written notes in Chinese and his books.

INSIDE KUNG FU: Master Chen, can you start by telling us the origin of Chen style tai chi chuan?

CHEN XIAOWANG: We can start with my ancestor Chen Bu, the first generation. He was originally from Shanxi Province. Nearing the end of the Ming dynasty, more than 500 years ago, Chen Bu migrated to Henan Province and moved his family to the present-day Chenjiagou Village in the county of Wenxian. At that time, the village was called Changyang Village (mainly consisting of people with the surnames Chang and Yang). When the Chen clan prospered and its population increased, the village name was changed to Chenjiagou (*Chen*—surname; *jia*—the family of; *gou*—gully or ravine, because the village lies in a gully not far from the Yellow River). Chen Bu was an accomplished martial artist, so everyone in my village has been practicing kung fu since then. Nothing very much happened until the ninth generation; Chen Wang Ting was an outstanding scholar and martial artist.

IKF: I have heard that Chen Wang Ting was a fearsome fighter. Was there anything written about him in the family record?

CXW: Yes, in our "Genealogy of the Chen Family," it was recorded: "Wang Ting, alias Zhouting, was a knight at the end of the Ming dynasty and a scholar in the early years of the Qing dynasty. He was known in Shandong Province as a master of martial arts, defeating once more than a thousand bandits. He was the originator of the bare-handed and armed-combat boxing of the Chen school. He was a born warrior, as can be proved by the broadsword he used in combat."

IKF: Is the sword still there?

CXW: No. It was a long time ago . . . besides, the cultural revolution has destroyed most of the relics.

We are lucky to have kept some of the written records of the family.

IKF: So, Chen Wang Ting invented tai chi chuan?

CXW: Yes. Between 1930 and 1932, Tang Hoa, a well-known and respected martial arts historian, was commissioned by the government to find out the truth. He came to our village three times, went through our family records, and did a lot of research. He determined that tai chi chuan originated from Chen Wang Ting from Chenjiagou in the middle of seventeenth century.

IKF: Do you agree with him?

CXW: Yes, I do. After the downfall of the Ming dynasty, the political scene was volatile, and the society was in turmoil. Chen Wang Ting withdrew from public life and retired to live in the village. He wrote not long before his death: "Recalling past years, how bravely I fought to wipe out enemy troops, and what risk I went through. All the favors bestowed on me are now in vain! Now old and feeble, I am accompanied only by the book of Huang Ting (a classic on *chi kung*). Life consists of creating actions of boxing when feeling depressed, doing field work when the season comes, and spending the leisure time teaching disciples and children so they can be worthy members of society."

Because Chen Wang Ting had fought in many battles and had traveled and read widely, he was able to combine many good points from other schools and from his experience, and to build on what was passed down by Chen Bu to create a unique system of martial arts.

IKF: What was so special about Chen Wang Ting's tai chi chuan?

CXW: One: He synthesized many forms of boxing into one system. He was especially influenced by the writing of General Qi Jiguan ("The Thirty-Two Forms of the Canons of Boxing"—a collection of forms from sixteen schools). Two: He utilized the theory of yin and yang as the theoretical basis of his martial arts. Three: He combined traditional Chinese medical theories (e.g., *Jingluo* and acupuncture) and techniques of *daoyin* (the concentrated exertion of inner force) and *tuna* (deep breathing exercises) into his system. Four: He invented the *chanxi* ("reeling silk") techniques and the push-hand exercises.

IKF: What was the content of Chen Wang Ting's tai chi chuan?

CXW: It had:

- five sets of tai chi chuan
- one set of *pao chui*
- one set of *chang quan*, consisting of 108 movements
- all types of weapons
- five methods of push-hands
- two-person "sticky spear" and other types of practice routines with weapons

IKF: Is there anyone still practicing these routines?

CXW: No, not the fist forms, anyway. During the fourteenth generation, Chen Chen Xing(1771–1853) condensed all the fist forms into two sets. We now call them "*laojia*" (the "old family" sets) to distinguish them from the "*xinjia*" (the "new family" set) created by my grandfather, Chen Fake (1887–1957). The first set of *laojia* is quite slow; it can be used to train the student to awaken and to get a feel of the *chi*. The second set, also called *pao chui*, is fast and powerful, where the student is taught *fa jing* ("explosive power"). The two sets of *xinjia* are similar to the *laojia* except that they require more subtle use of energy and dynamic force and are generally more difficult to perform well. The push-hands and

the weapons routine remain much the same to this day.

IKF: I understand that you have now further condensed the *laojia* and *xinjia* forms into one "thirty-eight" form. Can you tell us something about this new creation?

CXW: In the "thirty-eight" form, I have tried to do away with all the repetitions and to simplify the too-difficult moves, without destroying the characteristics of Chen style tai chi chuan, especially the attack-defense content and the *chanxi* techniques. It takes three to four minutes to perform. You can practice it either in a slow and gentle way or in a fast and vigorous fashion with jumps and *fa jing*; it all depends on your age or inclination. It's quicker and easier to learn, and I think it is a good way to popularize the Chen style tai chi chuan.

IKF: We all know that the Yang, the Wu, and the Sun styles evolved from the Chen. Can you tell us the main differences between Chen and the other styles?

CXW: They all have unique characteristics. Generally speaking, the names of the movements are different and sometimes the intentions are different. Chenjiagou tai chi has more weapons forms—apart from the sword and the saber, there is the spear, the staff, the *kwan do*, and the two-person weapons forms. In Chen style tai chi chuan, all the sets have *fa jing* movements which other styles tend to neglect or not show at all. Chen style tai chi chuan is for fighting as well as for health.

IKF: What about *chanxi jing* ("reeling silk energy")?

CXW: *Chanxi jing* is a unique characteristic of Chen style tai chi. The other styles don't have much of this spiral-like spinning and twisting movement.

IKF: And push-hands?

CXW: Chen style push-hands tended to be done in a moving fashion. One attacks forward while the other retreats backward, front on or side on, and so forth. The other styles like to do it more in a stationary manner, with less *fa jing* and less aggressive moves. We also tend to use *chin na* and takedowns a lot. We treat push-hands as a mock fight rather than an exercise. You have to be thrown around a lot to know what your *chi* or your *jing* is doing.

IKF: Speaking as one who has done only Yang style, is it possible to achieve mastery of tai chi by doing any one of these styles?

CXW: Of course. They all come from the one source. The principles are the same. What style you do is immaterial. With a good teacher, hard work, and perseverance, everything is possible.

IKF: Master Chen, you are making it sound so easy. I have also heard that you are a keen calligrapher and that you apply the same tai chi principles to your calligraphy. Is that so?

CXW: Yes. Both tai chi and calligraphy involve the same "transportation of *chi*" (*yun chi*) in our body. When I fight, I try to "transport" my *chi* to the point of impact without friction, still maintaining maximum efficiency. When I write, I try to do the same, except it's to the tip of my brush. I practice my calligraphy the same way I do my tai chi—with correct postures, relaxation, and efficient *yun chi*. Both activities complement each other.

Howard Choy is an architect and a practitioner of tai chi chuan and Choy Li Fut kung fu. He lives in Sydney, Australia. This interview appeared in the October 1991 edition of Inside Kung-Fu *magazine.*

35

Daniel Lee
The Harmonious Synthesis of Jeet Kune Do and Tai Chi

Richard Imamura

Across the spectrum of the kung-fu way of life, no two arts appear more dissimilar than jeet kune do and tai chi chuan. Thousands of years stand between the two, yet even that gap is dwarfed by the void separating the devastating and lightning-quick fighting art of Bruce Lee from the graceful, slow-motion exercises of the health-conscious Taoists. Fundamentally different, if tai chi chuan were day, then jeet kune do (JKD) would have to be night.

But day and night exist in harmony. With each morning, night yields to day—only to return with the sunset to prevail over day and begin the cycle anew. Day and night coexist in a yin-yang harmony, and in much the same way, within Professor Daniel Lee, the violence of JKD merges harmoniously with the passive philosophies of tai chi chuan.

An electrical engineer and college Chinese language and culture instructor, Professor Lee was the first student admitted to the Los Angeles *gwun* to study the newly developed JKD under Bruce Lee and

his assistant, Danny Inosanto, in 1967. He still values the "freedom of expression" he found through that association. Sure, the offense-oriented principles unleashed a most effective fighting system, but for Lee, "It's a means of expressing myself without artificiality."

He explains. "It is an all-out fighting art, and I like it. To me, it's like watching a football game, You don't see the one who falls down, you see the one who faked him out and went on to score the touchdown. That's what I enjoy in JKD—sharpening my skills and techniques so I can cope with the changing situations present in combat. I never go out with the intention of hurting someone, and though the [free] sparring has a lot of body contact, our protective gear and awareness prevent injuries."

However, while he still works out once a week at the JKD *gwun* (now operated by Inosanto), Lee devotes the majority of his time and interest to the gentler art of tai-chi chuan. "When I'm working out in JKD, I'm very physical and intense," he notes, "but

I don't want to remain in that mental state all the time. I want to be calm, quiet, relaxed, and centered. I want to be gentle and at peace with myself. Tai chi helps me reach these goals. We all have our emotional ups and downs, but practicing tai chi stabilizes me and provides evenness. I guess what it boils down to is yin and yang—the JKD training me to be effective in combat, honing the fighting reflexes; and the tai chi chuan promoting tranquility and harmony within myself and oneness with the world around me. I'm a firm believer in nonviolence, and yet I feel strongly that only a person who has undergone the discipline of training to master himself can truly be in charge of any situation that might arise. One who is truly strong can afford to be gentle."

And gentleness is the way of tai chi chuan. True tai chi is hard to come by outside of China, but in the eight years that he has studied the art, Lee has had the good fortune to study under a number of masters. "I'm continually searching for good teachers I can learn from, masters who are willing to teach with openness," he explains. "I don't jump around. When I stick with a teacher, I stick for many years, and I associate with them for life."

New Dimensions to Learning

Lee's first exposure to a genuine master of tai chi chuan was in 1966, one year prior to the opening of the Los Angeles JKD *kwoon*. At that time, Master Tung Fu Ling visited Los Angeles to try to drum up interest in the then-unknown (outside of the Orient) art. One of the world's foremost masters of the classical Yang style, Master Tung "was very discouraged because very few people knew about tai chi," Lee recalls. "He tried to open up a school, but there wasn't any interest in tai chi then. When I started learning from him, it was three times a week. I knew it would be only a short stay, so I dropped all other training in order to learn." Then, after one discour-

aging year, Master Tung returned to Hong Kong. (He subsequently relocated in Honolulu).

Finding himself without a teacher who could even come close to Master Tung—Tung Fu Ling is the son of the Grand Master Tung Yen Jet, probably the greatest tai chi chuan practitioner of modern times—Lee's tai chi training was sustained only through correspondence with his mentor and his own daily practice. When the opportunity was opened for him to learn the JKD process under Bruce Lee himself, Professor Lee responded immediately.

For two years, Daniel Lee's tai chi chuan practice paralleled the four workouts a week in JKD, but in 1969, he was able to study again under a tai chi chuan master with the arrival of Master Mary Chu.

"When Mrs. Chu came over here, I was really excited," Lee notes. "You see, back in China, Mrs. Chu had studied for many years with Grand Master Tung—so she and Master Tung Fu Ling were on the same level. In China, within the school system, family titles like "brother" and "sister" are used instead of ranks. So, since I had studied under Master Tung Fu Ling in 1966, when Mrs. Chu came over, she was considered as my "aunt." She liked me very much, right from the start, and took me in like a son." He studied with her for almost three years, firming up his movements and weapons skills in the Yang style and becoming the senior student in her class.

In 1972, he was given permission by Mrs. Chu to conduct tai chi chuan classes—something absolutely required if proper protocol and respect for a teacher is followed. "I treasure this privilege very much. It offers me a new dimension in my learning," Lee adds. And although he no longer attends Mrs. Chu's classes, he still has deep respect and affection for her. "I will always consider Mrs. Chu my teacher," he emphasizes. "I still go back to visit sometimes, and we keep in touch on the phone."

Since he is ever on the lookout for new directions to explore, recent months have found Lee again studying under someone he considers "a great master," Y. C. Chiang. Accomplished in the lesser-known northern Kuang Ping style of tai chi chuan and kung fu, too, Master Chiang is again widening Lee's totality of experience—the new and unfamiliar element being the rigorous, almost contortionist, stretching exercises typical of the northern systems. "The northern systems use all high kicks, which is why they emphasize stretching," Lee explains. "Their flexibility is so good that they can develop faster kicks and recover faster."

The Discipline of Tai Chi Chuan

Beyond merely becoming more flexible in order to kick faster or higher, Lee sees a deeper benefit in the practice of tai chi chuan. "All that we do here is really discipline of the mind and body," he says. "To accomplish anything in life, you've got to discipline yourself, keep your mind on what you're doing, in order to be successful. If your mind's wandering off, occupied with different things here and there, you'll never get anything done. So, tai chi chuan is a means of discipline. It takes thirty-five minutes to do the whole set. Slowly and persistently—that's discipline!"

With the slowing down comes even greater benefits. "It is actually achieving balance—mind, body, and spirit," Lee points out. "People say, 'Take it easy,' but they don't spell out how to do it. Well, you can't take it easy if your body's too tense or if your mind's still in tension. Tai chi chuan puts your mind in neutral gear and relaxes your body."

The slow-motion movements, developed to emulate the give-and-take harmony of the yin and yang, recall the wisdom of the ancient sages. "You see, Lao-tzu, in the Tao Te Ching, said rigidity is the symbol of death, and suppleness and softness are the symbols of life," Lee points out. "The flexible bamboo bends with the wind; the rigid branch snaps. In the same way, the tai chi chuan movements are varied so as to put into play every part of the body, from the smallest joint to the largest muscle, with harmonious design and graceful patterns. The result is glowing health—suppleness in the joints, your blood circulation is stimulated, the nervous system is activated, and the respiratory system is exercised. On top of all this, the body is so strong and healthy that sickness and disease are held off more easily. In other words, tai chi chuan refreshes your body so that every cell feels charged with new energy and vitality."

Along with the exercise benefits, changes come over the practitioner, according to Lee. "You gain a feel for the correct use of the body's energies without waste. With this new sensitivity, you learn to apply it in your everyday life so that in any task, you spontaneously employ the right amount of energy for the job at hand, thus decreasing tension and fatigue." Relaxation of the mind and body frees one from many of the trivial day-to-day irritations that can sometimes accumulate and make life miserable. Instead, fresh energy and a relaxed mind open new avenues of interest.

"From my long practice of tai chi chuan, I found that my interest began to grow beyond the physical movement, and into the realm of cosmology and reflection of the yin-yang principles underlying universal activity," Lee adds. "I began my deep study into Chinese philosophy. I have since built up a library of Chinese philosophy—I-Ching, Lao-tzu's Tao Te Ching, Zen discipline, Chinese literature devoted to hygienic and meditative techniques, and of course, books on tai chi chuan and all branches of the Chinese martial arts."

A teacher of Chinese language and culture at Pasadena City College for the past twelve years, Professor Lee is able to integrate the purely physical aspects of the art with the undiluted wisdom and reflections contained in the original Chinese manuscripts.

"In the Chinese way of life," he points out, "mental, physical, and spiritual development are all valued equally. Tai chi chuan has been regarded as a unique meditative art which satisfies the needs of people on these three levels of existence. It is often referred to as Chinese yoga—"mind in action, meditation in motion." It is a meditative art for achieving the harmony of the mind and body.

"The harmonious development of the body and mind are essential if one is to realize the profound possibilities of one's life. With the harmony of body and mind, the *chi* [life energy] begins to flow. When the flow of *chi* through one's body is free and uninhibited, spiritual energy begins to develop, which ultimately leads one to the attainment of spiritual enlightenment. Through practice of tai chi chuan, one develops a deep inner awareness; one is in touch with oneself and with the universe."

He adds, "As you establish harmony within yourself, you become calm and balanced. You are no longer selfish or self-centered. Loving and sharing become your way of life, and in your mind there is joy and peace. Myself, I feel I'm headed in the right direction, although I'm not anywhere near where I would ideally like to be."

Honing the Combat Instincts

Born in Shanghai in 1930, Lee always had more than a normal amount of drive. Coupled with a sharp mind and a naturally athletic body, the young Lee often pursued goals beyond the aspirations of his peers.

Once, two Russian brothers from his neighborhood attacked him and tried to steal his bicycle. Saving his bike with the aid of a bystander, Lee nevertheless took a pretty good beating. With a twelve-year-old's vow to avenge the wrong, he proceeded to the nearest gym to learn Western boxing. "I figured I should beat them at their own game," he remembers. "But after an afternoon of terrible beatings, the coach must have taken pity on me. He came up to me and asked, 'Why do you want to learn so

fast? Why don't you start off with the beginners?' It was then that I found out that this was the professional's class! The beginner's class was the next day."

From that point, Lee pursued his goal with determination. After training hard enough to settle his score with the Russians, he found that the physical sport of boxing held an appeal for him that went beyond revenge. Diligent training sharpened his skills and honed his combat instincts, and by 1948, he had become the Amateur Welterweight Champion of China. Following the Communist Revolution, Lee's family moved to Taiwan in 1949. Three years later, he emigrated to the United States to further his education.

Studying at Utah State University and UCLA, Lee earned his advanced degrees in electrical engineering—a profession he has practiced to this day at the Jet Propulsion Lab of Cal Tech. He currently resides in Altadena, California, with his wife and four children. At this point, none of his children has taken up either of his martial arts. "I don't want to pressure them," he explains. "I encourage them, and they've been exposed to it, but I'm not going to force them."

Describing himself as a family man, Lee makes a point of setting aside Sunday of each week for religion and "a family afternoon outing or home entertainment. I want to make sure that I have some time set aside from my busy schedule to communicate with my children, too. My family is very important to me."

The Liberating Impact of Bruce Lee

It's plain that Lee hopes that someday his children will take up the arts that have given him so much. "Bruce Lee had a great impact on my life," he states. "I worked out with him quite a bit, and I consider myself very fortunate. You know, it's just a handful of people who eventually encountered him." Recalling the early days of the JKD *gwun* in Los Angeles's Chinatown, Lee states, "This was the time [1967–1968] when Bruce was uncommitted to the movies or television. He spent more time to train us, and he set such high standards for our training that he gave everyone a special prescribed supplementary fitness program. He'd look at you and say, 'You've got to work on this area, that area, stretching, and so on.' He really meant business, and he worked very hard—four times a week. That's dedication."

Inspired by Bruce Lee's example, those who studied under him stand in awe of his greatness. "He was probably the one person I respected the most," says Professor Lee of his mentor. "Bruce Lee was a very straightforward person—very intense, but most of all, very honest. If he liked you, he liked you. He didn't hold back any punches; if he didn't like you, he said so—and that's the kind of person you like because you know he's going to say exactly the same thing behind you as he would to your face."

This honesty that Bruce Lee lived also permeates the principles of his fighting art, jeet kune do, which means "the way of the intercepting fist." Just as Bruce Lee would never think of applying fixed formulas or ideas to his honest approach to life, the principles of JKD depend on total freedom.

Developing from Bruce Lee's conviction that actual combat rarely, if ever, conformed to the dogmatic "dos and don'ts" of systematized styles, JKD's only bounds and limits exist in the individual abilities of the practitioner. It is an art in which the only rule is that there are no rules. "Bruce Lee wanted to liberate us from a fixed pattern—period," Lee recalls of his instructor. "He told us, 'I am no style, but I'm all styles; you don't know what I'm going to do, and I don't even know what I'm going to do. My movement is the result of your movement; my technique is the result of your technique.'"

The resulting art is one of simple and remarkably efficient techniques, honed to a razor's edge and guided by an intuitive combat awareness developed during all-out sparring. "You really go right in," says Lee, who feels that most other martial arts could do themselves good by incorporating more realistic conditions into their training. "You put all the body protectors on and go at it: that's the only way. When it's going to be all-out, your frame of mind changes because you know if you make one mistake, your opponent will be coming right at you. And then you really begin to respect his punch as the real thing."

Emphasizing large doses of almost-real combat to teach calm and quick reaction under pressure, JKD is most effective in actual use. In the advanced practitioners, punches and other attacks become reflex actions, guided solely by senses heightened through countless hours of almost-real sparring—the instant an opening occurs, the attack is already on the way. Because of the simplicity of the techniques, the attack is extremely powerful and effective.

Yet, beyond the techniques and their infinite variations and applications, JKD is not a style, but rather a transcendence of style. Removing the bonds of set patterns and fixed responses gives you a freedom to flow with reality. The closer you get to reality, the less you need complicated devices and techniques as crutches.

Recalling the words of his mentor, Lee explains the simplicity of JKD: "We didn't have many complicated techniques. Bruce Lee believed and said that 'In JKD, one does not accumulate, but rather, one eliminates the nonessential. It is not daily increase, but daily decrease. The height of cultivation always runs to simplicity; it is the halfway cultivation that runs to ornamentation. So, it is not how much fixed knowledge one has accumulated; rather it is what one understands and can apply that counts. *Being* is far more valued than doing. That's all there is. It is indeed difficult to convey simplicity.'"

Bruce Lee, in many ways, *was* jeet kune do. His leadership and his innovation provided much of the soul and spirit of the free-form principles at the heart of the art, and he will be missed. Daniel Lee felt the loss on a personal level, in losing a friend, as well as professional, in the art's loss of its founder and leader. "We are saddened beyond words by his passing, but the philosophy and principles he left behind for us will be cherished forever, Lee says. "It was always Bruce's wish that his art never be commercialized or exploited. We shall honor that wish."

Lee now devotes the majority of his time to tai chi chuan. Convinced that the JKD method of free-sparring to develop combat skills is very effective, Lee has of late been applying those techniques to tai chi. "I hope if I ever contribute to tai chi," he says, "one way is, in a general sense, to help people to find these exercises as a means of relaxation, finding calmness and the center within yourself. On the other hand, I would like to explore why tai chi has been called the superior fighting art. I haven't met a master yet who practices this aspect of the art."

Rediscovering Tai Chi's Fighting Artistry

Many tai chi instructors refuse to discuss the fighting aspects of their art, claiming that the techniques are either too dangerous or just plain unimportant, while others make the claim that practice of the solo form, coupled with the push-hands practice (sport tai chi), is all that is needed. Lee disagrees. "If a so-called master pushes his beginning student around in push-hands practice while the student only acts as a passive dummy, not trying to counter or even defend, then the so-called master has not convinced me that he knows anything about reality in combat. As Bruce Lee once said, 'He is like a man swimming on dry land.'"

However, says Lee, "Tai chi chuan is an effective fighting art. It's been proved through history. Master Yang Lu-Chan, nicknamed Yang Wu Ti, or 'Yang the Unsurpassable,' was once asked by the court to teach tai chi. Because of that, kung-fu masters challenged him from all over China—and couldn't beat him. But Master Yang didn't learn how to fight just by doing tai chi every day. He gained his experience through his

fighting. He used tai chi both offensively and defensively, but that art is lost. All you see in tai chi demonstrations are merely prearranged and fixed attacks and responses. But fighting is dynamic, so if you want to be good, you have to use it in a more live situation. Push-hands, also called 'joint-hands,' is only the beginning."

Applying JKD training methods to the forms of the solo form, Lee is trying to rediscover some of the lost art. "Now when I try to work on some of my tai chi self-defense techniques," says Lee, "I put on my JKD protective equipment and spar." Lee learned from experience. He explains: "Once I asked a friend of mine to attack me whatever way he wanted to, and I would try to defend myself. It was difficult to cover myself completely all the time, and I got clobbered many times. What was wrong was that my opponent knew that I was only going to try to *block* his attack, and he became fearless and kept charging toward me. Finally, I said to myself, 'Hold it, I'm going to use offensive movement as well,' and I did. All of a sudden, the picture changed: my opponent didn't come in wildly any longer, because he realized he would get hit as well."

The lesson: "I was no longer totally passive in my mind. I was now applying the yin-yang principle by using both offensive and defensive movement. With my mind open and my body relaxed, I was able to sense his movement, fitting in with his attack and using whatever technique I found appropriate. Eventually, I was able to handle his attacks with ease. I realized again that what Bruce Lee had said was right: 'Totality and freedom of expression toward the ultimate reality in combat is the key.'"

Fluid and quick, fighting ability demands all of the conditioning, flexibility, and agility provided by the solo form, plus much more. "You've got to have that intuitive feeling of timing," Lee believes. "A sense of distance and knowledge of your own limitations you can learn, rhythm you can train for, but not timing: you've got to work on it all the time."

The Interchangeability of Yin and Yang

Comparing his tai chi to JKD, Lee remarks, "Tai chi is circular movement, spiral movement, on and on, keep going in. I find a total harmony when I blend tai chi and JKD principles in combat. They all express the interchangeability of yin and yang. There is a place for straight line, and there is a place for circular line. Applying tai chi and JKD principles opens up new dimensions and latitude in combat. I could use circular movement to neutralize the straight aggressive punch, thus nullifying its power, or I could use a straight-line punch to intercept a straight-line punch, a hook, or a roundhouse kick. To cling stubbornly to the straight line and reject the circular line, or vice versa, is to become forever bound by their limitations."

So, even in combat, the yin-yang harmony holds appeal for Daniel Lee—engineer, philosopher, and martial artist. Combining the offense of JKD and the health and yielding of tai chi chuan, he has found a truly harmonious balance of opposites. And, in the process, he has expanded his knowledge and skills just a little bit more.

"To me, a person has to be dedicated to the art because of love. Through my daily practice of tai chi and deep reflection on the philosophy, I hope to reach the understanding and appreciation of my own cultural heritage. I do not want to reside only at the conceptual level. By experiencing the operating yin-yang principles in my own body and mind, I will be able to bring my understanding of principles to bear upon my daily life as a whole, thus living every moment in total harmony with myself and with the universe. I hope to be a clear channel of blessing to the people that cross my path, through my teaching; to instruct the correct use of one's energy without waste, to draw, to conserve, and channel one's energy that is normally untapped; and to promote to the public body vitality, well-being, and spiritual renewal."

He concludes, "I haven't reached the final blooming yet in my learning. I don't think I ever will, but the journey itself has been exciting and joyful."

This material appeared in the March 1974 edition of Inside Kung-Fu *magazine.*

36

Dan Lee Today

Steve Smoke

Dan Lee spent half his life in China, where he received his university education, and half his life in the United States, doing his advanced schooling and working in a scientific vocation. In his daily activity, Lee represents both Eastern and Western ideals.

By day, he works for the Jet Propulsion Lab in the Telecommunications division, where magnetic tape and mathematical calculations are the order of the day. His current assignment involves him with the orbiting and landing functions of the Viking spacecraft. By night, Lee teaches tai chi chaun, an aesthetic and consciousness-expanding art that could be considered paradoxical to his daily routine. Yet, the closest points on a circle are also the farthest from one another, and so it is with Lee, as the two systems of thought blend to form a complete and satisfyingly patterned lifestyle.

"A logical and analytical mind is required to work with precision instruments," explains Lee. "All activities are conducted with order and proper sequence of execution. The success of a project often depends on much planning and preprogramming as well as continual checking and rechecking. We are in the scientific forefront here because everything we learn on these missions can directly affect people all over this planet. It's very rewarding and exciting."

In those hours that follow such logical activities come pursuits of "detached calmness" through tai chi. Lee draws the parallel between the hemispheres of the brain (the right being the creative, nonrational, and the left being the logical and analytical) and the hemispheres of the world; the Eastern more subjective while the Western is oriented toward logic and analysis.

East, Meet West

A good portion of Lee's thinking has been shaped by his study of the Tao Te Ching. He sees much pertinence of the Tao to today's ecological, sociological, and scientific problems, noting that certain passages actually describe an electromagnetic field of force and the quantum theory. "Some psychologists appear to be fond of it as well," says Lee, "because the text seems to be describing consciousness itself."

He believes that while tai chi is a very healthy, understandable, holistic approach to the body, an understanding of traditional Chinese philosophy, particularly the Tao, is essential to fully understanding tai chi's method of movement and finding the harmony inside oneself.

He notes that such philosophy is traditionally a guideline for students learning tai chi. The books used for instruction have usually been written by people who lived the tai chi way of life, practicing endless hours every day, for twenty years or more. "Such writing crystallized all the tai chi principles for the sincere student," says Lee. "Without such understanding, the goals attained become severely limited in comparison."

Lee has studied the *T'ai Chi Ch'uan Classics* and says, "These are as important as the Tao and must be studied by any serious tai chi student." He contends that the bridge between East and West is not as large as some would imagine and is becoming even smaller. This is because as technology in the West increases, so does its interest in the philosophies of the East, such as yoga, martial arts, and meditation. The same is true of the East, which seeks and actively pursues Western modes of thinking and Western technology.

Says Lee, "We live in two universes, the inner and the outer. The body goes through changes of rhythm as well as other cyclical changes, just as the outer world goes through its seasonal changes. In tai chi, I want my students to feel what's happening. Sometimes we move so fast that the mind does not have time to comprehend what is happening, so we slow down in order to really feel what is going on inside us when we go through our movements—all the subtle changes with the relationships of the joints and muscles. Find that relationship; find the center. Therein a student will find a dynamic balance which will be flowing, moving and not static."

An important aspect of the two-universe concept is the difference between tension and pressure: pressure comes from without, while tension exists within. In his work at the Jet Propulsion Lab, Lee is constantly under pressure yet claims he is rarely tense, which he attributes to the relaxation inherent in his tai chi training and discipline.

Throughout the years, Lee has received many benefits from his tai chi practice. Among them is the cultivation of a meditative state of consciousness. "When my intellectual mind is quieting down and I allow the body to move with spontaneity, I feel peace and serenity pervade my whole being. I experience harmonious existence between the body and the mind."

He explains the progression: "In my tai chi, I find a way to put the Taoist philosophy into action. During my first year of training, I could relax neither my mind nor my body, and I usually shed a trail of sweat wherever I practiced. As I learned the movements of tai chi, I truly learned to relax my body and calm my mind. As I went through the movements, I began to see how each part of the body was interrelated to the other. Through my practicing, I gradually began to move more effortlessly and naturally and to breathe deeper and more naturally with the lower abdomen. This was a beautiful experience because I sensed the harmonious existence between the mind and the body."

This is very much the Taoist mode of exercise that the Chinese call *hsiu yang sheng hsin* (to cultivate and nurture the body and mind), which teaches that one must employ techniques that will promote a unified development of the body and mind. Lee quotes his favorite Lao-tzu saying : "Knowing others is wisdom; knowing yourself is enlightenment. Mastering others requires force; mastering the self requires strength."

Tai chi as taught and expressed by Lee is a mechanism by which one can sense the idea of the "here and now," that it isn't so much getting to a point, as it is experiencing how one gets there; the here and now is all there is. To relegate living to the future or the past is to never live. The philosophy behind tai chi describes such insight, and its movements facilitate a direct experience of that wisdom.

Lessons from Bruce Lee

The most influential teacher in Dan Lee's life was Bruce Lee. In him, Dan Lee found a man he could trust and learn from, in whom the wisdom of the East was matched with the pragmatism of the West, and who had a passion for life and a thirst for knowledge. He shares his favorite quotes collected from his instruction with Bruce Lee:

- Sharpen your tools. A JKD man faces reality and not crystallization of form. His tool is a tool of formless form.

- My followers in *jeet kune do*, do listen to this: All fixed set patterns are incapable of adaptability or pliability. The truth is outside of all fixed patterns.

- When one has reached maturity in this art, one will have the formless form. It is like the dissolving of thawing ice into water that can shape itself to any structure. When one has no form, one can be all forms; when one has no style, one can fit in with any style.

- While being trained in JKD, the student is to be active and dynamic in every way. But in actual combat, his mind must be calm and not at all disturbed. He must feel as if nothing critical is happening.

- In JKD, all techniques are to be forgotten, and the unconscious is to be left alone to handle the situation, when the technique will assert its wonders automatically or spontaneously. To float in Totality, to have no technique, is to have all techniques.

- The JKD man should be on the alert to meet the interchangeability of the opposites. As soon as his mind "stops" with either of them, it loses its own fluidity. A JKD man should keep his mind always in the state of emptiness so that his freedom in action will never be obstructed. When there is no obstruction, the JKD man's movements are like flashes of lightning or like the mirror reflecting images.

- When you perceive the truth in *jeet kune do*, you are at an undifferentiated center of a circle that has no circumference.

- Learn the principles, abide by the principles, and dissolve the principles—in short, to enter a mold without being caged in it, and to obey the principles without being bound by them.

- Utilize the art as a means in the study of the way (Tao).

- Ultimately JKD is not a matter of technology, but of spiritual insight and training.

Dan Lee looks at his martial arts training as being three-directional: First, from above, he seeks instruction from masters. Second, on an even level, he seeks exchange with his peers in sharing ideas. Third, he passes on knowledge below to others, especially perpetuating Bruce Lee's JKD philosophy.

Reaching for the Top in Teaching

Lee taught tai chi at UCLA extension, Claremont Men's College, and Cal Tech, as well as conducting private classes. His approach is hands-on: "I always teach my classes personally, especially beginning classes. A new student is like a piece of white paper, totally blank. It is an honor and a responsibility to teach new students. I am strongly opposed to the practice of many commercial establishments that advertise that you will learn from a certain instructor, when in fact, you rarely even see him."

When Lee has new students simply relax their shoulders, they are often surprised at how difficult it is to do. Most new students are also shocked to realize how awkward they really are. But with such knowledge comes new insight and a legitimate starting point for improvement. Lee teaches tai chi mostly out of his love for the art. He often refers to this pursuit not as teaching, but as sharing, in light of the personal growth it brings for himself as well as his students.

To Lee, form is a mechanical movement, and in order to truly learn a form, it is necessary to understand what is *behind* the movements. In tai chi, it is sometimes considered disrespectful or untraditional to ask questions of one's teacher; a respectful student simply mimics the movements handed down by the instructor. Lee notes that in contrast, a key aspect of the Western mind is that it questions why a thing is done. "This is a healthy point of view and one that I not only encourage, but insist on both for myself and for my students," says Lee.

He adds, "Bruce Lee once told me, 'Dan, always strive for understanding. Find the root, then you can see the flower.' Without knowing the relationship of the timing, space, and function, the form can degenerate quickly. If it is not functional, it is merely ornamentation, and the martial art aspect of tai chi is lost."

Technology is advancing, sports are advancing, records are breaking. Why? Are bodies stronger? Perhaps, but Lee believes that the real reason is that training methods have improved. Thus, he is constantly searching for the best, most applicable, and most understandable methods to teach the art. Being an engineer in the West, and having been raised in the East, Lee tries in his classes to make the Oriental arts vital and interesting to the Western mind. "How can a student apply what he learns to his daily life?" he asks himself. "If he can't, what he is learning is purely academic, partial and limited."

On training, Lee says that everything physical

must follow physical laws. Tai chi thus follows the laws of leverage, gravity, and so forth. Essential to training in and learning tai chi is sensing body movement. An axiom is that "if your arms moved independently of the body movement, it was not real kung fu."

Often, he notes, a new student observing a form sees appearances and not what is actually taking place. For instance, many forms appear to comprise a multitude of hand movements, so the novice then concentrates on imitating those movements without realizing that there is a subtle body movement that must precede them.

"One way I try to illustrate this," says Lee, "is by likening the movement of 'brushing the knee' to a baseball pitcher throwing a ball. A person who is familiar enough with baseball to perform the pitching motion can better understand the body movement involved in the tai chi form." Lee feels it is necessary to draw a Western parallel not only to bring home the point but also to illustrate pertinence to the student. His classes take place in what he calls a "nonjudgmental, noncompetitive environment."

The early awkwardness experienced by tai chi students is manifested by wobbliness while doing the exercises. "When you're centered," explains Lee, "your movements become smooth and graceful. But how do I explain such an abstract concept to my students?" Congruent with his illustrative teaching methods, Lee produced two toy "tops" to demonstrate the principle of "centering." After putting an extra weight (a piece of metal) on the bottom of one top, he set both of them spinning, with the inevitable result that the weighted one tipped over while the unobstructed one spun, perfectly centered and balanced, for a considerable time.

By way of further explanation Lee says, "If we are driving on the freeway and the car starts shaking, we know that something, usually the tires, must be out of balance and requires adjustment in order to run at optimum efficiency. The same is true of ourselves: balance and centering are most important."

Another key principle of tai chi is that of "yielding." For example, when an attacker comes at you and lands an effective blow to a rigid area, you're usually knocked off balance. Conversely, if you are fluid and yielding, the blow will be as though striking thin air, and often the mere momentum of an unlanded punch will throw the attacker off balance enough to make him hopelessly vulnerable. "Such examples," says Lee, "provide just enough of a learning tool so that students see these things for themselves as a flash of insight."

Such concepts as "yielding," says Lee, often strike the Western mind the wrong way. The popular view is that strength always wins out. To counter that viewpoint, he offers the example of the tough cowboy in the rodeo riding the broncos and bulls. If the cowboy were to remain tough and rigid while trying to ride a bucking bull, he would be thrown immediately to the ground. Successful riders move as if they are riding a wave—moving as it moves, following it, going with it, riding it out without resis-

tance. "The important point is to be 'one' with the hostile force," says Lee, "and not to resist it. Go with it, and don't use force; blend with it. It is like a pliable reed in the wind: it neither opposes nor gives way. That is the essence of tai chi."

Bruce Lee once cautioned him, "Dan, never talk of 'maturity', but rather of 'maturing,' because a person is constantly maturing and blossoming. Never stop being a student. Life is always a learning, searching, and finding experience. A teacher is not a giver of wisdom but simply a guide." To many, Daniel Lee is just such a guide: inspiring and setting a glowing example, and teaching tai chi out of his love and desire to share his art.

This material appeared in the August 1976 edition of Inside Kung-Fu *magazine.*

Pan Wing Chow
Original Chen Style: A Generation from Extinction?

Dave Cater

Master Pan Wing Chow has reached the twilight of his life, yet is the portrait of health as he performs the first section of the thirteen-section original Chen style tai chi chuan form. He is among the last of a dying breed who have remained true to master Chen Fake's original form. Sadly, the days of Pan Wing Chow and his art are numbered. With only six masters of original Chen style tai chi alive—and just three who studied with Chen Fake—the foundation of the popular form is destined to be lost with time. In this rare interview, Pan Wing Chow talks about his introduction to the art, his experiences with the great master, and the bleak future of this pure tai chi form.

INSIDE KUNG FU: What attracted you to the Chen style?

PAN WING CHOW: At the time I started, I learned Wu style tai chi from Mr. Liou, who told me if I really wanted to learn tai chi, I should study from the master himself—Chen Fake.

IKF: How was studying under him different from what you'd previously experienced?

PWC: The difference between Chen and Wu style tai chi is that Chen style is passed from generation to generation. Also, in the Chen style, you must learn "reeling out the silk," or the inner energy *jing*.

IKF: Were the techniques more to your liking? Did they fit you better?

PWC: At that point, all forms of tai chi were about the same—for health and the techniques—except for the Chen style, which is special for its "reeling out the silk," *jing*, and health. The techniques are superb.

IKF: The tendency of many martial artists is to experiment, to create new from old. But you have maintained the original style. Why?

PWC: Chen style mainly has had two big sets. The first big set has thirteen sections. The reason for my maintaining the tradition of Chen tai chi is that I want to study why there are thirteen sections. The hand movement is like flowing water and is one complete movement. Inside the thirteen sections are many different hand movements that make up the first form. The Chen style of tai chi was developed by many generations until it became a fixed form. The whole set also has a fixed name and fixed form. The reason for my dedication to the traditional Chen tai chi is that the final fixed form is complete. No change is necessary.

IKF: Chen tai chi has been altered by today's practitioners. Is there anything wrong with it? Why don't you try it?

PWC: There's nothing really wrong with those non-traditional forms. I just think I kept the same pattern because I'm over ninety years old and am not willing to learn any new forms. But if someone can take the best out of the Chen style and make the learning process shorter, it is possible to maintain the old while adding the new. The tai chi can be good.

IKF: How long should it take to learn the basic form of Chen tai chi?

PWC: It depends on the individual. The time can vary. A fast learner can learn the set in about three months. A slow learner, maybe six months. It all depends on how hard you practice.

IKF: During your early time with Chen Fake, how many hours did you practice?

PWC: At that time, I was studying hard at the university. Since I was not doing it professionally, I would not repeat it more than ten times a day.

IKF: What was Master Chen like when you first met him? What was he like as a teacher?

PWC: When I first met Master Chen Fake, he was only forty-four years old. He was very warm-hearted, willing to help people, humble, kind, and very patient. He died at 71, but he would have been 100 years old this year.

IKF: What did you think of his techniques? Did they astound you?

PWC: At the time, I was surprised. He was very powerful. And his techniques were very good.

IKF: How many instructors like you are still doing the old form?

PWC: There are six of us who know the traditional Chen style, but only three of us learned from Master Chen Fake. And we all learned at different times.

IKF: Do you worry that with so few true instructors left, traditional Chen style will die in a generation or two?

PWC: Yes, I am very worried about its dying.

IKF: How does it make you feel knowing that something you've practiced for more than fifty years is on the verge of extinction?

PWC: I am very sad to think this might happen. Because of my age, I don't teach it much anymore. And the rest of the group are also getting old and don't think much about teaching.

IKF: In the 1930s and '40s, were there large groups of people studying Chen tai chi? Was it a popular form?

PWC: No. In fact, few people studied Chen tai chi, because you could learn it only through private lessons. The reason Master Chen originally went to

Peking was that he was hired by a group of people to teach Chen tai chi on a private basis.

IKF: Did it make it difficult when there were so few people studying a martial art? Did you feel alone?

PWC: At the time, many people were interested in learning tai chi, but Chen tai chi was never very popular. I learned the style because I was introduced to master Chen Fake when he was in Peking. He did not teach publicly. The only other time it was taught was in the Chenjiagou Village, Henan Province, where Master Chen once lived. I was the only person outside Henan Province to learn Chen tai chi at the time.

IKF: When you studied with Chen Fake, where were your classes?

PWC: Master Chen lived at the Henan Association Headquarters. I learned at the home of Mr. Liou, who belonged to the Henan Association. He was a very good Wu style tai chi teacher. They were good friends, and although Mr. Liou learned some of the Chen style forms, he was known for his Wu style and couldn't change.

This material was published in the April 1987 edition of Inside Kung-Fu *magazine.*

38

Master Ni Ua-Ching
True Taoist Master

Suzanne Soehner

Master Ni represents a direct and continuous lineage of thirty-seven generations of Taoist tradition, dating back to the Tang Dynasty of China (A.D. 677). He is also the heir and embodiment of the wisdom and experience that has been transmitted in an unbroken succession for seventy-four generations, dating back to the Han dynasty (216 B.C.).

As a young boy, he was chosen to study with Taoist masters in the high mountains of mainland China. After more than twenty years of intensive training, he was fully acknowledged and empowered as a master of all traditional Taoist disciplines, including tai chi chuan, kung fu, meditation, acupuncture, and herbal medicine. Master Ni has taught and practiced these arts on the island of Taiwan for twenty-seven years and has written more than fifty books on Taoist subjects.

Because of the social changes that have taken place in China in recent history, Master Ni is the last in his lineage to be taught by ancient traditional methods and is the only Taoist master with these credentials teaching in the United States. Until now, this knowledge has been virtually unavailable outside of China. Master Ni is here for a limited period to share his wisdom and experience with serious students who are willing to make the effort to cultivate and develop themselves to their fullest potential.

INSIDE KUNG FU: Would you tell us something about your own background and training?

NI UA-CHING: Traditionally, a Taoist does not like to talk about himself as a special individual existence. However, this is a special occasion.

First, let us understand that traditionally, the esoteric knowledge of the ancient Chinese was transmitted through an apprentice system and through family continuation. I was born into one of those families with a Taoist heritage and with the responsibility to preserve this culture. Besides my father, who was my first traditional teacher, I had the special opportunity to learn from three other great masters who lived as hermits at that time in some very beautiful, high mountains. They passed their traditional knowledge and techniques to me, making me one spiritual descendant of this prehistoric tradition: the Union of Tao and Man.

This mainstream of Taoism maintains that man was born with the Tao as his inherent, true nature. However, he loses and separates himself from the Tao in his worldly life. Thus, our spiritual goal of life is to reunite ourselves with our true nature—the reunion of Tao and man.

Or we may put it this way: Mankind was born in a very balanced state. However, after living in the world, desire outgrew intelligence, causing imbalance and creating disaster, misery, and agony, taking us far away from our true nature. This is why we need the Taoist self-cultivation, to reconstruct within ourselves the image of the *shien*, or Immortal—a being united in body, mind, and spirit with nature. This is my simple background, as well as my tradition.

IKF: What is Taoism? How does it differ from other spiritual traditions?

NUC: First, I don't think it is appropriate to use "ism" to try to limit or title Tao. When we talk about a kind of "ism," we are generally referring to some kind of political principle, economic policy, or special view of life. Tao cannot be referred to as products fashioned from it. The Taoist tradition constitutes one branch or school of world knowledge which has accumulated over thousands of years. The title of "Taoism" was used only to differentiate it from other traditions.

You may say that Tao is the essence of the universe, which is pre-heaven and pre-earth, existing before anything became formed. It is the unmanifest potentiality from which all manifestations proceed. After things become mentally or physically formed, they then are given names or titles. The names and titles are not the Tao but are its descriptions.

This process can also be applied to describe our mind. When our mind is perfectly still and we have not yet formed it into any ideas, concepts, images, or attitudes, it is the true mind itself. This is so even if one is not aware of its existence. Actually, it is only when one is involved in something, excited or disturbed, that one is aware of the mind. Pure mind, in Taoist terms, is called *po*. This may be translated as "the original simplicity" or "the primary essence." It is the fundamental power of mind.

When pure mental energy connects with the universal, unmanifest, creative energy, it is also called *po* or Tao, the original simplicity. In its unmanifest aspect, the original simplicity is infinite. When it becomes manifest, it is finite.

Religions were originally created in human society out of mankind's mental need to understand and control its environment, as an expression of the evolution of human consciousness. Religions can take as many forms as man's mind may take. However, all theological inventions are of secondary importance and are not the original *po* itself, which should not be molded or distorted in order to worship its accessories.

Religion is the creation of the mind, and therefore, it relies upon psychological experience and intellectual discovery. Consequently, what religion is about is the worship of these experiences. But Taoism begins with the essential, intuitive understanding of the origin and nature of the universe.

The quality of Taoism is different from that of worldly religions, as Taoism doesn't emphasize worship. Worship is a secondary, mental activity. When you move your mind by creating the sentiment of worship, you fashion something outside of the mind as the object of your worship. By so doing, you trap your mind in the illusion of duality, which is against Tao.

Rather than invent an outside sovereignty to act as his authority, the Taoist perceives the worshipper and the worshipped as one. When a Taoist engages in worship, he is revering the objectivization of his own true nature. Relatively speaking, the goal of Taoism is the reunification of oneself with the great *po*, the primal, creative energy which is the essence of the universe.

The highest, most refined energy within us is of the same frequency as the primal energy referred to as *po*. Your life is one hand of the primal energy of the universe extending itself outward as your Self. It is not like one fish that jumped out of the ocean. We are an extension of the universal power which has stretched itself outward, not only into humankind but also into all manifestations. Since we have lost our *po*, our original simplicity or original essence, in our habitual mental perception of duality and multiplicity, we need to restore ourselves back to the great creative, original simplicity.

In Chinese, the original simplicity is called *yuen chi*, the "original, beginning energy." With *yuen chi*, we can do anything. If we disperse or scatter the *yuen chi*, we can do nothing.

So, the concept of original simplicity is not a doctrine; the original simplicity is the substance of all beings. The Taoist cultivates his energy in order to realize his true nature. The Taoist way is not merely a worship service or something like this. We just call it self-cultivation. As an aspect of self-cultivation, the Taoist tradition also includes the practice of certain rituals or formulas in order to bring about a response from the superphysical natural power. These are some of the activities and nonactivities that form today's Taoism.

The Taoist tradition in China has, over many years, gradually divided into two main groups, and even many smaller branches. One group preserves the original spirit of Taoism, while the other pays more attention to the ceremonies. I belong to the former, maintaining the original spirit of Taoism. My tradition is not connected with the local customs of different Chinese villages—the so-called Taoist folk religion.

IKF: Why have you come to America?

NUC: I came to the United States at the invitation of some American students who had come to Tai-

wan to study with me. Before coming here, I practiced traditional Chinese medicine on the island. I also taught tai chi chuan and passed on Taoism. While I was in Taiwan, I wrote many books on Taoism, with a wide readership interested in learning Taoism through me.

My accepting the invitation to come here was based on my own understanding of today's world crisis. The decisive power of human destiny is mainly mankind itself. There is a very old Chinese proverb that says: "When nature makes difficulties, mankind still has the opportunity to avoid the problem and survive. But when man himself creates disaster, it is hard for him to run away."

Today's international social conflicts are based mainly on the difference between, and error in, people's concept of God and the nature of life. The Roman emperors were the first to understand that Christianity could be used as a good ruling tool. Since then, Christianity has played an important part in all of Western society. The root of the problem is that the true quality of Christianity is more sociological than spiritual. The foundation of present-day Christianity is based on the shallow, emotional level of understanding. Today's church leaders emphasize emotional force such as faith, hope, and love, but they use Christianity to blind the directing eye of reason. Thus, strong prejudice was nursed and was made a persecution force for the free soul.

We all know that one's view of the universe influences his view of life. This view of life can influence a person's personality. Besides Christianity and Christianity-type religions, what other view of the universe does Western society hold? One can look in a college astronomy textbook and find that there are two main theories of the beginning of the universe. One is that the universe had no beginning at all:

what exists now is the same thing that has always existed. The second main theory is what is called the big bang theory, which states that there originally existed a "cosmic egg" of primordial energy, and then there was a big explosion and many smaller galaxies resulted. This is the Western society's heritage and culture.

From a Taoist perspective, the big bang theory presumes the existence of time and space prior to the creation of the universe, whereas the Taoist sees time and space as one of the developmental attributes of the universe. But I would rather discuss Taoist cosmology. I just mentioned this because the view one holds of the universe is so important in influencing one's activities and the whole of human society.

Through Taoist cosmology, one may know the universal law. You may call it Tao. Tao is the substance of the universe. As it extends, develops, and evolves, yin and yang manifest as the tai chi principle, which then splits and becomes three levels of existence, manifesting as the spiritual, mental, and physical planes. You might say as a way of physics, mind is the most sensitive energy, spirit is the most subtle, and physical energy is the grossest.

The Taoist cosmology holds a peaceful and orderly view of the universe. Such a view can bring a peaceful mind and a creative attitude. You may also know that to connect yourself with the deep root of the universe, the highest subtlety, utilizes your calm mind, your high-level energy, not the lower, emotional energy. Emotion is mostly a product of your relative activity. It is not the deep mind of the absolute world.

I came to America with the hope that through my teaching, people will be able to see a reasonable and integrated view of the universe. Through such reasonable understanding, the development of mankind's future will be bright. An individual life, with the foundation of understanding the origin and nature of the universe, can know that life does not finish at the end of the physical life. Life is connected with the whole universe. This understanding can help to eliminate the conflict in the world's thinking, the conflict that arises out of different, erroneous views of God and the nature of life.

Generally, all religions are a kind of logic. If you follow an incorrect logic, you will arrive at an incorrect result. The religion and culture of a people are the manifestation of the mental energy of the people. If the correct logic is applied, the resulting manifestations will be harmonious.

IKF: What is the I-Ching?

NUC: The I-Ching is the foundation of all Chinese intellectual systems. All eminent achievements of Chinese acupuncture, geomancy (the energy arrangements and relationships of one's environment), military philosophy and strategy, Chinese architecture, and so forth, are derived from the I-Ching.

The study of the I-Ching has reaped an abundant harvest of knowledge throughout its long history, which dates back more than five thousand years. However, even a native-born Chinese scholar has difficulty comprehending its profound imminence. I, as heir to the heritage of the mainstream of Taoism, in order to create other Taoist spiritual heirs, lead students whom I choose to the profound secrets of the I-Ching, which are the foundation upon which Taoism is developed.

Originally, the *Book of Changes* [the English translation of *I-Ching*] contained no written words at all. It had only signs made up of three or six lines, either broken, representing yin energy, or unbroken, representing yang energy. Originally, the signs were composed of three lines. All of the possible combinations of three yin and/or yang lines resulted in eight main signs known as the *bagua*. As time passed, some later stages doubled the signs, making six lines, which had sixty-four possible combinations. These signs are a concrete indication of all the energy manifestations of the universe, how they are formed and how they function.

The basic principles are the yin and yang, displaying duality. Yin and yang have many translations, such as the two sides of positive and negative, expansion and contraction, construction and destruction, masculine and feminine. Yin and yang are not two separate energies or activities. The activity of one is inherently contained within and created by the other. For example, a symphony is composed not only of musical sounds. The silent pauses between the sounds are also an intrinsic aspect of the composition.

In the English language, the contradictory sense of positive and negative is strong. But in the Chinese way of thinking, the yin and yang may unite themselves, and through this union, the existence of all things is made possible. If one side is excessive, its state of balance is lost, thereby creating the possibility of destruction. In Western thinking, positive and negative must fight each other on opposite sides, but the Chinese concept of yin and yang shows us that the great harmony of the universal development is based on the cooperation and union of apparent opposites.

The I-Ching shows that the universe is one whole but with two wings, like man with two legs. In order to function effectively, the two legs don't fight each other, but work together to help each other. For example, in movement, when you produce one kind of force to push yourself up and forward, at the same time you also produce a kind of rejecting force.

This principle can be applied to everything, with yin and yang united as a tai chi. The tai chi then evolves into three levels of existence: physical existence, spiritual existence, and the combination of the two, which is mental existence. Human beings are one manifestation of mental existence, and are a good example of the unification of the physical and the spiritual. Through the study of the I-Ching, one may come to know and experience the mysterious generating origin of the universe, achieve spiritual development, and keep pace with the evolution of the universe.

IKF: Why do you teach the I-Ching?

NUC: Some of my students have brought translations of the I-Ching to me. It is very difficult to make a translation—especially since the Chinese mental structure is so different from that of Westerners. Even excellent translators have trouble. So, none of the translations are perfect. There are many mistakes, and most of the translations are superficial. Only one who is born into this tradition has had his mind molded by it. With the added advantage of Taoist enlightenment training comes the development of high comprehension and familiarity with all of the historical aspects involved, thereby deepening the understanding of exactly what is meant in the *Book of Changes*.

You do not have many translations here in America, but in China we have maybe a thousand famous books discussing it. However, one must have excellent training in order to distinguish the true information from the false. The reason I think the *Book of Changes* is worthy of teaching is that when one practices the I-Ching, one can find external evidence showing the connection between oneself and the universal subenergy—the melting of subjectivity and objectivity. This evidence can guide you and encourage you to move forward into the mysterious realms. Through the practice of the I-Ching, one may prove the possibility of uniting subjectivity and objectivity into one whole.

This material appeared as "Interview with Master Ni Ua-Ching" in the May 1978 edition of Inside Kung-Fu *magazine.*

39

Lien Ying Kuo
The Living Legend of San Francisco's Chinatown

Rick Shively

Lien Ying Kuo's name has been bandied about the international Chinese martial arts community for so long that it's become legendary.

An undisputed master of tai chi chuan, the eighty-four-year-old sifu holds court in a small, practical studio perched across the street from Portsmouth Square in San Francisco. A one-square-block park tucked incongruously between the aged yet quaint buildings of Chinatown and the imposing sterility of the TransAmerican Pyramid which guards the boundaries of the city's financial district, Portsmouth Square is referred to by many natives as "Tai Chi Park."

An Open Invitation

The name is fitting, as any early-morning visitor would agree. As early as 5 A.M., anywhere from twenty to forty people can be seen performing a ghostly ballet in the cold, damp fog. Usually at the head of this group, a spry, smiling man runs through a set of exercises to loosen up. After completing a number of forms on his own, he begins to wander through the group, correcting a posture here, flashing an encouraging smile there, directing a mild look of reprimand every now and then.

It's Lien Ying Kuo in his element—teaching. Even though he can speak only a bare amount of English, the aged instructor seems to have little difficulty imparting even the most complicated moves to an eager class of American students. Members of the early-morning group in the park are representative of the people who straggle into the studio at other times of the day and evening. And, even though the master and his family retire to their apartment behind the studio at an early hour, the school is open to any students who want to use it.

"We want people to be happy here," Ein Gru, Master Kuo's pleasant-faced, thirty-one-year-old wife says. "That's why we're open all the time. Otherwise, what good is it?"

Kuo's Tai chi Chuan Academy is a family operation. Aside from acting as interpreter, wife, and mother to Kuo's nine-year-old son Chung Mei, and official greeter to the seemingly hundreds of people who wander into and out of the school all day, Ein is also an instructor and mother-confessor to many of the students who attend the academy. "We like to help all over," she says. "Tai chi can help many things, make a person feel very good in all ways, not just physical. And sometimes, just talking makes people feel good. So, we do that too."

Most of the regulars at the early-morning ritual are relatively longtime students of the Kuos. Most are well educated professionals and would be classified as nonviolent people who find hard-style martial arts contrary to their nature.

Kuo is one of the major theorists of the Chin school, which purportedly offers the closest blend of the hard and soft styles. Chin stylists claim there is a fifty-fifty blend of the two because while you are "yielding," you are most conscious of the "unyielding," and that is the only way you can take advantage of all things.

The one benefit virtually all of the students tout is the health aspects of the art. To a man, they all claim they've never felt better since taking up the predawn exercise class. All of Kuo's students are heavily encouraged to attend the sessions, and according to the veterans, new faces drift into and out of the class on a regular basis.

"I notice a difference doing it at this time," says one enthusiastic practitioner. "For some reason, it doesn't feel as good at 9 or 10.

When I first started coming, it was a lot later than this, and the sifu would say, 'I thought you were coming in the morning,' and I'd say, 'This is the morning—it'd be 10 o'clock. Then he'd say, 'This is not the morning.' So, I started coming about 8, but I was told that still wasn't morning. Finally, I got it down to about 6 and that was a little better. Now," he adds with a laugh, "I get here at 5, and I never felt better."

Old Ways Give Way to the New

According to Kuo's wife, people don't start the early classes until they've taken tai chi for at least six months. The Kuos are aware that the average American finds it difficult enough to master the intricate forms in the art and doesn't have the patience required to learn tai chi in the traditional manner. Consequently, they make an attempt to simplify the initial learning process as much as possible.

"We teach the beginning class only the five basic exercises," Mrs. Kuo explains, "rotating the waist, feet, and knee, putting hands together, and stretching. This is enough for beginning. Even the fourth and fifth exercises take a long time to learn, so we don't want to give them too much. In the old days back in China, they taught five basic exercises every day until you learned them all, and then you had to put teeth to toe before learning the rest of tai chi. But those were the old days. We don't do that anymore. It is more important now for people to think for themselves. Too many people are in a hurry, then too many forms get mixed up. You can finish the beginner's course here in six months, but it takes three years to get all sixty-four forms down real well."

Another quality that all the students also seem to share is a sense of serenity rarely seen in the average dojo or *gwun*. Despite the early hour, for instance, there is no sign of temperament or grumpiness, and everyone is very much awake. A first-time observer would walk away convinced that these people were involved more in an exercise of the senses rather than a physical one. Of course, in same ways, tai chi is a sensory exercise.

"It's so relaxing," says one student, a member of the faculty at a San Francisco school of psychology. "Ideally, you have to be able to do the tai chi and have the thought inside of the form, concentrating and sending it through the body. All the ideas that usually run through your mind, you put at rest and when you do tai chi, so that you can think about every individual movement of your body. It is a very relaxing thing: you have to relax to do the forms, and the single thought is relaxing. After your body gets real strong and you have the confidence that when you take one step, the body will go right there, then you are even more relaxed. That way, the older you get, the stronger you get, rather than weaker. Your body looks different, and you look different. People will comment on it."

The therapeutic effect is one incentive for a student to continue for the period of time required to really learn the art of tai chi. The soothing aspects of the art attract many people involved in high-pressure jobs. But there is another appeal for many of San Francisco's young Chinese—the cultural aspect. "At one time," says one young Chinese student, "I was interested in a lot of things, but I got away from Chinese culture. But I guess I was ready to get back into it, so I took a course in Eastern philosophy and started looking around. I just happened to stumble in here, and I've been doing it ever since."

Master Kuo, without a word to any of the students, begins to gather up whatever he had brought outside with him and heads back across the street. Informality is stressed, and class doesn't ever really start or end at any particular time. If students have a question, they all know where to find the Kuos. "There's no problem here," Mrs. Kuo says. "Most people come here, and as soon as they do the exercise and relax the body, they have no problem."

This material was published in the December 1976 edition of Inside Kung-Fu *magazine.*

Appendix

Practical Applications of Form Techniques

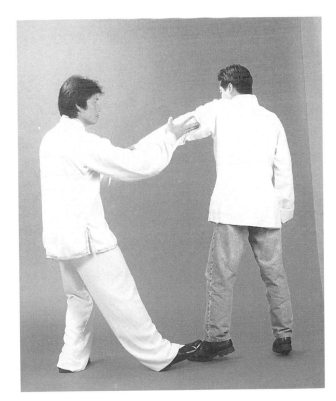

Raise hands—A lifting elbow lock

"Part the wild horse's mane"—An upper-body strike and push, using waist motion

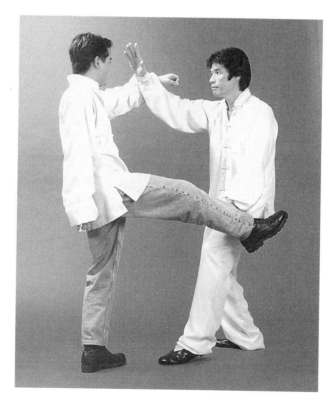

"Stork spreads its wings"—Stopping a fist and kicking attack, while preparing for a countering kick

"Brush knee and twist step"—Simultaneously blocking and kicking and countering with a straight push

"Repulse the monkey"—Escaping a grab with one hand while striking to the throat with the other

"Needle at sea bottom"—Countering a wrist grab with a wristlock and takedown

Rollback—A shoulder lock using the waist for leverage

Press—Straight push

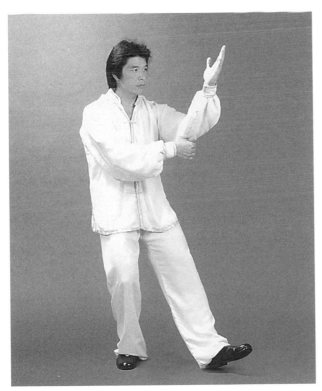

Elbow over fist—An elbow strike to the back of the neck

"High pat on the horse"—A strike to the jaw while holding one of the opponent's arms down

"Golden rooster stands on one leg"—Deflecting a punch with one hand, while kicking to the opponent's groin

"Lotus kick"—A cross-kick to the back while pulling the opponent backward into the kick

Punch down—A downward punch to the face of a prone opponent

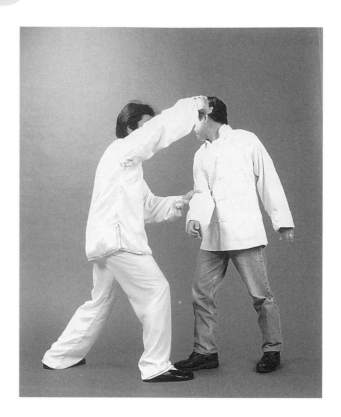

"Hit the tiger"—A fist strike to the side of the head, while holding one arm down

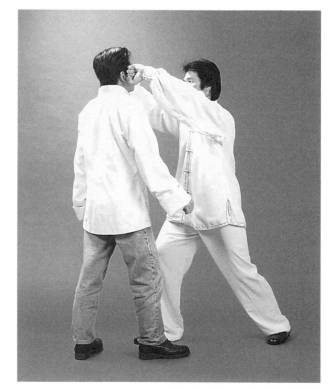

Double strike with fists—A double knuckle strike to the opponent's temples

Separation of left toe—A simultaneous block and kick to
the groin

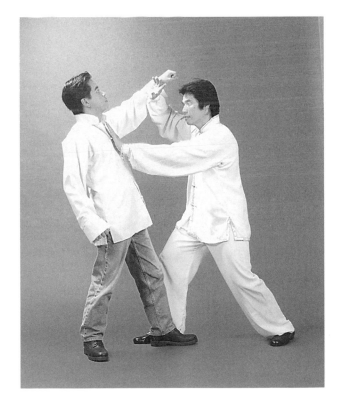

"Fair lady works the shuttle"—A simultaneous upward
block and straight push

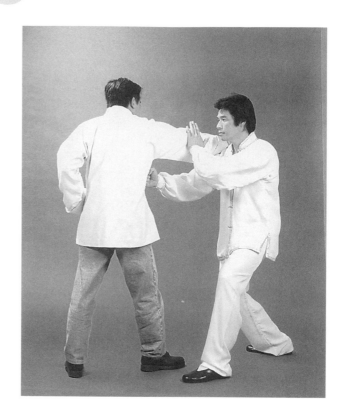

Parry and punch—A deflecting block and punch to the body

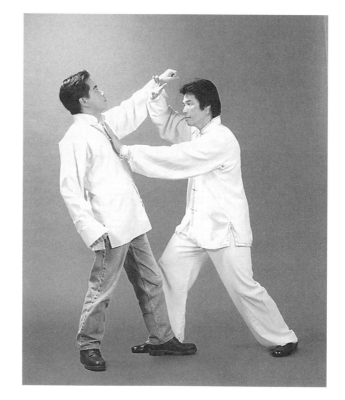

Fan through the back—An upward block and push to the body (the block can also be a grab)

Plain cross-hands—A finger jab to the throat while pressing down with the blocking hand

About the Editors

John Little's articles have been published in every major martial arts and health and fitness magazine in North America. He is considered the world's premier scholar on martial artist/philosopher Bruce Lee, having written more than fourteen books on Lee, his training methods, and his philosophy, including *The Warrior Within: The Philosophies of Bruce Lee* (NTC/Contemporary Publishing Group, Chicago), *The Tao of Gung Fu*, *The Art of Expressing the Human Body*, *Jeet Kune Do: Bruce Lee's Commentaries on the Martial Way*, and *Words of the Dragon* (Charles E. Tuttle, Boston). Little is the editor of the prestigious *Inside Kung-Fu* series (NTC/Contemporary) and *Bruce Lee: Words from a Master* (NTC/Contemporary), in addition to being the coauthor of *Power Factor Training*, *Static Contraction Training,* and *The Golfer's Two-Minute Workout* (NTC/Contemporary). Little received his B.A. in philosophy from McMaster University in Hamilton, Ontario, and spent his formative years in Agincourt and Muskoka. He is happily married and the proud father of four children.

Curtis Wong is the publisher of many of the world's leading martial arts magazines, including *Inside Karate*, *Inside Kung-Fu*, *Inside Kung-Fu Presents*, *Martial Arts Legends*, *Martial Arts Illustrated*, *Action Film*, *Paintball Games*, and the *Bruce Lee Quarterly*. He is the president of CFW Enterprises, a magazine and book publishing company in Burbank, California.